GBBHunter

A4L

Øgen 729

# WILLIAM GODWIN

WILLIAM GODWIN
*From the portrait by James Northcote*

[*Frontispiece*

# WILLIAM GODWIN

*A biographical study*

by

GEORGE WOODCOCK

*With a Foreword by*
*Herbert Read*

THE PORCUPINE PRESS
LONDON

FIRST PUBLISHED IN NOVEMBER MCMXLVI
BY THE PORCUPINE PRESS LTD.
10 BAYLEY STREET, BEDFORD SQUARE, W.C. I
PRINTED IN GREAT BRITAIN AT
THE WHITEFRIARS PRESS LTD., TONBRIDGE

# CONTENTS

# ILLUSTRATIONS

# FOREWORD

IN a famous letter, Shelley confessed to Godwin that he had enrolled his name in the list of the dead, and he described "the inconceivable emotions" with which he learnt of his continued existence. "I had felt regret that the glory of your being had passed from this earth of ours. It is not so. You still live, and I firmly believe are still planning the welfare of human kind."

Godwin had, indeed, outlived his fame, and for the reasons which it is easy to estimate, there has been no substantial revival. But if the modern reader, inspired by Mr Woodcock's new study, will take the trouble to read Godwin's works (and some trouble it will be, for they are not readily accessible), he too may experience feelings not unlike Shelley's. For these works, especially *Political Justice* and *The Enquirer*, are still alive, and even a romance like *Caleb Williams* has a vigour and significance that can still move us, though hardly "as a wind that tears up the deepest waters of the mind," which is Shelley's description of it.

Although Godwin's fame had faded even before Shelley discovered him, Shelley himself is partly the explanation of his darker eclipse. No philosophy was ever so entirely taken over and transmuted into the finer texture of poetry as Godwin's by Shelley. Shelley absorbed Godwin's philosophy not merely as an influence, but rather as a mental possession, and though Shelley, as he developed, was to owe more and more to Plato, it was never to the detriment of his original master. Shelley reconciled what he took from Plato with what he retained from Godwin : and what he retained from Godwin was the whole system of *Political Justice*—

" the first moral system," as he defined it, " explicitly founded upon the doctrine of the negativeness of rights and the positiveness of duties—an obscure feeling of which has been the basis of all the political liberty and private virtue in the world."*

The other explanation of Godwin's eclipse must be sought in the character of his rationalism, or intellectualism. Godwin thought that men could be persuaded into a rational mode of conduct and a rational order of society. He believed that a rational " education " was a sufficient instrument of change. Even Shelley was doubtful on this point, and saw the necessity of a change of heart, of some sudden emotional convulsion. Godwin's persistent rationalism (which is a characteristic of his period rather than of his personality) is never merely jejune : it is various, ingenious and profound. But it is fatally omniscient, and omniscience, in philosophers, is pretentious, and finally boring. I do not believe that in this respect *Political Justice* is more at fault than other systematic treatises on human nature ; but it is one explanation of its undeserved neglect.

Such neglect is undeserved because the book does express, more eloquently than any other work of its kind, certain truths about man and society which have been ignored for a century and a half. In spite of all his rationalism—and because he had his deeper intuitions—Godwin realised that any society compatible with human happiness must be a living body, a natural growth ; and that opposed to society in this sense was a rational concept, the State, which if applied in ignorance of natural laws and limitations, could only lead to the enslavement of the human mind. If the organised State is now omnipotent over the greater part of the globe, and if the people are more enslaved and oppressed than they were a century ago, it is because the truths expressed by Godwin have been forgotten. In this respect, Godwin was the precursor of De Tocqueville and Burckhardt, Acton and Croce— of all those philosophers who, in opposition to the scientific

* " Remarks on Mandeville and Mr Godwin," 1816.

materialism of the nineteenth century, have dared to affirm the priority of certain absolute values—values to which they give the names Freedom and Justice. "Justice" is peculiarly Godwin's value, and Justice, in this political context, as Coleridge recognised in his Sonnet to Godwin, spelt Happiness :

> For that thy voice in passion's stormy day
> When wild I roamed the bleak heath of distress
> Bade the bright form of Justice meet my way,
> And told me that her name was Happiness.

Mr Woodcock's study of Godwin is timely. An increasing number of people, especially of the younger generation, are turning away in disillusionment from the dreary world created by authoritarian or State socialism, and being in no mood for reaction or despair, they discover that there is another and more revolutionary concept of socialism, libertarian socialism, which is still untried, and in detail largely unformulated. Godwin was the first and most eloquent prophet of this social philosophy, and in the years that lie immediately ahead of us, his name and his message will be reanimated.

HERBERT READ

# SHELLEY ON GODWINISM

AND behold, thrones were kingless, and men walked
One with the other even as spirits do,
None fawned, none trampled ; hate, disdain, or fear,
Self-love or self-contempt, on human brows
No more inscribed, as o'er the gate of hell,
" All hope abandon ye who enter here ; "
None frowned, none trembled, none with eager fear
Gazed on another's eye of cold command,
Until the subject of a tyrant's will
Became, worse fate, the abject of his own,
Which spurred him, like an outspent horse, to death.
None wrought his lips in truth-entangling lines
Which smiled the lie his tongue disdained to speak ;
None, with firm sneer, trod out in his own heart
The sparks of love and hope till there remained
Those bitter ashes, a soul self-consumed,
And the wretch crept a vampire among men,
Infecting all with his own hideous ill ;
None talked that common, false, cold, hollow talk
Which makes the heart deny the *yes* it breathes,
Yet question that unmeant hypocrisy
With such a self-mistrust as has no name.

      .      .      .

The loathsome mask has fallen, the man remains
Sceptreless, free, uncircumscribed, but man
Equal, unclassed, tribeless, and nationless,
Exempt from awe, worship, degree, the king
Over himself ; just, gentle, wise : but man
Passionless ?—no, yet free from guilt or pain,
Which were, for his will made or suffered them,
Nor yet exempt, though ruling them like slaves,
From chance, and death, and mutability,
The clogs of that which else might oversoar
The loftiest star of unascended heaven,
Pinnacled dim in the intense inane.

*Prometheus Unbound*

## PART I

# The Early Years
## 1756-1783

I

WILLIAM GODWIN was born in 1756, a year that might well be taken to represent the beginning of the change from the mercantile and aristocratic society of the seventeenth century to the industrial, plutocratic and imperialist society of the nineteenth century. He died in 1836, so that his life had comprehended all the major changes, industrial, political, literary and philosophical, which marked the age of Queen Victoria from that of the early Georges. He, perhaps more than any of his contemporaries, realised how these changes in human environment could have led to the ultimate happiness and freedom of all men ; having failed in his task of enlightenment, he lived to see them become the determining circumstances of a slavery of the mind and a drudgery of the body as thorough and as degrading in their results to mankind as almost any preceding condition of human bondage.

In 1756, these social changes had scarcely begun. In that year began the Seven Years War ; during a series of unsuccessful campaigns in Europe, the first markets for the industrial era were acquired, as if by an afterthought, through the tiny expeditions of Clive in India and Wolfe in Canada. The major inventions of the Industrial Revolution were still to come, and the factory system had appeared only in isolated districts. Indeed, the few slight changes that had already taken place in industry and farming can hardly have been observed by most of the people of the 1750's. The society in which they lived was still based on peasant cultivation and hand crafts operated by small masters, working on their own or controlling very small workshops.

Politically, this was a time of apparent stagnation, when the

structure of landed oligarchy imposed in 1688 seemed to be set
immoveably over the backs of the common people. It is true
that, only ten years before, the last feudal army had marched
down into the heart of England under the Young Pretender. But
it had affected in no way the tendency of the ideas or lives of the
people—even of those who still maintained a sentimental
adherence to the lost Stuart cause, and when this little ripple of
the past ebbed back into the North, the vestiges of feudal society
that remained in Scotland were ruthlessly crushed, and the clan
chieftains turned into eighteenth-century squires who even anticipated their southern fellows in instituting a thorough process
of enclosure of the communal lands and depopulation of the
Highland countryside.

In England, the landowners ruled the country effectively,
through their control of the House of Lords by their own presence, and of the House of Commons by proxy through the
restricted electoral system and the network of purchaseable
boroughs, which assured a majority to the party willing and able
to spend most freely on buying votes and constituencies. The
governmental system was entirely corrupt ; it was efficient only
in its provision of sinecures and pensions for thousands of supporters of the government in power. Its very corruption, however, led to a comparative laxness in the persecution of individuals. This fact, and the steadily increasing material prosperity
which benefited relatively large sections of the community, were
probably the principal reasons for the inertia of the common
people, who stood aside from the political scene in almost complete neutrality. It was not until seven years later that the
activities of John Wilkes stirred the people of London into a
social consciousness they had not demonstrated effectively since
the days of Lilburne, and initiated an era of social struggle yet
unfinished.

In the intellectual life of the capital, the celebrated Dr Johnson
was rising to the zenith of his influence. Johnson professed to be
a Tory and a High Churchman, but it was characteristic of his
age that his bombastic exterior covered a genuine independence
that prompted him to denounce slavery and patriotism, and to
treat with contempt the advances of aristocratic patrons. Among
other writers of the day there was evident an even more lively
tendency to socially critical and destructive thought, and in the

circles of literature and theology the battle against the old society first began. The political ideas of John Locke, the merciless social satire of Swift a generation before, had never completely lost their influence, and now there were added to them the nihilistic attitude implicit in the philosophical idealism of David Hume and the radical influence of the new social philosophy that was being elaborated in France by Diderot, D'Alembert and the other members of the group gathered round the *Encyclopédie*.

## 2

Thus, William Godwin was born at the very outset of the era of change which was to determine the character of his life and work, and whose nature he was to define so much more ably than any of his contemporaries.

His birthplace was Wisbech, in the Fenland, a part of the country where the old mercantile society still survived in its most happy form. The district was then among the most prosperous in England. Its wheatlands were fertile, even under the wasteful old farming system that preceded the four-field rotation, and the land supported an independent peasantry. In its principal city of Norwich, the weaving of woollen worsteds was still the most important textile industry in the land ; Norwich itself was one of the three great cities of England. Its woollen industry was carried on by small weavers, who worked in long garrets above their houses and sold their products to the prosperous local merchants. Among these workers there was a tradition of freedom surviving from the mediæval city, and they were always ready to show their independence of the merchants and of the authorities.

Even today there lingers in Norwich a social consciousness which has long died out in the surrounding country districts. In Godwin's day the local peasantry and artisans must have retained much more of the fervour for independence which had made them the nucleus of the New Model Army of the Commonwealth, had formed from among them the Independent movement and had caused them to listen willingly to the teachings of the Levellers. Among them religious dissent remained in its strongest forms, and theological discussions of predestination and free will, of Arianism and Trinitarianism, were still vigorous and uncompromising. No better environment could have been provided for the breeding of a great philosopher of liberty, who would carry to their logical conclusions the ideas that had motivated for centuries the actions of the peasants and artisans among whom he was born.

Godwin, like many of the writers of his time, was born into a respectable Nonconformist family of the middle class, among whom the ministry had been for generations a favoured occupation. Edward Godwin, a paternal great-grandfather, was an attorney, sufficiently respected by his fellow citizens of Newbury to be elected, successively, Mayor and Town Clerk of the small Berkshire borough. His son Edward, Godwin's grandfather, was a dissenting minister who gained a deserved celebrity in his profession. He studied in the seminary of Samuel Jones at Tewkesbury ; among his fellow pupils were Isaac Watts, the hymn writer, Thomas Secker, later Archbishop of Canterbury, and Bishop Butler, the author of the *Analogy*. Edward Godwin married the widow of his tutor, and then became a preacher at the chapel in Little St Helens, Bishopsgate Street, where he ministered to a fashionable congregation for the remainder of his days. He seems to have been an upright and straightforward man who endeavoured to live according to his own teachings. In dissenting circles he was considered a man of intellect and discrimination, and such celebrated religious poets as Philip Doddridge and Robert Blair sought his assistance in the publication of their literary works.

Edward Godwin had two sons. The elder, also Edward, indulged in his early years in " a certain career of wildness and dissipation," but later redeemed himself and " became a convert to the tenets and practices of Mr George Whitfield. He was for a short time, for the thread of his life was soon broken, a distinguished preacher in the Methodist Connection, and an eager publisher of experiences, devout allegories and hymns." This is the account given by William Godwin in a short autobiographical sketch, which he wrote in 1800 and which remains almost the only reliable document giving any extensive information concerning his family and his own early years.

The younger son of Edward Godwin was John, the father of William Godwin, who became a pupil of Dr Doddridge and entered the ministry without indulging in any of the " wildness " that had begun his brother's enthusiastic career. He seems to have been a colourless character, as devoid of ennobling passion as he was of perceptible vice. In Godwin's references to him there appears a constant hostility :

My paternal grandfather, as I have said, was esteemed a man of learning ; my father was certainly not a man of learning. . . . I scarcely ever heard him read anything but expositions and sermons. His study occupied but little of his time. His sermon, for in my memory he only preached once on a Sunday, was regularly begun to be written in a very swift short-hand after tea on Saturday evening. I believe he was always free from any desire of intellectual distinction on a large scale ; I know that it was with reluctance that he preached at any time at Norwich, in London, or any other place where he suspected that his accents might fall on the ear of criticism. He was regarded by his neighbours as a wise as well as a good man, and he desired no more.

John Godwin, aspiring to no high position in the ministry, contented himself with the small livings which he could enjoy without mental exertion. He spent his life moving from one to another of these tiny congregations. At no time was his income greater than £60 a year—and at times it was considerably less. At this period the income of a skilled London artisan was about £40 a year, while, on the other hand, the livings of Anglican clergymen were frequently ten times this figure.

While he was minister at Wisbech, John Godwin married Anna Hull, the daughter of a shipowner of King's Lynn. Of this marriage were born some thirteen children ; William was the seventh and middle child.

Almost the only bitter thing Godwin says of his mother is that she did not suckle her own children ; he seems to have felt some peculiar slight to his future dignity in that he was " sent from home to be nourished by a hireling." For the rest he speaks of her in terms of high appreciation, quite unlike the frequently contemptuous references he makes to his father.

I was brought up in great tenderness, and though my mind was proud to independence, I was never led to much independence of feeling. While my mother lived, I always felt to a certain degree as if I had somebody who was my superior, and who exercised a mysterious protection over me. I belonged to something.

This close relationship lasted well into Godwin's manhood, and there are extant many letters which his mother wrote to him, in a hand and spelling which showed a scanty education.

However, in spite of her lack of learning, Anna Godwin appears to have been a smart and witty woman.

She was facetious, and had an ambition to be thought the teller of a good story, and an adept at hitting off a smart repartee. She was a most obliging, submissive and dutiful wife. She was an expert and active manager in the detail of household affairs.

Godwin's childhood was dominated by the gloomy Calvinist atmosphere of the home. His father was strict and scrupulous in the details of pietistic austerity. Apart from the reading of sermons and expositions, already mentioned, he allowed little relaxation among his family. He was particularly exact in his observance of the Sabbath, which he carried to a somewhat absurd extremity, for Godwin tells us :

One Sunday, as I walked in the garden, I happened to take the cat in my arms. My father saw me, and seriously reproved my levity, remarking that on the Lord's day he was ashamed to observe me demeaning myself with such profaneness.

William was a delicate child, whose sensitiveness was perhaps increased by his bodily awkwardness and frailty. In this religious home there seems to have been a general contempt for the body ; little attention was paid to physical weaknesses, and William's childhood was varied by few of the comforts or amusements which in our day are habitually given to children. His mother was tender, and would probably have been kinder had she dared, for she is described as " the qualifier and moderator " of her husband's austerities, but his father was so harsh in his attitude that years later William had the feeling that he had been selected for especially strict treatment—" to me, who was perhaps never his favourite, his rebukes had a painful tone of ill humour and asperity."

This real or imagined injustice aroused an antagonism in the child, which remained in the thoughts of the man long after his father was dead, and there is little doubt that this circumstance had a profound effect in shaping Godwin's later life. The resentment bred of religious servitude in childhood produced eventually a stubborn independence and a passionate desire for freedom. Having been in youth the victim of physical austerity and of the tyranny of ideas enforced by others, William Godwin took as his life's work the liberation of man from the slavery of the mind and thence from the bondage of material coercion. Above all, he struggled for the freedom of children from the dominant opinions of their parents and masters, and sought to evolve an attitude towards education based on the natural development of inherent capacities rather than the coercive imposition of a mental pattern designed to turn the child into what his parents would like him to be. In his manhood he remembered clearly the unhappiness which, as a child, he had experienced from the ignorance of his parents. To the children who came under his care, whether they were his own or those of others, he acted according to the principles he had stated in his writings and endeavoured to build his relationships with them on a basis of equality, unhampered by the attempt to establish physical or intellectual domination. All these children seem to have regarded him with an affection and loyalty which could only spring from considerate treatment.

Thus the filial antagonism of young William Godwin resulted in an eventual and passionate denial of all the ideas which his father maintained. Only in the inflexibility with which he held the opinions he had formed for himself did Godwin later bear any resemblance to his Calvinist father. But during childhood open rebellion of this or any kind was hardly possible, and his hostility was manifested in an attitude of rivalry, a desire to be even more pious and austere than his father and thus to supplant him as the representative of moral rectitude and religious enthusiasm.

He was, intellectually, a very precocious child, and from his earliest days of articulate thought his concern was with matters of religious or literary interest. In manhood he could not remember ever having played any of the customary games of childhood, and, even though his memory may have been faulty in this respect, there is every reason to imagine him a solemn and contemplative child, given to reading and other serious activities rather than to the commonly light-hearted pursuits of childhood. Many years later he said, " I remember, when I was a very little boy, saying to myself, ' What shall I do, when I have read through all the books that there are in the world ? ' " This statement shows the importance of intellectual activity in the mind of this remarkable child. It also demonstrates the single-ness of purpose and the reliance on the products of the mind which supported Godwin throughout his career and led him to his feats of social thought and to the intellectual eminence which he eventually attained.

When Godwin was very young, a cousin of his father came to live with the family.  She had a small income of £40 a year, and out of this paid £16 a year for board and lodging, which supplemented substantially the small income on which this large family lived.  Miss Godwin, who had strong literary tastes and an even stronger Calvinist faith, undertook the education of William in literature and religion ;  at the time she seems to have wielded a much greater superficial influence than either of his parents. She varied his father's dry fare of sermons with a few profane works, but in general the reading she encouraged was of a religious nature.  The first books her pupil read were *Pilgrim's Progress* and *An Account of the Pious Deaths of Many Godly Children* by James Janeway.  Godwin was suitably impressed by these worthy examples.

Their premature eminence, suited to my age and situation, strongly excited my emulation.  I felt as if I were willing to die with them, if I could with equal success engage the admiration of my friends and mankind.

Though expressed in a different manner, Godwin's ambitions and objectives in later life changed very little from those he felt, or later says that he felt, as a small boy.  He was always concerned to " engage the admiration of my friends and mankind." Nor, when it finds expression in the performance of good actions or the production of valuable works, can this be regarded as a reprehensible motive.  It is largely on emulation of this nature, on the desire for the approval of one's fellows, that human achievement and progress are built.  Furthermore, the religious motives which were expressed so crudely in childhood were transformed into a concern for morality which was constant throughout Godwin's life.

Twice in these early years his education was interrupted by his father's removals from congregation to congregation.  In 1758 the family moved from Wisbech to Debenham, in Suffolk.  But here the worshippers were divided by a schism concerning the Arian doctrines, and the Arians became so strong during John Godwin's Trinitarian ministry that he was forced to retire, in

1760, to a small village, Guestwick, sixteen miles north of Norwich, which was unstirred by such theological strife.

The religious cast of thought imposed by his home life was confirmed at a dame's school at Guestwick, where William studied until the age of eight. The octogenarian mistress was " much occupied with matters of religion," and under her tuition he read the whole of the Bible, from Genesis to Revelation. In later years he considered that this instruction had a decisive effect on the formation of his character, and it is certain that, although afterwards he became a sceptic regarding religious forms and theological dogmas, the ethical standards underlying his ideas were essentially Christian.

At this time he first decided that his vocation was to become a dissenting minister, like his father. This was, perhaps, partly the natural consequence of the influence of so many religious people. But it was also a means to satisfy the " love of distinction " which he admits he possessed at an early age, and, perhaps more important still, it helped to balance his filial hatred by an imagined displacement of his father in the function wherein he appeared to wield most power. The boy could not wait until manhood to satisfy this desire, but already set up in rivalry, and " preached sermons in the kitchen, every Sunday afternoon, and at other times, mounted in a child's high chair, indifferent as to the muster of persons present at these exhibitions, and undisturbed at their coming and going."

When he was eight years old his schoolmistress died, and he was sent to a school conducted by a remarkable journeyman tailor, named Akers, who " had never had more than a quarter of a year's schooling in his life. The rest was the fruit of his own industry. . . . Few men ever excelled him in the rapidity and truth of his arithmetical operations," and he was " the best, or second best, penman in the county of Norfolk ".

At this school, attended by thirty boarders and seventy day scholars, William first came into close contact with children who had not been bred according to strict religious conventions. He was self-righteously appalled at their wickedness, and set out to convert a boy named Steele, to whom he preached of " sin and damnation " to such terrifying effect that he " brought tears to his eyes." He even obtained secretly the key of the chapel so that he could stand in his father's pulpit to preach and pray for his unfortunate schoolfellows whom he found so lacking in God's grace.

At this period his restricted experience was varied by a trip with Miss Godwin to Norwich, Wisbech and Lynn. This journey was attended by some surprising lapses into profane amusements. At Wisbech, for the only time in his life, Godwin watched the races with " great interest and passion." At Norwich he saw Otway's *Venice Preserved*, an experience which started an abiding passion for the drama and led him into the misapprehension that of all types of writing he was best fitted for the composition of plays. The results of this lapse of judgment were at once tragic and farcical, as will be seen in the history of his efforts to become a successful dramatist.

His present schoolmaster " soon openly declared that young Godwin was such a child as had never come under his observation before." This encomium, and their own closer observation of his erudite pursuits, soon led his parents to recognise that " the little Solomon," as Mrs Godwin called him, was no ordinary child, and at eleven he was sent to Norwich, where he became the sole pupil of Samuel Newton, the minister of the Independent congregation. Newton was a religious bigot, a disciple of Sandeman, " a celebrated north country apostle, who, after Calvin had damned ninety-nine in a hundred of mankind, has contrived a scheme for damning ninety-nine in a hundred of the followers of Calvin." In later years Godwin regarded his old schoolmaster with the greatest repugnance, but at the time of his pupillage he was sufficiently influenced by Newton's teachings to accept his peculiar religious beliefs and to benefit from his efficient teaching. It is also probable that Newton's extreme Wilkesian radicalism had a delayed influence on Godwin's own orientation towards radical thought, and helped to break the early pietistic attitude that might well have made him little more than a theological pedant.

Of his own character at this time, Godwin leaves a self-complacent description :

It was scarcely possible for any preceptor to have a pupil more penetrated with curiosity and a thirst after knowledge than I was when I came under the roof of this man. All my amusements were sedentary ; I had scarcely any pleasure but in reading ; by my own consent, I should sometimes not so much as have gone into the streets for weeks together. It may well be supposed that my vocation to literature was decisive, when not even the treatment I now received could alter it. Add to this principle of curiosity a trembling sensibility and an insatiable ambition, a sentiment that panted with indescribable anxiety for the stimulus of approbation. The love of approbation and esteem, indeed, that pervaded my mind was a nice and delicate feeling, that found no gratification in coarse applause, and that proudly enveloped itself in the consciousness of its worth, when treated with injustice.

Godwin received little in the way of " coarse applause " from Newton, who always regarded him as a victim of intellectual arrogance. On the other hand, he received not a little injustice, for Newton, according to the foolish custom of the time, felt it necessary to exorcise Godwin's self-approbation by a timely application of the birch. Godwin was justly indignant.

It had never occurred to me as possible that my person, which hitherto had been treated by most of my acquaintances, and particularly by Mrs Sothren and Mr Akers, who had principally engaged my attention, as something extraordinary and sacred, could suffer such ignominious violation. The idea had something in it as abrupt as a fall from heaven to earth. I had regarded this engine as the appropriate lot of the very refuse of the scholastic train.

It would seem that, if Godwin at this time suffered so much surprise at the application of corporal punishment, his father's austerities can rarely have been expressed in active physical cruelty.

Godwin's education under Newton was devoted principally to the expansion of his intellectual powers. He was introduced to a comparatively wide selection of literary works, for which he developed an enthusiasm that almost prompted him immediately to make literature rather than religion his chosen career. His earlier impulses prevailed, and he retained his determination to succeed in his father's profession. The cultivation of his physical powers was neglected, but this was due mostly to his own passion for study. He was sent to dancing classes in Norwich, but did not enjoy himself, displaying the clumsiness which is frequently shown by persons of intellectual inclinations.

Towards the end of his life, when he was over seventy, he published an essay " Of Youth and Age " (*Thoughts on Man*, 1831), in which he gives a picture of youth that confirms the impressions he had recorded thirty years before, in his middle age.

I find then in myself, for as long a time as I can trace backward the records of memory, a prominent vein of docility. Whatever it was proposed to teach me, that was in any degree accordant with my constitution and capacity, I was willing to learn. . . .

The thoughts that occurred to me, as far back as I can recollect them, were often shrewd ; the suggestions ingenious ; the judgments not seldom acute. I feel myself the same individual all through. Sometimes I was unreasonably presumptuous, and sometimes unnecessarily distrustful. Experience has taught me in various instances a sober confidence in my decisions, but that is all the difference. . . .

That Godwin had, indeed, changed very little in the essentials of his character during the passage from boyhood into manhood is shown by one piece of external evidence from the pen of the same Samuel Newton. Many years after Godwin's schooldays, a correspondence arose between the master and his former pupil over certain disagreements which the old Sandemanian not unnaturally held with parts of *Political Justice*. Godwin's dignity was affronted by a report of the strictures which Newton was said to have made, and he wrote to him in indignation. In one of his replies, which were couched in the most courteous phrases and can hardly be regarded justly to have merited the anger Godwin appears to have felt, Newton remarked,

Viewing it altogether, I own it is a wonderful production ; but I must confess that it has such a cast of character in it from its author, that I am inclined to think I should have known it to have been yours, had not your name stood in the title page.

From the tone of these letters one gains the impression that Newton was a man of moderate expression, if of fervent opinions, and it seems in fact that in boyhood Godwin did not regard him with quite so great an aversion as he felt in later years. Once, for instance, when he was taken for a while to live at home, he himself asked to go back to resume his studies with Newton. He rapidly and willingly took for his own the opinions of his master —" I was his single pupil and his sentiments speedily became mine." It is possible that Godwin unconsciously transferred to Newton the repugnance he felt for the opinions which Newton professed and to which he himself adhered firmly for some years. It is never easy to regard dispassionately either the opinions one has discarded or the people with whom one has shared them in the past.

3

Godwin's education under Newton terminated in 1771, when he had reached the comparatively early age of fifteen. Then, for a short period, he returned to his old school at Hildolveston and acted as usher to Mr Akers. This was the only period when he had actual experience of scholastic teaching, but, young as he was at the time and brief as was his employment—it lasted little more than a year—he was sufficiently observant of the effect of educational methods on the children under his charge to be able, some years later, to use this experience effectively in the development of his own theories.

At this period he continued and even increased his study of literature. He read through the works of Shakespeare, and planned an epic poem on the threadbare theme of Brute—which does not appear to have been completed. He began also to show signs of the scepticism which later characterised his approach to all established systems of thought or convention. The objects of his early doubt were not, however, religious or political, but the scientific theories then becoming popular, and particularly the conjectures of the astronomers. It is curious to notice that the future author of *Political Justice* should have based his criticisms largely on religious arguments. In *Thoughts on Man* (1831) he records a conversation with Mrs Akers on this subject :

I find that we have millions of worlds round us peopled with natural creatures. I know not that we have any decisive reason for supposing these creatures more exalted than the wonderful species of which we are individuals. We are imperfect ; they are imperfect. We fell ; it is reasonable to suppose that they have fallen also. It became necessary for the second person in the trinity to take upon him our nature, and by suffering for our sins to appease the wrath of his father. I am unwilling to believe that he has less commiseration for the inhabitants of other planets. But in that case it may be supposed that since the creation he has been making a circuit of the planets, and dying on the cross for the sins of rational creatures in uninterrupted succession.

It is possible that after the lapse of sixty years Godwin's memory made his comments on this occasion appear more mature and rational than they were in reality. Nevertheless, the attitude they express anticipates the analytical method by which Godwin was later to judge and reject all the beliefs he had previously taken for granted.

In November, 1772, while he was still teaching at Hildolveston, his father died, but this does not appear to have caused him any great sorrow.   His record of the event is laconic and even humorous :

He died at fifty years of age, but it was with considerable reluctance that he quitted this sublunary scene.   The last time I stood by his bedside, two or three days before he expired, he repeated with an anxious voice a hymn from Dr Watts' collection, the first stanza of which is as follows :—

> When I can read my title clear
>   To mansions in the skies,
> I'll bid farewell to every fear
>   And wipe my weeping eyes.

His mother was left with sufficient money to maintain herself modestly, and also to provide for William's further education. Her character, during her widowhood, became " considerably changed.   She surrendered herself to the visionary hopes and tormenting fears of the methodistical sect, and her ordinary economy became teazingly parsimonious."

Early in 1773 Godwin left the rural school and went to London, where he applied for admission to Homerton Academy. This was one of the dissenting colleges which, at a time when the entry of Nonconformists into the old universities was still made difficult by the requirements of orthodoxy, provided an inexpensive education, surprisingly sound and comprehensive, and in some respects even better than that dispensed at the conservative institutions of Oxford and Cambridge.

Homerton Academy, however, maintained an orthodoxy of its own, and Godwin was refused admission because of his adherence to the Sandemanian heresy.   After this failure he spent some months with relatives in Kent, where he planned further poetic masterpieces, and reinforced his theological attitude by studying anew the works of Sandeman.   In September, 1773, he applied to the dissenting college at Hoxton, and here there appears to have been no objection to his peculiar beliefs, for he was admitted without question.   Here the next five years of his life were passed in continuous study.

His tutor at Hoxton was the famous Dr Kippis, a philologist and classical scholar of high standing.   Kippis had long rejected Calvinism and now adhered to the doctrines of Arminius ; he had also a tendency to be sympathetic towards the Socinians. In politics he was an uncompromising radical, and played an active and prominent part in the various liberal and reformist movements of his day. There is no doubt that he had a profound, if delayed influence on Godwin's thought, but for the time being Godwin chose to assert his independence by acting contrarily to the general opinion of the college. Everybody else was an ardent Whig ; he became a Tory.

The prevailing opinions were those of Arminius and Arius, but I endured the fiery trial, and came out in my twenty-third year as pure a Sandemanian as I had gone in.

Although the college was small—it had only three tutors—its syllabus included " the classics, Hebrew, logic, ethics, divinity, rhetoric, the mathematics, natural philosophy and pneumatology." In addition, Godwin pursued his own studies in literature, and in order to assimilate all his learning thoroughly he worked continually and with a strict adherence to system.

. . . there was not a day passed in which I did not read a portion, first of the Greek, then of the Roman classics, another part of the day was appropriated to metaphysics, theology, and books of reasoning, a third to history, and so forward.

He maintained this systematic method throughout life.

His description, written more than twenty years later, of his activities during his college life, is not altogether modest, but significant of the thoroughness with which he always worked :

During my academical life, and from this time forward, I was indefatigable in my search after truth. I read all the authors of greatest repute, for and against the Trinity, original sin, and the most disputed doctrines, but I was not yet of an understanding sufficiently ripe for impartial decision, and all my enquiries terminated in Calvinism. I was famous in our college for calm and impassionate discussion ; for one whole summer I rose at five and went to bed at midnight, that I might have sufficient time for theology and metaphysics. I formed during this period, from reading on all sides, a creed upon materialism and immaterialism, liberty and necessity, in which no subsequent improvement of my understanding has been able to produce any variation. I was remarked by my fellow-collegians for the intrepidity of my opinions, and the tranquil fearlessness of my temper.

A further account, written towards the end of his life, gives a rather more sober account of the evolution of his thought without, however, contradicting the main tendency of the passage quoted above :

One of the earliest passions of my mind was the love of truth and sound opinion. " Why should I," such was the language of my solitary meditations, " because I was born in a certain degree of latitude, in a certain century, in a country where certain institutions prevail, and of parents possessing a certain faith, take it for granted that all this is right ? " This is matter of accident. " Time and chance happeneth to all " : and I, the thinking principle within me, might, if such had been the order of events, have been born under circumstances the very reverse of those under which I was born. . . .

During my college life, therefore, I read all sorts of books, on every side of any important question, or that were thrown in my way, that I could hear of. But the very passion that determined me to this mode of proceeding, made me wary and circumspect in coming to a conclusion. I knew that it would, if anything, be a more censurable and con-temptible act to yield to every seducing novelty than to adhere obstin-ately to a prejudice because it has been instilled into me in youth. I was therefore slow of conviction, and by no means " given to change." I never willingly parted with a suggestion that was unexpectedly furnished to me ; but I examined it again and again, before I consented that it should enter into the set of my principles.

Here, if we are to accept this as a faithful portrayal of Godwin in his adolescent years—and he was too conscientious in record-ing events and thoughts to be suspected of conscious deception—we see already at work the analytical mind which required only the impulse to make it turn to the systematic destruction of previously accepted systems of thought, in order to create in their place a way of thinking which seemed to follow from the natural processes of the unrestricted human reason. An important point, which also tends to confirm the authenticity of Godwin's account, is that this passage actually shows the conflict between the two sides of Godwin's reaction to his home influence, which in his father assumed a hostile form, to be countered at once by resistance and by emulation. The young man tells himself that he cannot accept any belief merely because it was the belief cultivated in his native environment, i.e., the belief of his father. He has therefore to examine such a belief thoroughly in order to find whether it really conforms to the findings of his own inde-pendent judgment. Nevertheless, he is reluctant to give up this belief, or to replace it by any new belief, until his examinations have left him no shred of reason on which to base its retention.

While, therefore, he wishes to destroy them, at the same time he has an impulse to vindicate his father's beliefs, and thus, vicariously, to become his father.

That, by the end of his college years, his faith in the religious precepts of his youth was not so completely unshaken as he would have us believe, and as he himself probably believed, is shown by a passage from his autobiographical fragment :

In the last year of my academical life I entered into a curious paper war with my fellow student Mr Richard Evans, an excellent mathematician, and a man of very clear understanding. The subject, the being of a God. Our papers were, I believe, seen by no person but ourselves. I took the negative side, in this instance, as always, with great sincerity, hoping that my friend might enable me to remove the difficulties I apprehended. I did not fully see my ground as to this radical question, but I had little doubt that grant the being of God, both the truth of Christianity, and the doctrines of Calvinism, followed by infallible inference.

The young man was playing with intellectual fire, and we know Godwin's sincerity too well to believe that, even in pretence, he would deny a belief of which he was thoroughly convinced. The fact that the existence of God was the main subject of his doubts is significant. Granted the existence of God, he did not choose to deny the validity of any detail of the religion which he and his father had up to then upheld, although in reality it is by no means sound philosophically to state that " the truth of Christianity and the doctrines of Calvinism " necessarily follow " by infallible inference " from a belief in the existence of God. It is perhaps not an unjustifiable suggestion that our argument should be extended, and that " God " should be regarded as being in Godwin's mind identical with his father. The statement then assumes a deep psychological significance, for if the authority of the father and the need to emulate him are granted, then the son must necessarily accept his beliefs in both Christianity and Calvinism. The inner struggle was not terminated when Godwin left Hoxton in 1778.

4

On leaving Hoxton, Godwin followed his plan of entering the ministry. After rejection by a congregation to whom he made a trial sermon at Christchurch, he was accepted as minister at the quiet little Hertfordshire town of Ware. He had now attained his desire to assume the profession and position of his father, and from this point onwards the tendency to rebel against the beliefs of his youth began to grow steadily stronger. He had proved himself as good as his father. Now, having assumed his father's authority, he was free of its domination, and could proceed to destroy the whole edifice of belief on which that authority had been based.

I had no sooner gone out into the world than my sentiments on both these points began to give way ; my toryism did not survive above a year, and between my twenty-third and my twenty-fifth year my religious creed insensibly degenerated on the heads of the Trinity, eternal torments, and some others.

Of his activities as a minister, and of the events which took place during this period, Godwin left little account, and it is possible that in this reticence we see the measure of his later repugnance for the values of his youth, against which he eventually revolted so violently. Almost the only important detail recorded concerning his residence at Ware is that here he encountered the Rev. Joseph Fawcet, a man whom Hazlitt described as " the most candid and unsophisticated of literary acquaintances " and whom Wordsworth took as his model for " The Solitary." Godwin regarded Fawcet as " one of the four principal oral instructors to whom I feel my mind indebted for improvement." The others were Thomas Holcroft, George Dyson and Samuel Taylor Coleridge.

Mr Fawcet's modes of thinking made a great impression upon me, as he was almost the first man I had ever been acquainted with, who carried with him the semblance of original genius.

One of Fawcet's topics of discussion was apparently " a declamation against the domestic affections," a contention which he held in common with the theologian Jonathan Edwards, and which so impressed Godwin that he used it extensively in the first edition of *Political Justice*. Later, having learnt from experience the positive value of these affections, he was to modify his ideas to such an extent that he ended by believing very nearly the opposite of what Fawcet had helped to teach him.

In August, 1779, he left Ware. Already he must have had doubts as to fitness for his profession, if not yet of the validity of the major items of his beliefs, for instead of taking up another living, he went to London and lived penuriously for four months in a little lodging near Cripplegate. No details remain concerning his immediate reason for leaving Ware, or what he hoped to accomplish by going to London. It is probable, however, that during this period he was again engaged at least in planning, if not in writing, future literary works, and that he was making contacts in the literary world of London. No doubt he also read widely, and we know from his own account that he studied with admiration the works of Burke and Fox, then the leaders of political radicalism.

His months in London do not appear to have brought him to any definite decision regarding his vocation, for early in 1780, probably when his funds had run low, he took a living at Stowmarket, in Suffolk. It was here that his early beliefs suffered the destructive blows from which they never recovered. " In 1781 there came to reside at Stowmarket Mr Frederic Norman, deeply read in the French philosophers, and a man of great reflection and acuteness." Norman introduced Godwin to the writings of Rousseau, Helvétius and d'Holbach, and the reading of these authors so severely shook his faith in the existence of God that he was glad to take advantage of a dispute " on a question of Church discipline " and resign his living.

He returned to London, where he took lodgings in Holborn and began to write for a living. He planned a series of biographies of English political figures, which he intended to publish periodically, but the first of these, of Lord Chatham, became so long that finally he decided to complete it as a separate volume. The remaining biographies in the series were never written.

He published the *Life of Chatham*, anonymously and at his own expense, in the spring of 1783. It was a dull and pedestrian work, written in an affected style and giving no indication of the profundity of thought which Godwin was later to demonstrate. Few writers at the age of twenty-seven have made a less promising start, and we can only echo Godwin's own words, that it was a " very wretched attempt."

Godwin's doubts on the validity of his ministry do not appear even at this time to have brought him to a satisfactory decision, for early in 1783 he resumed his profession by becoming a candidate at Beaconsfield, where he remained for some seven months. There his religious conflict continued. Finally, through the influence of Dr Priestley's writings, he abandoned the Calvinism of which he had been so vigorous an advocate, and adopted Socinianism, a doctrine which denied the divinity of Christ; " . . . my mind rested in that theory, to which I remained a sincere adherent till the year 1788."

The acceptance of this change in beliefs finally decided Godwin to leave the ministry. The ideas inculcated in his youth had been successively destroyed, he had outlived the need to emulate his father, and when, in the summer of 1783, he left Beaconsfield, it was to start on a career devoted to the education of humanity in order to make them fit to accept a freedom that contradicted the ideas in which he had been reared. The last traces of Calvinism were purged away, and the development of a libertarian philosophy now began. It was a development that embraced the next ten years of Godwin's life.

## PART II

# Years of Preparation
## 1784–1793

### I

APPROPRIATELY enough, for one who was to become primarily an advocate of the moral and social education of mankind to make them fit for a life of freedom, Godwin's first attempt to form a career was directed towards teaching, rather than literature. He planned a small private school, to consist only of twelve pupils, and, with financial assistance from some source which he does not specify in his autobiographical notes, he hired a furnished house at Epsom, and published a small prospectus, in which he set out his theory of education. The reply to his announcement was meagre and disappointing. " I never secured a sufficient number of pupils at one time to induce me to enter upon actual business."

It is, perhaps, not surprising that few people were attracted to support the project by giving their children into Godwin's charge, for the pamphlet, *An Account of the Seminary that will be opened on Monday the Fourth Day of August at Epsom in Surrey*, contains few of the practical and concrete details which are usually expected by parents looking for a school where they can send their troublesome children.

It is true that in the latter part of the prospectus Godwin makes certain vague propositions concerning the syllabus, stating that emphasis will be laid on the teaching of the Latin, Greek, French and English languages and literatures. He contends that the teaching of languages should start at the age of ten, but that earlier the pupils should receive moral training to induce an appreciation of voluntary benevolence and a sympathy for the oppressed. These he hopes to attain largely by means of a proper introduction to history.

21

Throughout the pamphlet, however, the stress is always laid on his theory of education, which is developed at length, and whose colouring of French revolutionary philosophy was likely to deter many of his possible clients.  To conventional parents of the eighteenth century there must have been something frightening in experimental ideas on education, and probably even the enlightened were less eager than their modern descendants to send their children to schools whose principal attraction is the theory of freedom on which their teaching is based.

If, however, the *Account of the Seminary* did not attract the parents of Godwin's day, it is nevertheless of some interest, because it is the first publication in which his leading ideas on society and education are sketched and presented to the public eye.  Here we find already the outline of the ideas that were expressed ten years later in *Political Justice*.  When the pamphlet was written, Godwin was still much under the influence of French thinkers, such as Rousseau and Helvétius, but he showed an independence of attitude which made him subject even such recent masters to his habitual criticism and analysis, so that in a number of points he rejected their ideas and adopted an independent viewpoint.  He was already involved in that intellectual process by which he tested every thought he expressed so thoroughly that, even if it had already been expressed by another, it seemed in a peculiar sense his own and fitted integrally into his philosophic scheme.

The pamphlet begins with a brief analysis of the nature of government, and a comparison of government and education, demonstrating that the latter is more important in human and social development.

The state of society is incontestably artificial ; the power of one man over another must be always derived from convention, or from conquest ; by nature we are equal.  The necessary consequence is, that government must always depend upon the opinion of the governed. Let the most oppressed people under heaven once change their mode of thinking, and they are free. . . . Government is very limited in its power of making men either virtuous or happy ; it is only in the infancy of society that it can do any thing considerable ; in its maturity it can only direct a few of our outward actions.  But our moral dispositions and character depend very much, perhaps entirely, upon education. . . . To mould these pliant dispositions, upon which the happiness of multitudes may one day depend, must be infinitely important.

Here, in the questioning of the value of government and the proclamation of the uses of education, we see already in formation the social attitude which was later to be developed in *Political Justice*. Later, Godwin was to estimate more highly the *power* of government to influence the lives of man, but he never ceased to deny its *value* or to uphold the usefulness of education. The first part of this quotation is, indeed, paraphrased with comparatively little alteration in *Political Justice*, where he says :

All government is founded in opinion. . . . Destroy this opinion and the fabric which is built upon it falls to the ground. It follows therefore that all men are essentially independent.

Later, Godwin discusses the ideas of Rousseau. He acknowledges the importance of many of his ideas, but contends that his system of education is made defective by its " inflexibility."

He then criticises the pedantry of conventional education, and from this proceeds to attack the idea of educating a child by means of severity and punishment.

He advocates that, instead of forcing the child, by moral or physical coercion, to learn what he is unwilling or unable fully to understand, the teacher should seek to gain his interest and confidence by a simple method which aids rather than stifles his natural development, and which gives him the greatest possible independence of action. In this way the child will be given no inducement to embrace falsehood.

Into the government of youth passion and caprice should never enter. The gentle yoke of the preceptor should be confounded as much as possible with the eternal laws of nature and necessity. . . .

His general criticism of the educational methods of his day is expressed in terms which might well be applied to the methods still frequently used in our own time, more than a century and a half afterwards.

Modern education not only corrupts the heart of our youth, by the rigid slavery to which it condemns them, it also undermines their reason, by the unintelligible jargon with which they are overwhelmed in the first instance, and the little attention that is given to accommodating their pursuits to their capacities in the second.

The moral virtues cannot be implanted in children ; they arise naturally and can only be encouraged by the teacher. On the other hand,

The vices of youth spring not from nature, who is equally the kind
and blameless mother of all her children ; they derive from the defects
of education.

This is an argument repeated on a larger scale in *Political Justice*,
with mankind in the place of the child, and the institution of
government in the place of the bad teacher.

As he contends that government should not interfere in the
moral regeneration of man, but should leave truth to fight its
own battles, so in this early essay he recommends the teacher to
foster the natural benevolence of the child, to encourage him in
co-operation, but to avoid the nurturing of a competitive feeling.

Emulation is a dangerous and mistaken principle of constancy.
Instead of it I would wish to see the connection of pupils consisting only
of pleasure and generosity.   They should learn to love but not to hate
each other.   Benevolent actions should not directly be preached to
them, they should strictly begin in the heart of the performer.   But
when actually done, they should receive the most distinguished applause.

For its time, this was a valuable and enlightened little manual
on sensible education, however unsatisfactory it may have been
as the prospectus of a progressive school.   Even today, in a large
number of schools, many of its ideals have still not been put into
practice.   But, in our study of Godwin's development as a
political thinker, it is most important because it marks how early
the main ideas of *Political Justice* had formed in his mind, and how
long he spent in their elaboration before they were finally
published to the world ten years later.

2

Having been forced to abandon his model school, Godwin
finally adopted literature as his regular profession.   Already he
had a number of literary acquaintances, including Fawcet and
Kippis, who had given him encouragement, and, although he
had yet no record of impressive achievements, it was evident to
those who encountered him that he was possessed of considerable
intelligence, erudition and tenacity.

He settled in London, and took lodgings near St Mary-le-
Strand.   He had little money, having lost the mysterious
" pecuniary assistance which had in some degree smoothed for
me the difficulties of the two preceding years, and enabled me

to publish on my own account the *Life of Chatham*, the friend who assisted me going abroad at this period, and leaving me forty pounds in his debt."

His old tutor, Dr Kippis, came to his assistance, by sending him a pupil, who paid a small but regular fee, and by introducing him to some of the London publishers. Of these, Stockdale gave him five guineas for a pamphlet supporting the Coalition Government which came to power in February, 1783. This, like other of Godwin's slighter and earlier works, appears to have vanished.

Another publisher, John Murray, accepted a pamphlet called *The Herald of Literature*, which was hardly more than a publisher's catalogue extolling the merits of *The Most Considerable Productions that will be made in the Course of the Ensuing Winter*. It is written pompously, but shows a certain development in the vigour of Godwin's style. Its judgments are unreliable and valueless, largely because all the works mentioned are praised indiscriminately. It is sufficient to mention that Gibbon is ranked below Hume as a historian, and also presumably below Robertson, the forgotten historian of America, since Godwin places the latter " second to Hume," an honour which " might satisfy the ambition of a Livy or a Tacitus." Moreover, he says of Fanny Burney, " There scarcely seems to exist a more original genius in the present age than this celebrated writer." When it is added that he praises Sheridan's improvements on Ben Jonson, it will be seen how immature and unsure are the critical standards which Godwin shows at this period.

Godwin received no money for *The Herald of Literature*, but a short time after Murray gave him the opportunity of writing articles for *The English Review*, a political monthly of a radical tone. For this work Godwin received two guineas a sheet, " in which employment it was my utmost hope to gain twenty-four guineas per annum." This small sum represented Godwin's sole regular income for some years to come. The work on *The English Review* brought him into the circle of political journalists and into contact with many of the literary and political figures of the time. His articles, unfortunately, are so little distinguished in style from the remainder of the material in this review as to be virtually unrecognisable, and Godwin himself has left no record of their identity.

B 2

For the rest, Godwin managed to make up his living by a multitude of small literary employments, which consumed a great deal of energy, but brought him very little money.

This was probably the busiest period of my life ; in the latter end of 1783 I wrote in ten days a novel entitled *Damon and Delia*, for which Hookham gave me five guineas, and a novel in three weeks called *Italian Letters*, purchased by Robinson for twenty guineas, and in the first four months of 1784 a novel called *Imogen, a Pastoral Romance*, for which Lane gave me ten pounds.

None of these hastily written works has survived, and from Godwin's laconic references it is reasonable to imagine that he himself regarded them as of no great merit. Even this tedious work did not wholly provide the means of livelihood, and Godwin also undertook such indirectly literary work as translation, correcting the writings of illiterate radical politicians and preparing indices for other writers. " Notwithstanding these resources," he says with what seems exaggeration, " for the most part I did not eat my dinner without previously carrying my watch or my books to the pawnbroker to enable me to eat."

Godwin was probably thinking with bitterness of his own days of over-worked journalism when he wrote, in his *Memoirs of Mary Wollstonecraft*, an eloquent description of the evils of a hack writer's life, which his future companion also endured during these same years.

It perhaps deserves to be remarked that this sort of miscellaneous literary employment seems, for the time at least, rather to damp and contract, than to enlarge and invigorate, the genius. The writer is accustomed to see his performances answer the mere mercantile purpose of the day, and confounded with those of persons to whom he is secretly conscious of a superiority. No neighbour mind serves as a mirror to reflect the generous confidence he felt within himself ; and perhaps the man never yet existed, who could maintain his enthusiasm to its full vigour in the midst of this kind of solitariness. He is touched with the torpedo of mediocrity.

One other work was published in 1784, which brought him no money, but which has intrinsic interest for an indication it gives of Godwin's earlier intellectual development. It was the *Sketches of History*, a volume of sermons. These appear to have been prepared some years earlier, for they represent an almost orthodox attitude to religion, which Godwin himself tells us he had already abandoned some considerable time before the publication of this volume. It is difficult to see why he should have chosen to publish the sermons when he did, unless it was from a desire not to waste anything he had written, akin to the motive which caused him in later years to preserve carefully every letter and scrap of paper that had some documentary bearing on his life. The book received some praise from the critics who specialised in religious writings, but this would seem to be rather an embarrassment than an advantage to one who was setting out to become a radical political writer.

In style and content the sermons are little better or more intelligent than many of the hundreds of similar and contemporary volumes from the pens of literary clergymen, and they have a dull and clumsy rhetoric which makes them tedious to read. In general their thought is of a kind to which few Calvinist adherents could easily have objected, except for a single statement, in which we can detect the beginning of the development that eventually caused Godwin's abandonment of Calvinism and orthodox religion in general.

In the first place, we may remember that God is our master, and proprietor, and may do what he will with his own. This observation asks one word by way of explanation. The creator may place his creature in a high or a low station ; he may make of some vessels to honour, and of others vessels to dishonour. But the right of the creator does not extend to the making an innocent being, in a comprehensive sense, and with a view to the whole of his existence, miserable. God himself has not a right to be a tyrant.

It is evident that the latter part of this statement invalidates the remainder, for if we allow that predestination can in any way be incomplete, or that there can be a limitation of the power of God, then, in effect, we destroy these beliefs, for they can survive only as complete and unconditional dogmas. There cannot be partial predestination, nor can there be any curtailment of the might of an Almighty. Admit the first doubt as to the complete applicability of either of these concepts, and it is inevitable that a process of thought conducted with intellectual clarity must eventually reach a complete rejection of both. This had already happened in Godwin's case by the time these words came from the press.

This sermon, then, might well be taken as marking symbolically the turn in Godwin's life that changed him from the strict Calvinist, the follower and rival of his father, into the equally

uncompromising libertarian whose resentment of the authority
he had experienced in childhood led him in manhood to fight
fearlessly against the very idea of authority, in the attempt to root
it from the minds of men and so banish it from the world of
material fact.

3

In 1785 Godwin's material fortunes improved, and he gained
both an established reputation as a political journalist and the
basis of a regular income which relieved him of the necessity of
uncongenial hackwork for the publishers.

In that year Sheridan and his associates founded a new Whig
review, *The Political Herald*. To this periodical Godwin contributed a series of pedestrian articles on such themes as "Sketches
of the Present Times" and "The Present State of Civil Liberty
in the World." His work was not remarkable, but the association
brought him the friendship of men like Sheridan and Curran. In
the following year the review failed, and an attempt was made
by Fox's supporters to revive it. Godwin was offered the editor-
ship, but refused it, having already developed that desire for
independence of party alignments which later he expressed
uncompromisingly in his criticism of political associations.

The second event that helped to establish him as a writer, and
to provide for his material welfare, was due once again to his old
tutor, Dr Kippis, who seems to have had considerable faith in
Godwin's potentialities. Kippis had become the editor of a
yearly publication, *The New Annual Register*, which was intended
by the Whigs to offset the influence of the Tory *Annual Register*,
and at his instance Godwin was entrusted with writing the
historical section. This was a publication of a much higher
standard than the reviews for which he had written previously,
and his work involved much research that was to be valuable in
his later writing. Also, by assuring him an income of sixty
guineas a year, it removed the need to do so much journalistic
work, and thus enabled him to devote more time to preparation
for future writing by means of reading and leisurely thought.
His work on *The New Annual Register* gave him a basic living for
some years, until he began writing *Political Justice* in 1791.

At this time his religious beliefs were again changing gradually,
and during 1785 he was sufficiently troubled with doubts to enter

into a correspondence with Dr Priestley, the Unitarian, on the subject of the existence of God. " But," he tells us, " I was not a complete unbeliever till 1787." A note which was apparently written at this time conveys the impression that the state of his religious thought was of a pantheistic and almost mystical nature, and that he had finally abandoned institutionalised religion.

> Religion is among the most beautiful and most natural of all things ; that religion which " Sees God in clouds and hears Him in the wind," which endows every object of sense with a living soul, which finds in the system of nature whatever is holy, mysterious, and venerable, and inspires the bosom with sentiments of awe and veneration.
> But accursed and detestable is that religion by which the fancy is hag-rid, and conscience is excited to torment us with phantoms of guilt, which endows the priest with his pernicious empire over the mind, which undermines boldness of opinion and intrepidity in feeling, which aggravates a thousand-fold the inevitable calamity, death, and haunts us with the fiends and retributory punishments of a future world.

It was to a very similar belief that he returned in his old age, when he wrote *The Genius of Christianity Unveiled*.

During these early years in London his personal life under-went a series of changes, which it will not be amiss to mention here.

He maintained his connection with his family, but it appears from surviving letters that they regarded with disapproval his retirement from the ministry and his abandonment of Calvinist beliefs.

One letter shows that Godwin already regarded himself as blessed with a vocation for the regeneration of humanity, though he does not appear ever to have been quite so impervious to the disapprobation of others as he would have us believe. It also illustrates the affection which existed between mother and son and which was to prevail until the mother's death, unaffected by the differences of opinion that arose between them on the most fundamental questions of belief.

> I am exceedingly sorry [he wrote to his mother] that you should suffer yourself to form so unfavourable an opinion of my sentiments and character as you express in your letter. Not that I am anxious so far as relates to myself what opinion may be formed of me by any human being : I am answerable only to God and conscience. But I am sorry, even without deserving it, to occasion you with the smallest uneasiness.
> You seem to regret my having quitted the character of a dissenting minister. To that I can only say, with the utmost frankness, whatever

inference may be drawn from it, that the character quitted me when I was far from desiring to part with it.

. . . If I could ever hope for his [God's] approbation, I have now more reason to hope for it than ever. My views, I think, were always right, but they are now nobler and more exalted. I am in every respect, so far as I am able to follow the dictates of my own mind, perfectly indifferent to all personal gratification. I know of nothing worth living for but usefulness and the service of my fellow creatures. The only object I pursue is to increase, as far as lies in my power, the quantity of their knowledge and goodness and happiness. And as I desire everything from God, I hope the situation in which I am now placed is that in which I am most likely to be useful. . . .

Godwin's early years in London, living in cheap lodgings and providing for his own needs, must have been very lonely, and although he was given to habits of solitary study, it is evident that there were times when he felt the need for some form of regular companionship. Thus during 1784 and 1785 he corresponded with his sister Hannah, with a view to obtaining a satisfactory wife. This curiously cold-blooded transaction, however, failed because Miss Gay, whom his sister recommended as " in every sense formed to make one of your disposition really happy," did not appear, on inspection, to suit Godwin's taste. He was " not struck with her," and did not again engage his sister as a potential matchmaker.

Some time later he solved the problem of companionship in a limited way by sharing a house with James Marshal. He had met Marshal as a fellow indexer in the days of literary drudgery. While Godwin soon abandoned this type of work, Marshal never rose above it. He seems to have been a loyal friend and a man of intelligence and good humour. Lamb said of him : " I have seen that man in many situations, and from my soul, I think that a more god-like honest soul exists not in the world." He remained Godwin's close friend for the rest of his life, and rendered him considerable services in the writing of some of his works, such as *Political Justice*.

In these days, Godwin rapidly increased the number of his friends and acquaintances. He was a man to whom friendship was of the greatest importance. His earlier biographer, Kegan Paul, remarks that :

Except the one great passion of his life, and even this was conducted with extreme outward and apparent phlegm, friendship stood to him in the place of passion, as morality was to him in the room of devotion.

All the jealousies, misunderstandings, wounded feelings and the like, which some men experience in their love affairs, Godwin suffered in his relations with his friends. Fancied slights were exaggerated ; quarrels, expostulations, reconciliations followed quickly on each other, as though they were true *amantium iræ*. And his relations with women were for the most part the same as those with men. His friendships were as real with the one sex as with the other, but they were no more than friendships.

Principal among the friends he made in these years were Thomas Holcroft and George Dyson, respectively the second and third of his " oral instructors." Holcroft was one of the strangest and most colourful figures of his time. The son of a shoemaker, he had started life as a stable boy, and eventually became a successful author, actor and impresario. Byron said of him that he had a strength of endurance " worth more than all the talent in the world," and Hazlitt wrote an admiring and admirable memoir of his life.

Vitality and irritability were Holcroft's two outstanding characteristics. These qualities resulted, during their twenty years of friendship, in many quarrels between him and Godwin. On the other hand, they made him an excellent foil for Godwin's arguments. Godwin himself frankly owned his intellectual debt, when he admitted :

My mind, though fraught with sensibility, and occasionally ardent and enthusiastic, is perhaps in its genuine habits too tranquil and unimpassioned for successful composition and stands greatly in need for stimulus and excitement. I am deeply indebted in this point to Holcroft.

It was through Holcroft's arguments that Godwin finally abandoned his Socinian beliefs and became an agnostic. Godwin, in his turn, converted Holcroft to radical political beliefs and made him one of the most enthusiastic antagonists of the prevailing social order.

George Dyson was a man some years younger than Godwin, who had enthusiasm and literary promise, but whose intemperance neutralised all the talents nature had given him. He was a good conversationalist and a penetrating thinker, from talking with whom Godwin considered he had gained a considerable improvement in his own mental resources. He was afflicted by an even more violent temper than Holcroft, and Godwin inevitably quarrelled with him frequently, often because he found it his duty to remonstrate with Dyson on the irregularity of his ways. In the end their differences of character forced them apart, and Dyson appears only in these early years of Godwin's literary life. Nevertheless, the place which Godwin accords him among the influences of his intellectual development is sufficient proof of his mental vigour.  Godwin's esteem, severely qualified by the circumstances, is shown in a letter of remonstrance which he wrote to Dyson towards the end of their friendship.

I hope, and still strongly incline to believe, that I shall one day see you, complete in talent, and free from every stain of those vices which I have always suspected, and now vehemently disapprove in you.  You have been one of my prime favourites, and whatever may be the vicissitudes of your character, the deviousness of your conduct, or the fermentation of your uncontrollable passions, they will all be watched by me with affectionate anxiety.  You may grieve me, but you cannot inspire me with anger.

Among the other friendships which Godwin began at this time were those with Fenwick and Fell, which lasted for many years. Of acquaintances he made many, particularly in political circles, of whom perhaps the most strange was Canning, then an Eton schoolboy, whom he met at Sheridan's and who, Godwin remarks somewhat complacently, " was very pressing on me for the cultivation of my acquaintance."

A relationship of a rather different character, which developed into a comparatively successful experiment in education, began in 1788, when his second cousin Thomas Cooper, then twelve years old, was orphaned by the death of his father, a ship's surgeon, in the East Indies.  Godwin, despite his own precarious circumstances, took the boy to live with him and undertook his education.  Mary Shelley suggests that this venture was a failure, and blames Godwin's deficiencies as an instructor.  Her note is of interest as an illustration of Godwin's method and character, but it should be remembered that Mary, an irrational and unstable woman, was not given to scrupulous exactitude in her reports, which should always be treated with reserve.

Godwin, who, from the very nature of his opinions, was led to analyse mind and draw conclusions as to character, had a sanguine faith in the practicability of improvement, and entertained rigid opinions on the subject of education.  Tom Cooper was a spirited boy, extremely independent and resolute, proud, wilful and indolent.  Godwin, conscientious to the last degree in his treatment of everyone, extended his utmost care to the task of education ; but many things rendered him unfit for it. His severity was confined to words, but these were pointed and humiliating. His strictness was undeviating ; and this was more particularly the case in early life, when he considered the power of education to be unlimited in the formation of character, the understanding and temper. He took great pains with his kinsman, and devoted attention and care to his instruction. To further his endeavours, he kept notes of the occurrences that disturbed their mutual kindness, evidently as appeals to the lad's own feelings and understanding, endeavouring to awake in him a desire of reparation when he had done wrong, and also of detailing and remarking on any defects in his own behaviour. These papers throw light on his own views of education, and show the conscientious and persevering nature of his endeavours. At the same time they display his faults as a teacher. He was too minute in his censures, too grave and severe in his instruction ; at once too far divided from his pupil through want of sympathy, and too much on a level from the temper he put into his lectures.

It must be borne in mind, even granting Godwin's failure to gain a completely successful result, that Thomas Cooper did not come under his care until he was already twelve. And it is by no means proved that the attempt was so great a failure as is assumed by Godwin's detractors. Godwin certainly demonstrated what Kegan Paul justly calls " extreme kindness and forbearance," and there is an indication of success in the frank and equal friendship which developed after Cooper reached maturity. Cooper became an actor, following Holcroft's advice, and for a while lived the miserable existence of a wandering player. During this time he sent Godwin many vivid and cordial letters telling his adventures and troubles. Eventually he emigrated to America, where he had some dramatic success, but finally declined into poverty.

4

The external event which had the most profound effect on Godwin's opinions and on the course of his life was the outbreak of the French Revolution in 1789. His philosophical and political theories and his hope for the future happiness of mankind had grown from his reading of the French thinkers of the eighteenth century. And now, suddenly, a whole nation had risen, had cast off its despotic king and privileged aristocracy, and had declared, through the mouths of its revolutionaries, an intention to build a community founded on the principles enunciated by Godwin's French masters. As yet the revolution was untainted by its later perversions, and the magic slogan of *Liberty, Equality, Fraternity* seemed to represent a glowing reality, instead of being recognised as a tinsel symbol whose meaning its users soon ceased to comprehend. It was natural, therefore, that at this time of apparent triumph for his own conceptions of truth and justice, Godwin should have been moved deeply ; indeed, there were few on whom the French Revolution had a more permanent effect.

My heart beat high with great swelling sentiments of Liberty. I had been for nine years in principles a republican. I had read with great satisfaction the writings of Rousseau, Helvétius and others, the most popular authors of France. I observed in them a system more general and simply philosophical than in the majority of English writers on political subjects, and I could not refrain from conceiving sanguine hopes of a revolution of which such writings had been the precursors.

Yet Godwin was not one of those who accepted the Revolution with wholly uncritical enthusiasm. There were points, both of practice and theory, on which he disagreed with his fellow radicals, and there were certain circumstances in the revolution whose possible development he regarded with the greatest disquiet. In 1801, when replying to his antagonists, he recapitulated his thoughts on this subject :

I never went so far, in my partiality for the practical principles of the French revolution, as many of those with whom I was accustomed to converse. I uniformly declared myself an enemy to revolutions. Many people censured me for this lukewarmness ; I willingly endured the censure. (*Thoughts Occasioned by Dr Parr's Spital Sermon.*)

In his autobiographical fragment he states clearly the reason for these reservations :

I never for a moment ceased to disapprove of mob government and violence, and the impulses which men collected together in multitudes produce on each other. I desired such political changes only as should flow purely from the clear light of the understanding and the erect and generous feelings of the heart.

The events of the French Revolution led to a great increase of radical activity in England. Old political societies were renewed, and many new associations were formed to profess sentiments for the French Revolution and to put forward various vague programmes for the regeneration of humanity.

Among the intellectuals there was a general enthusiasm for the Revolution and a new interest in political matters. But none among the writers of this period was more aware than Godwin of the possibilities implicit in the social changes that were taking place, and for some years his activity and thought were devoted almost completely to social concerns. He maintained a close observation of events, and mixed freely in political circles, where he met all the leading radicals. His principles did not allow him to join political associations, because he refrained from accepting any partisan doctrine that might interfere with his freedom of judgment. Nevertheless, he maintained contact with the radical societies, was present at the meeting of the Revolution Society on November 4th, 1789, when Dr Price preached his famous sermon celebrating the fall of the Bastille, and even went so far as to draft an address of congratulation from English Republicans to the French Revolutionaries.

He and Holcroft belonged to a small debating society, and of their activities therein John Binns, the political writer, says in his memoirs :

So prolix were these gentlemen, that a committee of the society was instructed to buy and did buy two fifteen-minute glasses, the society having adopted a rule that no member should speak for a longer time. I have no recollection to have seen either of these glasses turned when any member other than Godwin or Holcroft rose to speak.

Godwin appears, indeed, to have done much talking in these days, for Sheridan told him, probably in jest, " You ought to be in Parliament," and Godwin seriously considered following the suggestion. But it was by no means useless talk, for in those days there were great subjects for discussion, and it was by continual conversation with his friends, and particularly with Holcroft, that he developed the ideas later embodied in *Political Justice*.

My mind became more and more impregnated with the principles afterwards developed in my Political Justice ; they were the almost constant topic of conversation between Holcroft and myself ; and he, who in his Sceptic and other writings had displayed the sentiments of a courtier, speedily became no less a republican and reformer than myself.

During 1790 Godwin was still unsure of his future. Apart from his political journalism, he wrote " a tragedy on the story of St Dunstan, being desirous, in writing a tragedy, of developing the great springs of human passion, and in the choice of a subject of inculcating those principles on which I apprehend the welfare of the human race to depend." The play was not published and the manuscript has not survived, but the quality of the plays which Godwin wrote in later years gives little reason to suppose that it would have added to the value of his writings.

His circumstances, even after he had secured his small regular income from *The New Annual Register*, remained insecure and difficult, and at times he seems to have desired an escape from the vagaries of hack journalism, for he played with various ideas of gaining a regular employment, and applied unsuccessfully for a post in the Natural History Department of the British Museum. Towards the end of 1790, however, there occurred the circumstance that decided finally the course of his life.

5

Up to 1790 the predominance of Jacobin ideas had been undisputed in the intellectual world. But the ruling class had never paid more than lip service to the Revolution, which they regarded correctly as an indirect threat to their interests, and by the end of 1790 the defenders of reaction, who would have received scant hearing in the previous year, had rallied and, led by the renegade liberal, Edmund Burke, were conducting an anti-Gallic and anti-Jacobin campaign. This had, for its principal weapon, the terror it could induce in a bourgeois audience by vilification of the revolutionaries and exaggerated stories of the atrocities said to have been perpetrated by the Jacobins. The reactionary campaign had the full support of the court and the Tory leaders, and Burke's *Reflections on the French Revolution*, published in November, 1790, crystallised the alarm of the upper and middle classes and set on its way the swing of opinion that eventually involved England in the most bloody and expensive war it had yet endured.

Burke's *Reflections* were the first serious blow at the ideas of the revolution, and the Jacobins immediately realised the necessity of refuting them. Godwin was sufficiently concerned to form, with Holcroft and Thomas Brand Hollis, a small committee which undertook the publication of the most famous of the replies to Burke, Tom Paine's *The Rights of Man*, which appeared in March, 1791. The difficulty experienced by the committee in persuading a publisher to undertake the work showed the effect Burke's writings had already produced. At last, however, Paine's book appeared, to be greeted by a whimsical note from Holcroft to Godwin :

> I have got it—If it do not cure my cough it is a damned perverse mule of a cough—The pamphlet—From the row—But mum—We don't sell it—Oh, no—Ears and Eggs—Verbatim, except the addition of a short preface, which, as you have not seen, I send you my copy—Not a single castration (Laud be unto God and J. S. Jordan !) can I discover—Hey for the New Jerusalem ! The millennium ! And peace and eternal beatitude be unto the soul of Thomas Paine.

Tom Paine's book was one of many replies to the *Reflections ;* the others included Mary Wollstonecraft's *Vindication of the Rights of Man.* To Godwin all these replies seemed at best superficial. He saw that the real refutation of the established order of property and government must rest on a stronger basis than the mere answer to debating points, and he decided to write a work that would consider the whole field of politics and endeavour to establish the permanent and fundamental principles on which a just society could be founded.

With the maturing of events in France and of their influence on his English contemporaries, it became clear to Godwin that none of the radicals had realised completely the conclusions implicit in the French Revolution. To destroy monarchy and aristocracy as governmental institutions was a good thing, and on this point all the supporters of the Revolution, and many, like Mackintosh and Wordsworth, who later became its bitter enemies, were agreed. But that was as far as most of them went. Yet to evolve no clear idea of the society that should follow the abolition of such tyrannical institutions was to leave the way open for a return in some form to the oppression from which men had been relieved. Therefore Godwin felt that Paine and his followers did not, in fact, go nearly far enough in their condemnation of what he called " positive institution."

It is true that Paine had at least a glimpse of the true character of the state when he wrote his celebrated, but isolated, passage on government :

> Society is produced by our wants and government by our wickedness ; the former promotes our happiness positively by uniting our affections ; the latter negatively by restraining our vices. The one encourages intercourse, the other creates distinctions. The first is a patron, the last a punisher. Society in every state is a blessing ; but government even in its best state is a necessary evil. . . . Government, like dress, is the

badge of our lost innocence ; the palaces of kings are built on the
ruins of the bowers of paradise.

Paine, in this flash of insight, had epitomised the argument
against government which was later to sustain the libertarian
tradition down to our own day.  But it remained only a flash of
insight ;  in the remainder of his writings he was willing to suppose that a form of government could actually exist that might
be beneficial to humanity.  It was left to Godwin to carry the
condemnation of government and all other " positive institutions " to its logical and extreme conclusion.

It had become clear to him, as it was to no other man of his
day, that the real core of the problem of social misery lay not in
the superficial aspects presented by such questions as parliamentary representation and methods of taxation, but at a deeper
level, in the relations between men in society, and particularly
in the vital matter of property relationships, to which none of the
English followers of the Revolution had given serious consideration.  Accumulated property, he realised, was the basis of the
whole edifice of government and tyranny, at once its reason for
existence and its means of perpetuation.  Government was merely
the means by which the control of property remained in the
hands of the few ;  the privileged class which governed a country
was always the class that enjoyed the fruits of accumulated property.  Therefore, while Godwin recognised the evils of existing
forms of government, and went beyond his contemporaries even
in this matter in recognising the injustice of the very institution
of government, he was most sharply distinguished from them in
the fact that he laid his great stress on the need for the abolition
of accumulated property.  For, he realised, unless it were
abolished, a formal termination of government would still leave
power in the hands of those who controlled property and would
allow the resurrection of governmental forms and the continuance
of the social evils, such as war, which arise from property.

Already in 1791 he had written a letter to Sheridan from which
we see that he was approaching the anarchism that characterised
*Political Justice* and had already reached the conclusion that men
allowed to grow in freedom will naturally tend to be virtuous.

Liberty strips hereditary honours of their imaginary splendour, shows
the noble and the king for what they are—common mortals, kept in
ignorance of what other mortals know, flattered and encouraged in folly

and vice, and deprived of those stimulations which perpetually goad the hero and the philosopher to the acquisition of excellence. Liberty leaves nothing to be admired but talents and virtue, the very things which it is the interest of men like you should be preferred to all the rest. Pursue this subject to its proper extent, and you will find that— give to a state but liberty enough, and it is impossible that vice should exist in it.

*Political Justice* was planned in May, 1791. An entry in Godwin's diary makes the following reference to his decision :

This year was the main crisis of my life. In the summer of 1791 I gave up my concern in the *New Annual Register*, the historical part of which I had written for seven years, and abdicated, I hope for ever, the task of performing a literary labour, the nature of which should be dictated by anything but the promptings of my own mind. I suggested to Robinson the bookseller the idea of composing a treatise on Political Principles, and he agreed to aid me in executing it. My original conception proceeded on a feeling of the imperfections and errors of Montesquieu, and a desire of supplying a less faulty work. In the first fervour of my enthusiasm, I entertained the vain imagination of " hewing a stone from the rock," which, by its inherent energy and weight, should overbear and annihilate all opposition, and place the principles of politics on an immovable basis. It was my first determination to tell all that I apprehended to be truth, confident that from such a proceeding the best results were to be expected.

The arrangement with Robinson, with whom Godwin had already negotiated unsuccessfully for the writing of a Naval History, was finally concluded on July 10th. The agreement was relatively generous, and Godwin eventually received one thousand guineas for the book. Robinson advanced him the money to live during the period of writing, so that he would have no need to waste his time on hack journalism.

Godwin's decision was followed by long discussions with his friends, particularly Holcroft and Marshal, during which the detailed structure of the book was planned and elaborated. The actual work of writing did not begin until September, and took some sixteen months to complete. Godwin worked slowly and thoroughly, never writing more than six or seven pages a day, and often less.

Even as he wrote, his ideas were maturing steadily, and by the time of completion he emerged a far more convinced and thorough revolutionary than he had been at the start. The development is evident in the book itself, for the setting of the type and even the printing of the sheets were begun while he was still engaged on writing the latter part.

Godwin realised the unevenness arising from this circumstance, and gave an apology for this, as well as for the haste in which the whole book was written, a haste which indeed is hardly to be detected in his polished style and consummate argument.

The printing of the following treatise, as well as the composition, was influenced by the same principle, a desire to reconcile a certain degree of dispatch with the necessary deliberation. The printing was for that reason commenced long before the composition was finished. Some disadvantages have arisen from this circumstance. The ideas of the author became more perspicuous and digested as his enquiries advanced. The longer he considered the subject, the more accurately he seemed to understand it. This circumstance has led him into a few contradictions. The principal of these consists in an occasional inaccuracy of language, particularly in the first book, respecting the word " government." He did not enter upon the work without being aware that government by its very nature counteracts the improvement of individual mind ; but he understood the full meaning of this proposition more completely as he proceeded, and saw more distinctly into the nature of the remedy. This, and a few other defects, under a different mode of preparation would have been avoided. The candid reader will make a suitable allowance. The author judges upon a review that these defects are such as not materially to injure the object of the work and that more has been gained than lost by the conduct he has pursued.

In fact, to the student who wishes to observe the metamorphosis of Godwin's attitude from one very close to that of Jacobin radicals, like Tom Paine, to an anarchism ahead of the ideas of any of his contemporaries, the manner in which the book grows with the development of his theories is interesting and valuable.

6

Godwin discussed his work and ideas with all his friends and acquaintances, and the project aroused wide interest, at a time when new ideas and new philosophies were always subjects for lively discussion. In his diary of 1792 he records with a certain self-satisfaction :

During this year I was in the singular situation of an author possessing some degree of fame for a work still unfinished and unseen. I was introduced on this ground to Mr Mackintosh, David Williams, Joel Barlow, and others, and with these gentlemen, together with Mr Nicholson and Mr Holcroft, had occasional meetings, in which the principles of my work were discussed.

Mackintosh was the author of *Vindiciæ Gallicæ*, one of the replies to Burke, but later he became an apostate, and, for his criticism of the revolutionary ideas he had formerly held, obtained a knighthood. Joel Barlow was an American poet who at one time acted as Ambassador to Napoleon, and who, as a confidential friend of Thomas Jefferson, the radical President of the United States, represents a channel through which Godwin's ideas may have had a more or less direct effect on the native American anarchists and near-anarchists like Thoreau, Tucker and even Emerson.

Another celebrity whom Godwin met at this time was Horne Tooke, the former Wilkesian,

to whose etymological conversation and various talents I am proud to acknowledge myself greatly indebted, though these came too late to be of any use to me in the concoction of my work, which was nearly printed off before I had first the pleasure of meeting this extraordinary and admirable man.

Horne Tooke does not appear to have reciprocated Godwin's high opinion. According to contemporary reports, he treated him with a supercilious condescension. Coleridge says that he referred to him as " Little Godwin " and had no appreciation of the extent of Godwin's abilities. Years later, however, when Godwin had saved him from being hanged, Horne Tooke was to modify his attitude.

During this period, also, Godwin began that series of friendships with talented and beautiful women which was one of the remarkable features of his life. The reports that have come to us from a variety of sources suggest that he was possessed of no extraordinary personal attractiveness. He had a large head and —one gathers from Northcote's portrait—a high and well-formed brow. Southey spoke of his " noble eyes," but objected violently to his long nose, which Hazlitt, on the other hand, regarded with great admiration. His body was thickset, his legs short, and he was awkward and sluggish in his movements. He dressed usually in dull, clerical-looking clothes and retained the appearance of a clergyman—more than twenty years later Thomas Jefferson Hogg still found him looking like a dissenting minister. His voice was unimpressively thin, and he was reputed to be a poor and slow-witted conversationalist—though Holcroft disagreed with the general opinion on this subject.

He was nevertheless very vain, self-opinionated and pontifical in his expression of opinion, retaining the manner of an ineffective preacher, and was regarded by many as rude and abrupt in his contradiction of ideas with which he disagreed. Crabb Robinson was angry because Godwin treated him—deservedly but perhaps tactlessly—as a being of inferior intelligence, and Hazlitt said to Northcote :

> Like most authors, he has something of the schoolmaster about him, and wishes to keep up an air of authority. What you say may be very well for a learner, but he is the oracle. You must not set up for yourself, and to keep you in due subordination, he catechises and contradicts you from mere habit.

Godwin had also an irritable disposition, and was so sensitive to what he considered insults that he was continually taking offence at actions or statements of his acquaintances. The resultant quarrels he referred to in his diary as " démêlés," and the frequency with which this word appears is a measure of the instability of Godwin's temper, which earned him the title of Sir Fretful from Marshal and other friends.

Yet, despite these unattractive qualities, there is no doubt that Godwin attracted the affection and friendship of many men and women of uncommon ability and intellect. He had a fundamental soundness of thought and action, a forthright honesty which underlay his outspoken rudeness, and a kindness and sympathy for the unfortunate, expressed in a generosity that extended to the limit not only of his own purse but also of those from which he could borrow or beg. His awkward silences or pontifical speeches in the crowded drawing-room were balanced, for his intimate friends, by the genial companionship of more private intercourse. Above all, he seems to have had some charm which his enemies could not detect or his friends define, but which had a real influence on those who attained his close friendship. Nothing else will explain the fact that he enjoyed the affection of men as varied in their natures as Coleridge, Lamb, Hazlitt, Curran and Holcroft, that men like Samuel Rogers and Northcote spoke of him always with esteem, and that so many charming women should have been willing to accept his friendship.

In 1791, he encountered the most famous of these women, who was also to become the most intimately related to him. This was

Mary Wollstonecraft, whom he met at dinners given by the publisher Johnson in November of that year, at which Tom Paine also was present. The result of this first meeting appears to have been mutual dislike.

The interview was not fortunate. Mary and myself parted mutually displeased with each other. I had not read her *Rights of Woman*. I had barely looked into her *Answer to Burke*, and been displeased, as literary men are apt to be, with a few offences against grammar and other minute points of composition. I had therefore little curiosity to see Mrs Wollstonecraft, and a very great curiosity to see Thomas Paine. Paine, in his general habits, is no great talker ; and, though he threw in occasionally some shrewd and striking remarks, the conversation lay principally between me and Mary. I, of consequence, heard her, very frequently, when I wished to hear Paine. (*Memoir of Mary Wollstonecraft.*)

Godwin and Mary Wollstonecraft met again on several occasions before her departure for France in 1792, but their relationship did not improve through these early meetings.

The woman with whom Godwin was on the closest terms of friendship in these days was Mrs Inchbald, the actress and novelist, who was regarded as one of the best writers of her day, and whose novels are in some ways superior to those of writers, like Mrs Radcliffe, whose reputation has survived while hers has declined almost to nothing. Godwin became acquainted with her through having read manuscripts of her books for Robinson, and a close friendship ensued, which survived for some years.

Godwin could not fail to admire her [says Mary Shelley] ; she became and continued to be a favourite. Her talents, her beauty, her manners were all delightful to him. He used to describe her as a piquante mixture between a lady and a milkmaid, and added that Sheridan declared she was the only authoress whose society pleased him.

Among the other beautiful women whose society Godwin enjoyed were Amelia Alderson, the Belle of Norwich, for whom he developed a sentimental attachment, but who later married the painter John Opie ; Maria Reveley, the wife of a liberal architect who had become acquainted with Godwin through Holcroft —Godwin's visits to her became so frequent that Reveley's jealousies were aroused and Godwin had to abandon his attentions until, years later, they were renewed in somewhat dramatic circumstances ; " Perdita " Robinson, the famous Shakespearean actress whose portraits were painted by the most celebrated artists of her time, who became the mistress of the Prince Regent, wrote poor novels in the Godwinian manner, and died in poverty, comforted only by the stalwart adherence of a few old friends like Godwin and Peter Pindar ; and Mrs Siddons, the most accomplished actress of her time, immortalised by Reynolds as The Tragic Muse.

But the years during which Godwin was writing *Political Justice* were not merely a time of expanding fame for the author of this yet unpublished work. They represented a period of increasing anxiety for those who professed revolutionary beliefs and sought to spread them by means of their writing or speech. After Burke's attack on the French Revolution, there had been a steady increase in the forces both supporting and attacking the Jacobins, and an equally strong increase of acrimony between the two parties. The respectable middle classes became more and more alarmed with stories of the Terror, and the revolutionaries more bellicose in their attacks on the constitution.

The London Corresponding Society was founded early in 1792, and rapidly increased to a membership of 30,000, mostly among petty tradesmen and literate artisans. It was only the principal of many clubs and societies which arose and added to the alarm of the bourgeoisie and the Government. It was founded to advocate parliamentary reforms, but very soon its meetings became discussions at which every kind of revolutionary idea was promulgated. Holcroft was an enthusiastic participant, but Godwin, true to his principles, remained aloof, and learned from observation of this and other political societies that such associations are as useless in practice as he had before held them to be in theory. The revolutionism preached at the meetings of the Corresponding Society ranged from Holcroft's non-violent Godwinian anarchism, to the demagogic advocacy of Jacobin violence by such figures as Horne Tooke and Thelwall, who gained a satisfaction of their vanity in daring speeches full of sedition and " hanging matters." In spite of the talk of revolution, the Corresponding Society was relatively harmless, so far as its ability to carry out an insurrection was concerned. Nevertheless, it represented a tendency in thought which had become feared by Pitt and his fellows of the Government, who, rightly, regarded the free development of opinion as a danger to their own corrupt tyranny.

Burke's fulminations and the writing of various hacks hired by the Government had prepared the ground for a beginning of repression, and a favourable emotional atmosphere was created by the feeling of the imminence of war between England and revolutionary France. The attack on the radicals began on a small scale. Booksellers were prosecuted for selling seditious writings, like *The Rights of Man*. Small organisations for discussion were closed down through Government threats. In November, 1792, the little debating society to which Godwin belonged became a victim to the spreading oppression. In December the attack began to show its full savagery, when Tom Paine was sentenced to death for writing *The Rights of Man*. Paine, fortunately, had already escaped to the Continent, having been warned by William Blake that the officers of the Crown were about to apprehend him.

In such an atmosphere, it is natural that the writer of a political work which attacked the very basis of the existing governmental system should feel misgivings regarding the fate of his book and the kind of persecution to which he would be subjected. Godwin experienced such fears, but overcame them and proceeded with a high courage to write what was in his mind, and publish it regardless of consequences. In the preface to *Political Justice*, dated January 7th, 1793, barely a month after the sentence on Paine, he stated his position with a dignity which shows the calm bravery that lay behind the dull exterior of this quiet scholar :

The period in which this work makes its appearance is singular. The people of England have assiduously been excited to declare their loyalty, and to mark every man as obnoxious who is not ready to sign the Shibboleth of the constitution. Money is raised by voluntary subscription to defray the expense of prosecuting men who shall dare to promulgate heretical opinions, and thus to oppress them at once with the enmity of government and of individuals. This was an accident wholly unforeseen when the work was undertaken, and it will scarcely be supposed that such an accident could produce any alteration in the writer's designs. Every man, if we may believe the voice of rumour, is to be prosecuted who shall appeal to the people by the publication of any unconstitutional paper or pamphlet, and it is added that men are to be prosecuted for any unguarded words that may be dropped in the warmth of conversation and debate. It is now to be tried whether, in addition to these alarming encroachments on our liberty, a book is to fall under the arm of the civil power which, beside the advantage of having for one of its express objects the dissuading from all tumult and violence, is by its very nature an appeal to men of study and reflection.

It is to be tried whether a project is formed for suppressing the activity of mind and putting an end to the disquisitions of science. Respecting the event in a personal view the author has formed his resolution. Whatever conduct his countrymen pursue, they will not be able to shake his tranquillity. The duty he is most bound to discharge is the assisting the progress of truth ; and if he suffer in any respect for such a proceeding, there is certainly no vicissitude that can befall him that can ever bring along with it a more satisfactory consolation.

But exclusively of this precarious and unimportant consideration, it is the fortune of the present work to appear before a public that is panic struck, and impressed with the most dreadful apprehensions of such doctrines as are here delivered. All the prejudices of the human mind are in arms against it. This circumstance may appear to be of greater importance than the other. But it is the property of truth to be fearless and to prove victorious over every adversary. It requires no great degree of fortitude to look with indifference on the false fire of the moment and to foresee the calm period of reason which will succeed.

With this calm challenge to the enemies of liberty, *Political Justice* was published in February, 1793.

The following chapter will be devoted to a somewhat lengthy exposition of the main contentions put forward in *Political Justice*. This seems to me particularly necessary in view of the fact that there is now no edition of this book readily available in England, except on the more remote shelves of a few public libraries.

## PART III

# Political Justice

## 1793

### I

G ODWIN starts his enquiry from the assumption " that the happiness of the human species is the most desirable object for human science to promote, and that intellectual and moral happiness or pleasure is extremely to be preferred to those which are precarious and transitory." This object he finds to be intimately connected with the political functioning of society, in so far as " erroneous and corrupt government was the most formidable adversary to the improvement of the species." From this it follows that political enquiry is "the first and most important subject of human investigation." By *politics*, Godwin makes it clear that he means not merely the practical functioning of governmental institutions, but also the moral basis of human intercourse within society. Therefore he wishes to make his book " exclusively of its direct political use, an advantageous vehicle of moral improvement . . . from the perusal of which no man should rise without being strengthened in habits of sincerity, fortitude and justice."

He proceeds to examine the record of political institutions in their relationship to the happiness of men. In a few condensed pages he brings all history to support his contention that up to his own day governments have always bred terrible wars, when millions of men have died for causes in which they had not the least personal concern. " It is an old observation, that the history of mankind is little else than the history of crimes." Nor does the domestic policy of governments give any more satisfaction than their foreign transactions. In all countries men continue to live in poverty, and the only means by which their discontent is counteracted is not reason, but repression.

Such considerations show that government cannot be regarded as " a neutral and unimportant concern." It is possible that these evils are incapable of remedy, but it is nevertheless worth while to consider whether they cannot be extirpated.

Men may one day feel that they are partakers of a common nature, and that true freedom and perfect equity, like food and air, are pregnant with benefit to every constitution. If there be the faintest hope that this shall be the final result, then certainly no subject can inspire to a sound mind such generous enthusiasm, such enlightened ardour and such invincible perseverence.

Godwin bases his belief in the probability of the improvement of society on four considerations, which are discussed in turn.

1. *The moral characters of men are the result of their perceptions.* This contention is based on a belief that, while the physical nature of man may be determined by heredity and given him at birth, his moral and intellectual characters are shaped by the influence of environment, of impressions exerted after birth. Godwin does not go so far as Helvétius, who proclaimed the complete equality of all newly born children, and he agrees that some children will be physically better equipped than their weaker brethren to benefit from the impressions they receive. Nevertheless, the difference is of degree, not of kind, for

the moral causes that awaken the mind, that inspire sensibility, imagination and perseverance, are distributed without distinction to the tall or the dwarfish, the graceful or the deformed. . . .

As man's moral character is made by impressions received after birth, there is no such thing as an " original propensity to evil." " We are neither virtuous nor vicious as we first come into existence " and " our virtues and vices may be traced to the incidents which make the history of our lives." Hence it follows that if the environment in which men live can be changed, so can their moral nature, and that if certain kinds of external influences are eliminated, men can cease to be vicious.

Furthermore, while moral characters are determined by environment, men's voluntary actions originate in opinion. Godwin is careful to distinguish voluntary actions from the actions which, while not strictly involuntary, are based on habits or customs of thought. The voluntary action springs from a judgment of goodness or desirability, and is thus an act of the reason.

Men always act upon their apprehension of preferableness. There are few errors of which they are guilty which may not be resolved into a narrow and inadequate view of the alternative presented for their choice. Present pleasure may appear more certain and eligible than distant good. But they never choose evil as apprehended to be evil.

In so far as men's actions are based on reason, they can be changed by rational persuasion, and even the influence of environment can often be countered by the proper development of opinion.

2. *Of all modes of operating upon mind government is the most considerable.* Here Godwin shows that literature and education have a great influence over the minds of men, but that these influences are limited in comparison with that of political institutions. (Note the change in emphasis from the early pamphlet in which he gave education the higher place.)

. . . political institution is peculiarly strong in that very point in which the efficacy of education was deficient, the extent of its operation. . . . All the effects that any principle adopted into the practice of a community may produce, it produces on a comprehensive scale. It creates a similar bias in the whole or a considerable part of the society.

Thus a despotic government will render men pliant, but a society based on liberty and truth will render them " resolute and independent." In an imperfect society superstition, cruelty and falsehood flourish. " But however powerful these errors may be, the empire of truth, if once established, would be incomparably greater."

Error thrives only when it is encouraged and supported by positive institutions and governments. Left to its own operations the human mind would naturally tend to detect and reject error and approach steadily nearer to the truth.

Injustice therefore by its own nature is little fitted for a durable existence. But government " lays its hand upon the spring there is in society and puts a stop to its motion." It gives substance and permanence to our errors. It reverses the genuine propensities of mind, and instead of suffering us to look forward, teaches us to look backward for perfection. It prompts us to seek the public welfare, not in innovation and improvement, but in a timid reverence for the decisions of our ancestors, as if it were the nature of mind always to degenerate and never to advance.

3. *The good and ill effects of political institution are not less conspicuous in detail than in principle.* In support of this statement

Godwin gives a brief but vivid account of the principal social evil of his day, the vast inequality of property, which causes a minority to degenerate in ostentatious luxury and the great majority to live in toil and penury.

This condition is aggravated by " the luxury, the pageantry and magnificence with which enormous wealth is usually associated," and the " insolence and usurpation of the rich," all of which make poverty more bitter by emphasising the differences between the rich and the poor, the two nations of the nineteenth century radicals.

Existing political institutions favour these conditions in a number of ways. Firstly, legislation favours the rich against the poor. Their property is protected by unfair laws, taxation is contrived to favour them, and " offences which the wealthier part of the community have no temptation to commit are treated as capital crimes. . . . Monopolies and patents are lavishly dispensed to such as are able to purchase them ; while the most vigilant policy is employed to prevent combinations of the poor to fix the price of labour. . . ." Secondly, the law is generally administered in favour of the rich. Thirdly, the conditions associated with political institutions, which give to certain individuals power and privilege, tend " greatly to enhance the imagined excellence of wealth."

4. *Perfectibility is one of the most unequivocal characteristics of the human species, so that the political as well as the intellectual state of man may be presumed to be in a course of progressive improvement.* Godwin reinforces his statement by making a comparison between the primitive and the civilised states of man. He pays particular attention to the development of language and writing, as examples of consistent improvement, and then, referring in passing to the other achievements of human genius, the material victories over nature as well as " all the wonders of painting, poetry, eloquence and philosophy," concludes :

Is it possible for us to contemplate what he has already done without being impressed with a strong presentiment of the improvements he has yet to accomplish ? . . . Let us look back, that we may profit by the experience of mankind ; but let us not look back as if the wisdom of our ancestors was such as to leave no room for future improvement.

Some of the most violent criticism of *Political Justice* was based on Godwin's statement on the perfectibility of man, and in the third edition he gives a clearer definition of the term *perfectibility*.

By perfectible it is not meant that he is capable of being brought to perfection. But the word seems sufficiently adapted to express the faculty of being continually made better and receiving perpetual improvement ; and in this sense it is here to be understood. The term perfectible, thus explained, not only does not imply the capacity of being brought to perfection, but stands in express opposition to it. If we could arrive at perfection, there would be an end to our improvement. There is, however, one thing of great importance that it does imply : every perfection or excellence that human beings are competent to conceive, human beings, unless in cases that are palpably and unequivocally excluded by the structure of their frame, are competent to attain.

Having thus established his theoretical premises, Godwin now proceeds to his examination of the principles underlying social and political institutions.

2

The discussion of the principles of society opens with a statement of the difference between society and government.

Men associated at first for the sake of mutual assistance. They did not foresee that any restraint would be necessary to regulate the conduct of individual members of the society towards each other or towards the whole. The necessity of restraint grew out of the errors and perverseness of the few.

The study of social principles is " strictly speaking a department of the science of morals. Morality is the source from which its fundamental axioms must be drawn, and they will be made somewhat clearer in the present instance if we assume the term ' justice ' as a general appellation for all moral duty."

Justice is further defined as " a rule of conduct originating in the connection of one percipient being with another."

Towards other individuals it is incumbent on us to do all in our power according to their need and worth. This does not mean that we should neglect our own needs, for we ourselves are part of the whole, and, except in extraordinary circumstances, " it is just that I should be careful to maintain my body and my mind in the utmost vigour and the best condition of service."

Our property and our persons we hold in trust for mankind. "I am bound to employ my talents, my understanding, my strength and my time for the production of the greatest quantity of general good. . . ."

But justice is reciprocal. If it be just that I should confer a benefit, it is just that another man should receive it, and if I withhold from him that to which he is entitled, he may justly complain.

"Moral justice" is the "criterion for the investigation of political truth." What is just between men individually is just for society as a whole, for "society is nothing more than an aggregation of individuals. Its claims and its duties must be the aggregate of their claims and duties, the one no more precarious and arbitrary than the other." Society cannot "change eternal truth or subvert the nature of men and their actions," and it has therefore no right to demand that we should do more or other than justice. On the other hand, it is the purpose of society to do for its members "everything that can contribute to their welfare. But the nature of their welfare is defined by the nature of mind. That will most contribute to it which enlarges the understanding, supplies incitements to virtue, fills us with a generous conscience of our independence, and carefully removes whatever can impede our exertions."

In estimating our duty, a difficulty arises on "the difference that may exist between abstract justice and my apprehensions of justice. When I do an act wrong in itself, but which as to all the materials of judging extant to my understanding appears to be right, is my conduct virtuous or vicious?"

Godwin answers emphatically that

Morality is, if anything can be, fixed and immutable; and there must surely be some strange deception that should induce us to give to an action eternally and unchangeably wrong the epithets of rectitude, duty and virtue.

The fact remains that men are bounded in their apprehension of justice by the limits of their knowledge and ability. Duty therefore consists in serving the general good to the full extent of our capacities. It cannot command us to do what is beyond our powers. On the other hand, incapacity or ignorance cannot make an act unjust in itself partake of the nature of justice or duty.

Since men cannot, perhaps, be expected to be absolutely

virtuous, they should endeavour to form a virtuous disposition.

A virtuous disposition is of the utmost consequence, since it will in the majority of instances be productive of virtuous actions ; since it tends, in exact proportion to the quantity of virtue, to increase our discernment and improve our understanding ; and since, if it were universally propagated, it would immediately lead to the great end of virtuous actions, the purest and most exquisite happiness of intelligent beings. But a virtuous disposition is principally generated by the uncontrolled exercise of private judgment and the rigid conformity of every man to the dictates of his conscience.

This can be attained only if a moral equality of men is admitted. Physically and mentally, it must be granted that the circumstances of environment have created great irregularities among men. On the other hand, even these irregularities do not justify or enable one man to hold others in his power.

There is no such disparity among the human race as to enable one man to hold several other men in subjection, except so far as they are willing to be subject. All government is founded in opinion. Men at present live under any particular form because they conceive it their interest to do so. One part indeed of a community or empire may be held in subjection by force ; but this cannot be the personal force of their despot ; it must be the force of another part of the community, who are of opinion that it is their interest to support his authority. Destroy this opinion, and the fabric which is built upon it falls to the ground. It follows therefore that all men are essentially independent.

Even if physical equality has limitations, there can be none to moral equality. Justice must be applied to all men in equal measure, and opportunities and encouragement should be given without discrimination.

The same independence, the same freedom from any such restraint as should prevent us from giving the reins to our own understanding or from uttering upon all occasions whatever we think to be true will conduce to the improvement of all. There are certain opportunities and a certain situation most advantageous to every human being, and it is just that these should be communicated to all, as nearly at least as the general economy will permit.

The duties of man are governed by the natural laws of morality and truth. What of his rights ? Godwin exposes the unclearness of the idea of the " Rights of Man," which forms part of the stock of ideas common to all liberal movements, and denies its validity.

By right, as the word is employed in this subject, has always been understood discretion ; that is, a full and complete power of either doing a thing or omitting it without the person's becoming liable to animadversion or censure from another ; that is, in other words, without his incurring any degree of turpitude or guilt.

But if we grant a morality by which men's actions can be judged, then in this sense man has no rights, for morality already indicates what he should do. Except in insignificant matters where his actions can have no possible effect on the general good, he has no " right " of discretion, but should act according to his conception of moral action.

It is scarcely necessary to add that if individuals have no rights, neither has society, which possesses nothing but what individuals have brought into a common stock.

Men have claims, not " rights," over the assistance of their fellows, but society or government in themselves have no rights or claims over men. Thus, while men have no " right " to freedom of conscience or speech, morality demands that these should exist for the apprehension and spreading of the truth, and no aggregate has the right " to assume the prerogative of an infallible judge and to undertake authoritatively to prescribe to its members in matters of pure speculation. . . . But does all this imply that men have a right to act anything but virtue and to utter anything but truth ? Certainly not. It implies indeed that there are points with which society has no right to interfere, not that discretion and caprice are more free or duty less strict upon these points than upon any others with which human action is conversant."

There is a fundamental distinction between an absolutely just action and an action approved by " positive institution." In other words, moral justice is not necessarily the same as political law, and we must judge the rightness of an action by our internal understanding of morality rather than by the dogmas of an external institution.

The nature of happiness and misery, pleasure and pain is independent of all positive institution : that is, it is immutably true that whatever tends to procure a balance of the former is to be desired, and whatever tends to procure a balance of the latter is to be rejected. In like manner the promulgation of virtue, truth and political justice must always be right. There is perhaps no action of a rational being that has not some tendency to promote these objects, and consequently that has not a moral character founded in the abstract nature of things.

THOMAS HOLCROFT
*From the portrait by John Opie*

The tendency of positive institution is of two sorts, to furnish me with an additional motive to the practice of virtue or right, and to inform my understanding as to what actions are right and what actions are wrong. Much cannot be said in commendation of either of these tendencies.

The additional motive that positive institutions can offer is that of reward. But if an action is performed for any other motive than its moral value, it becomes, so far as the agent is concerned, a vicious action.

This is what is meant by the principle that we should do good regardless of the consequences ; and by that other, that we may not do evil from the prospect of good to result from it.

As for the contention that " positive institution may inform my understanding," this is palpably false, because a man can recognise truth only by his own understanding. A proposition is understood to be true not from the statements of authority, but from its intrinsic evidence.

But positive institutions do more than advise us regarding certain propositions. " In the very nature of these institutions there is included a sanction, a motive either of punishment or reward to induce me to obedience."

Godwin now criticises the idea that in certain departments of civil life governments have a right to our obedience. In reality, such limitations of private judgment are arbitrary, because " there are perhaps no concerns of a rational being over which morality does not extend its province, and respecting which he is not bound to a conscientious proceeding."

Punishment is evil not merely for its effect on the victim, but because it induces other men from fear to act against their own understandings or to accept without enquiry the opinions dictated by the government.

Reason, exercised independently in the discovery of justice, is the only true rule of conduct. None other is valid except in so far as it is consistent with justice. If every man listened with sobriety to the voice of reason, the result would be an unconstrained concord.

But it may be granted that in the present imperfect state of human judgment emergencies will arise in which these principles cannot be applied ; for example, " where the proceedings of the individual threaten the most injurious consequences to his neighbours, and where the instant nature of the case will not accord with the uncertain progress of argument and conviction addressed to the mind of the offender."

In such a case, where a man's private judgment is obviously faulty and the cure cannot be rapid, it may be justifiable to apply restraint. But its degree should be limited. Firstly, we must remember the fallibility of evidence. Secondly, we must consider that an action evil in its consequences can be committed for any number of motives, either vicious or virtuous. Thirdly, whatever restraint may be allowed, it must not partake of punishment.

Even if revenge is left out, punishment for correction is unsatisfactory, for it excites in the sufferer a feeling of injustice and often instils into him a sense of the rightness rather than the error of his actions.

Punishment is a specious name, but is in reality nothing more than force put upon one being by another who happens to be stronger. Now strength does not constitute justice. . . . He that has recourse to it would have no occasion for this expedient if he were sufficiently acquainted with the powers of that truth it is his office to communicate.

Equally, Godwin condemns punishment for example. This also is an attempt at persuasion by force, for instead of using reason to demonstrate injustice, it attempts to deter men by acting upon their fear. Such a method is unlikely to make men wise, " and can scarcely fail of making them timid, dissembling and corrupt."

Nevertheless, while men are imperfect, there seems little chance of abolishing punishment. But men are what they are because of the environment in which they dwell, and to talk of the abolition of punishment is useless unless we can abolish those social causes " that generate temptation and make punishment necessary. . . . He that would reconcile a perfect freedom in this respect with the interest of the whole, ought to propose at the same time the means of extirpating selfishness and vice."

3

The consideration that it may be necessary on occasion " to supersede private judgment for the sake of public good, and to control the acts of the individual by an act to be performed in the name of the whole," leads Godwin to enquire " in what manner such acts are to be originated." In other words, he is led " to ascertain the foundation of political government."

He mentions three hypotheses commonly held on this subject, and dismisses them in turn. The first, that of a system of force, " appears to proceed upon the total negation of abstract and immutable justice, affirming every government to be right that is possessed of power sufficient to enforce its decrees." The second, that of the origin of all government by divine right, " either coincides with the first, and affirms all existing power to be alike of divine derivation ; or it must remain totally useless till a criterion can be found to distinguish those governments which are approved by God from those which cannot lay claim to that sanction."

The third hypothesis is that of the social contract, commonly maintained by radicals in Godwin's day. Godwin begins with a series of minor objections. A contract made by our ancestors cannot justly be binding on their descendants. Nor can acquiescence in an existing state of society be interpreted as consent to an original contract, for " acquiescence is frequently nothing more than a choice on the part of the individual of what he deems the least evil." And how are we to determine the extent or duration of the obligation incurred by consent to a social contract ? But the principal objection to the social contract is that it negates the individual's private judgment of what is just.

The rules by which my actions shall be directed are matters of a consideration entirely personal, and no man can transfer to another the keeping of his conscience and the judging of his duties. But this brings us back to the point from which we set out. No consent of ours can divest us of our moral capacity. This is a species of property which we can neither barter nor resign, and of consequence it is impossible for any government to derive its authority from an original contract.

The whole principle of a social contract is based on the idea that we are under an obligation to fulfil our promises. But the fact that it has been promised does not endow any act with justice. We should perform acts, not because we have promised them, but because they are just.

But it will be said, if promises be not made, or when made be not fulfilled, how can the affairs of the world be carried on ? By rational and intelligent beings acting as if they were rational and intelligent.

In so far as government is admitted to be necessary, it is " a transaction in the name and for the benefit of the whole," and each man should have a share in its administration, because in this way we can approach nearest to "the uncontrolled exercise of private judgment."

Where measures are to be adopted for the good of the community, they should be deliberated in common. This is not incompatible with private judgment. Indeed, there is a striking analogy between common deliberation and private judgment.

No individual can arrive at any degree of moral or intellectual improvement unless in the use of an independent judgment. No state can be well or happily administered unless in the perpetual use of common deliberation respecting the measures it may be requisite to adopt. But though the general exercise of these faculties be founded in immutable justice, justice will by no means uniformly vindicate the particular application of them. Private judgment and public deliberation are not themselves the standard of moral right and wrong ; they are only the means of discovering right and wrong, and of comparing particular propositions with the standard of eternal truth.

From this it follows that no individual or body of individuals has the authority to make laws.

Legislation, as it has been usually understood, is not an affair of human competence. Reason is the only legislator, and her decrees are irrevocable and uniform. The functions of society extend, not to the making, but to the interpreting of law ; it cannot decree, it can only declare that which the nature of things has already decreed, and the propriety of which irresistibly flows from the circumstances of the case.

Thus the authority of the community is strictly executive, and is confined to "the public support of justice." When it deviates from this it is the duty of every man to resist its decisions.

The discussion of authority leads us to consider obedience. Godwin insists that the community as such has no command over our obedience.

The object of government, as has been already demonstrated, is the exertion of force. Now force can never be regarded as an appeal to the understanding ; and therefore obedience, which is an act of the understanding or will, can have no legitimate connection with it. I am bound to submit to justice and truth because they approve themselves to my judgment. I am bound to co-operate with government as far as it appears to me to coincide with these principles. But I submit to government when I think it erroneous merely because I have no remedy.

No truth can be more simple, at the same time that no truth has been more darkened by the glosses of interested individuals, than that one man can in no case be bound to yield obedience to any other man or set of men upon earth.

But, although we cannot obey other men, we may nevertheless benefit from " mutual communication " with those who are wiser or better informed.

Yet this practice of " confidence and delegation " should be used as seldom as possible.   We must use our own understanding and judgment as far as circumstances permit.

Man when he surrenders his reason and becomes the partisan of implicit faith and passive obedience is the most mischievous of all animals.   Ceasing to examine every proposition that comes before him for the direction of his conduct, he is no longer the capable subject of moral instruction.   He is, in the instant of submission, the blind instrument of every nefarious purpose of his principal ;   and when left to himself, is open to the seduction of injustice, cruelty and profligacy.

Godwin now reaches the  argument that has often been stated with great plausibility,  that the differing characters of nations suit them to different types of government, that while for one people a free system may be good,  for others despotism is most beneficial.   To a believer in the absolute nature of justice the answer is obvious.

Truth is in reality single and uniform.   There must in the nature of things be one best form of government, which all intellects sufficiently roused from the slumber of savage ignorance will be irresistibly incited to approve.   If an equal participation of the benefits of nature be good in itself, it must be good for you and me and all mankind.
The subject of legislation is everywhere the same, man.   The points in which human beings resemble are infinitely more considerable than those in which they differ.

It may be argued that man is not everywhere ready for liberty, and that he should be given only such  freedom as he is capable to bear.   This argument is dangerous,  because any restriction tends to hinder further development.   The principle of gradual improvement is indeed one which Godwin supports ;   his doctrine of perfectibility contends that man has a natural tendency towards progress.   But political institution,

. . . by its very nature . . . has a tendency to suspend the elasticity and put an end to the advancement of mind. . . . It were earnestly to be desired that each man was wise enough to govern himself without the intervention of any compulsory restraint ;  and since government even in its best state is an evil, the object principally to be aimed at is that we should have as little of it as the general peace of human society will permit.

The only sure way of improving men's minds is by the publication of truth. Here again government is fallible, because it will desire " by means of ignorance and implicit faith, to perpetuate the existing state of things." Truth can be propagated only by free discussion, " so that the errors of one man may be detected by the acuteness and severe disquisition of his neighbours."

### 4

It has been stated that every man is bound to resist an action that appears contrary to justice. How is this resistance to be performed ?

There are two modes, action and speech. Active resistance should be used only when the individual perceives that his action will have positive results and will not interfere with any better contribution he can make to the general good. It can take the form either of an example of martyrdom or of an appeal to force.

At the time when *Political Justice* was written, the possibility of martyrdom was near, and Godwin illustrates the courageous but balanced manner in which he and his friends regarded the dangers of their situation.

The question of martyrdom is of a difficult nature. I had rather convince men by my arguments than seduce them by my example. It is scarcely possible for me to tell what opportunities for usefulness may offer themselves in the future years of my existence. Nor is it improbable in a general consideration that long and persevering services may be more advantageous than brilliant and transitory ones. The case being thus circumstanced, a truly wise man cannot fail to hesitate as to the idea of offering up his life as a voluntary oblation.

Whenever martyrdom becomes an indispensable duty, when nothing can preserve him short of the clearest dereliction of principle and the most palpable desertion of truth, he will then meet it with perfect serenity. He did not avoid it before from any weakness of personal feeling. When it must be encountered, he knows that it is indebted for that lustre which has been so generally acknowledged among mankind to the intrepidity of the sufferer. He knows that nothing is so essential to true virtue as an utter disregard to individual advantage.

Godwin regards the use of force in general with disapprobation. It is no substitute for reason, and the fact that it is used by people who seek to establish justice does not make it better. It should never be used without prospect of success, and even when it is likely to succeed, it should only be used " where time can by no means be gained, and the consequences instantly to ensue are unquestionably fatal."

The resistance that must be opposed in every instance is "that of uttering the truth, of censuring in the most explicit manner every proceeding that I perceive to be adverse to the true interests of mankind."

The revolutions we should most desire are those which proceed by changing the opinions and dispositions of men, and whose methods are argument and persuasion.

We must . . . carefully distinguish between informing the people and inflaming them. Indignation, resentment and fury are to be deprecated ; and all we should ask is sober thought, clear discernment and intrepid discussion.

Used with sincerity and persistence, reason will accomplish all that violence can only attempt with the most dubious chance of success.

Political associations are injurious, because they seek to impress by weight of numbers and not by propagating the truth. Their appeals are concerned with the effect they will have on the people rather than with whether they are near the truth. But action which is not based on knowledge is unsure and equivocal in its nature.

In emergencies it may be necessary to form associations ; for instance, when new encroachments on freedom appear imminent. But these should confine themselves to appeals to reason and eschew any attempt to stir up hatred. Their existence should terminate as soon as the danger which caused their foundation is at an end.

But, although associations of this type are " of a very danger-ous nature," it is undoubtedly beneficial to maintain " unre-served communication" among groups of people awakened to the pursuit of truth. These small discussion groups might even-tually become universal, and then they would be a potent factor for both the improvement of individuals and the " amelioration of political institutions."

But these consequences are the property only of independent and impartial discussion. If once the unambitious and candid circles of enquiring men be swallowed up in the insatiate gulf of noisy assemblies, the opportunity of improvement is instantly annihilated. The happy varieties of sentiment which so eminently contribute to intellectual acuteness are lost, activity of thought is shackled by the fear that our associates should disclaim us. A fallacious uniformity of opinion is produced which no man espouses from conviction, but which carries all men along with a resistless tide. . . . Human beings should meet together not to enforce but to enquire. Truth disclaims the alliance of marshalled numbers.

By this means social reform will be gradual and tranquil. But this does not mean necessarily that " the revolution is at an immeasurable distance." " The kingdom of truth comes not with ostentation," and its growth may produce great results when these are least expected.

These thoughts lead Godwin to consider the nature and benefits of truth and its acquisition. Truth, considered abstractedly, " conduces to the perfection of our understandings, our virtue and our political institutions." " Virtue is the only state conducive to lasting human happiness," and virtue exists in qualitative proportion to the degree of knowledge of truth.

The pursuit of truth should not, however, be merely on the abstract plane. It must enter into our daily lives, which should always be governed by the observance of complete sincerity. Sincerity

compels me to regard the concerns of my species as my own concerns. What I know of truth, of morals, of religion, of government, it compels me to communicate. All the praise which a virtuous man and an honest action can merit I am obliged to pay to the uttermost mite. I am obliged to give language to all the blame to which profligacy, venality, hypocrisy and circumvention are so justly entitled. I am not empowered to conceal anything I know of myself, whether it tend to my honour or to my disgrace. I am obliged to treat every man with equal frankness, without dreading the imputation of flattery on the one hand, without dreading his resentment and enmity on the other.

The results of such vigorous plain speaking would be universally beneficial, to the individual as well as to the community. The individual would acquire fortitude, presence of mind, vigour and alertness of the understanding.

The community would benefit from the rigorous mental efforts of the sincere man, and from the moral courage with which he denounces injustice and vice wherever he encounters it. " If every man today would tell all the truth he knows," says Godwin with enthusiasm, " three years hence there would be scarcely a falsehood of any magnitude remaining in the civilised world."

Godwin carries his demands for sincerity to a logical but perhaps slightly extravagant extreme.  He regards with disapprobation the white lie told to spare a person to whom the truth might be painful, the strategic deceit to save one's life in time of danger, and the keeping of secrets which are supposed to be necessary for the welfare of individuals or of society.

We must not be guilty of insincerity.  We must not seek to obtain a desirable object by vile means.  We must prefer a general principle to the meretricious attractions of a particular deviation.  We must perceive in the preservation of that general principle a balance of universal good outweighing the benefit to arise in any instance from superseding it.

5

Having laid down the moral foundations of his argument, Godwin proceeds to discuss what he calls " the practical detail of political institution."

The different topics of political institution cannot perhaps be more perspicuously distributed than under the four following heads : provisions for general administration ; provisions for the intellectual and moral improvement of individuals ; provisions for the administration of criminal justice ; and provisions for the regulation of property. Under each of these heads it will be our business, in proportion as we adhere to the great and comprehensive principles already established, rather to clear away abuses than to recommend farther and more precise regulations, rather to simplify them than to complicate.  Above all we should not forget that government is an evil, an usurpation upon the private judgment and individual conscience of mankind ; and that, however we may be obliged to admit it as a necessary evil for the present, it behoves us, as the friends of reason and the human species, to admit as little of it as possible, and carefully to observe whether, in consequence of the gradual illumination of the human mind, that little may not hereafter be diminished.

General administration, the first of these departments of practical politics, includes :

. . . all that shall be found necessary of what has usually been denominated legislative and executive power.  Legislation has already appeared to be a term not applicable to human society.  Men cannot do more than declare and interpret law ; nor can there be an authority so paramount as to have the prerogative of making that to be law which abstract and immutable justice had not made to be law previously to that interposition.  But it might notwithstanding this be found necessary that there should be an authority empowered to declare those general principles by which the equity of the community will be regulated, in

particular cases upon which it may be compelled to decide. . . .
Executive power consists of two very distinct parts : general delibera-
tions relative to particular emergencies, which, so far as practicability
is concerned, may be exercised either by one individual or a body of
individuals, such as peace and war, taxation, and the selection of proper
periods for convoking deliberative assemblies ; and particular functions,
such as those of financial detail, or minute superintendence, which cannot be exercised unless by one or at most by a small number of persons.

Godwin distinguishes three types of government : monarchy,
aristocracy and democracy, and discusses them in turn. He
emphasises that he claims no positive merit for any of these
systems.

The corporate duties of mankind are the result of their irregularities
and follies in their individual capacity. If they had no imperfection, or
if men were so constituted as to be sufficiently and sufficiently early
corrected by persuasion alone, society would cease from its functions.
Of consequence, of the three forms of government and their compositions
that is best which shall least impede the activity and application of our
intellectual powers.

Godwin deals firstly with monarchy and aristocracy, and,
although his arguments against these two institutions are acute
and sound, I have chosen to omit them because of the virtual
non-existence of these forms of government—at least in the shape
Godwin knew—during the present age. I will therefore proceed
immediately to his discussion of the democratic form of government.

At the end of his consideration of the evils of an aristocratic
society, Godwin gives in vivid terms the picture of his conception
of a society unsullied by privilege and inequality.

Let us for a moment give the reins to reflection, and endeavour
accurately to conceive the state of mankind where justice should form the
public and general principle. In that case our moral feelings would
assume a firm and wholesome tone, for they would not be perpetually
counteracted by examples that weakened their energy and confounded
their clearness. Men would be fearless, because they would know that
there were no legal snares lying in wait for their lives. They would be
courageous, because no man would be pressed to the earth that another
might enjoy immoderate luxury, because everyone would be secure of
the just reward of his industry and prize of his exertions. Jealousy and
hatred would cease, for they are the offspring of injustice. Every man
would speak truth with his neighbour, for there would be no temptation
to falsehood and deceit. Mind would find its level, for there would
be everything to encourage and to animate. Science would be unspeak-

ably improved, for understanding would convert into a real power, no longer an *ignis fatuus*, shining and expiring by turns, and leading us into sloughs of sophistry, false science and specious mistake. All men would be disposed to avow their dispositions and actions ; none would endeavour to suppress the just eulogium of his neighbour, for, so long as there were tongues to record, the suppression would be impossible ; none fear to detect the misconduct of his neighbour, for there would be no laws converting the sincere expression of our convictions into a libel.

It is clear that the subjects of a monarchy or the serfs of an aristocracy are far from the attainment of such a condition, for their lives are condemned not only to bondage and poverty, but also to the stupidity and vice that arise from their degraded positions. Let us therefore dismiss these two pernicious systems from our minds and turn to consider how far democracy presents the necessary conditions for raising men to the heights of which they are capable in a sound and healthy society.

Democracy is defined by Godwin as " a system of government according to which every member of society is considered as a man and nothing more. So far as positive regulation is concerned, if indeed that can with any propriety be termed regulation which is the mere recognition of the simplest of all principles, every man is regarded as equal." This is nothing new in the idea of democracy, which has always been regarded in theory as a system based on equality. But in practice it has never been achieved, because its completion would lead to a revolutionary levelling identical with that envisaged by the anarchists. Godwin is willing to face the practical consequences of his direction of thought, so that in the end what he calls *democracy* becomes nothing short of what his modern spiritual descendants call *anarchy*.

There are two great objections which the supporters of other types of government have directed against democracy. Firstly, it is said that man is so imperfect that some authority is necessary to curb the vagaries of human nature. Secondly, it is contended that in a democracy the ignorance of the majority will outweigh the wisdom of the minority, that because of this political life will be unstable, and that the people will in general become hostile to good and easily led away into injustice by the ambitious demagogue.

It is to be admitted that in past democracies such faults have existed.  But even the most imperfect and turbulent democracies have been infinitely superior in their achievements to monarchies and aristocracies.  Let us only regard Athens.

Shall we compare a people of such incredible achievements, such exquisite refinement, gay without insensibility and splendid without intemperance, in the midst of whom grew up the greatest poets, the noblest artists, the most finished orators and political writers, and the most disinterested philosophers the world ever saw—shall we compare this chosen seat of patriotism, independence and generous virtue with the torpid and selfish realms of monarchy and aristocracy?  All is not happiness that looks tranquillity.  Better were a portion of turbulence and fluctuation than that unwholesome calm which is a stranger to virtue.

It is an erroneous argument of the enemies of democracy to take men as they are under tyranny and thence to judge their power to govern themselves.

The thing most necessary is to remove all those restraints which hold mind back from its natural flight.  Implicit faith, blind submission to authority, timid fear, a distrust of our powers, an inattention to our own importance and the good purposes we are able to effect, these are the chief obstacles to human improvement.  Democracy restores to man a consciousness of his value, teaches him by the removal of authority and oppression to listen only to the dictates of reason, gives him confidence to treat all other men as his fellow beings, and induces him to regard them no longer as enemies against whom to be upon his guard, but as brethren whom it becomes him to assist.

Godwin regards the faults of past democracies as due to neglect of sincerity, and here he rises to his most fervent advocacy of the omnipotence of truth.

If the error in their constitution which led to this defect can be discovered, if a form of political society can be devised in which men shall be accustomed to judge strictly and soberly, and habitually exercised to the plainness and simplicity of truth, democracy would in that society cease from the turbulence, instability, fickleness and violence that have too often characterised it.  Nothing can be more certain than the omnipotence of truth, or, in other words, than the connection between the judgment and the outward behaviour.  If science be capable of perpetual improvement, men will also be capable of perpetually advancing in practical wisdom and justice.  Once establish the perfectibility of man and it will inevitably follow that we are advancing to a state in which truth will be too well known to be easily mistaken, and justice too habitually practiced to be voluntarily counteracted.  Nor shall we see reason to think upon severe reflection that this state is so distant as we might at first be inclined to imagine.  Error is principally indebted for its permanence to social institution. Did we leave individuals to the progress of their own minds, without endeavouring to regulate them by any species of public foundation, mankind would in no very long period convert to the obedience of truth. The contest between truth and falsehood is of itself too unequal for the former to stand in need of support from any political ally. The more it be discovered, especially that part of it which relates to man in society, the more simple and self-evident will it appear ; and it will be found impossible any otherwise to account for its having been so long concealed than from the pernicious influence of positive institution.

Godwin considers that the imperfection of previous democracies may also have been due partly to the fact that they had no system of delegation. Delegation, or representation " within proper limits might be entitled to our approbation, provided the elector had the wisdom not to relax in the exercise of his own understanding in all his political concerns, exerted his censorial power over his representative, and were accustomed, if the representative were unable after the fullest explanation, to bring him over to his opinion, to transfer his deputation to another." It will be seen that what Godwin meant was a delegation much more radical than the parliamentary representation which has so far been the governing system of all modern democracies.

Having decided that democracy contains the necessary elements of a sound administration, Godwin proceeds to examine it in detail so as to arrive at the circumstances necessary for its satisfactory conservation of individual freedom and private judgment.

The first requisite of a good society is that it should be administered without the use of imposture and deceit. Men are not so unwise that they can only be induced by religious fantasies and political myths into accepting truth or goodness. The grim terrors of religious fiction serve only to frighten and stupefy the converted, and do not impress the unbelieving. The effect of political myths is similar. Men can only be brought to a true understanding of a good way of life by appeals to their reason. Truth should stand on its own feet.

Why divide men into two classes, one of which is to think and reason for the whole, and the other to take the conclusions of their superiors on trust ? This distinction is not founded in the nature of things ; there is no such inherent difference between man and man as it thinks proper to suppose. The reasons that should convince us that virtue is better than vice are neither complicated nor abstruse ; and the less they be tampered with by the injudicious interference of political institution, the more will they come home to the understanding and approve themselves to the judgment of every man.

Nor is the distinction less injurious than it is unfounded. The two classes which it creates must be more and less than man. It is too much to expect of the former, while we consign to them an unnatural monopoly, that they should rigidly consult for the good of the whole. It is an iniquitous requisition upon the latter that they should never employ their understandings, never penetrate into the essences of things, but always rest in a deceitful appearance. It is iniquitous that we should seek to withhold from them the principles of simple truth and exert ourselves to keep alive their fond and infantine mistakes. The time must probably come when the deceit shall vanish, and then the impostures of monarchy and aristocracy will no longer be able to maintain their ground. The change will at that time be most auspicious if we honestly inculcate the truth now, secure that men's minds will grow strong enough to endure the practice in proportion as their understanding of the theory excites them to demand it.

Another consequence of existing forms of government is the perennial incidence of war. Godwin devotes four chapters to the discussion of this subject, and much of what he says has been made obsolete by modern military and diplomatic practice. But his general analyses of the causes of war and the duty of the individual in war are of permanent value.

War occurs in society in so far as it tends towards authority and inequality. It is the result of a creed of selfishness that spreads from the individual and corrupts society.

Because individuals were liable to error, and suffered their apprehensions of justice to be perverted by a bias in favour of themselves, government was instituted. Because nations were susceptible to a similar weakness and could find no sufficient umpire to whom to appeal, war was introduced. Men were induced deliberately to seek each others' lives and to adjudge the controversies between them, not according to the dictates of reason and justice, but as either should prove most successful in devastation and murder. This was no doubt in the first instance the extremity of exasperation and rage. But it has since been converted into a trade. One part of the nation pays another part to murder and by murdered in their stead ; and the most trivial causes, a supposed insult or a sally of youthful ambition, have sufficed to deluge provinces with blood.

Godwin describes the physical horrors and moral subversion which are the consequences of war. War is incompatible with justice and truth, and there is no reason for its existence in a democratic society.

What could be a source of misunderstanding between states where no man or body of men found encouragement to the accumulation of privileges to himself at the expense of the rest? A people among whom equality reigned would possess everything they wanted where they possessed the means of subsistence. Why should they pursue additional wealth or territory? These would lose their value the moment they became the property of all. No man can cultivate more than a certain portion of land. . . . War and conquest cannot be beneficial to the community. Their tendency is to elevate a few at the expense of the rest, and consequently they will never be undertaken but where the many are the instruments of the few. But this cannot happen in a democracy till the democracy shall become such only in name. If expedients can be devised for maintaining this species of government in its purity, or if there be anything in the nature of wisdom and intellectual improvement which has a tendency daily to make truth prevail more over falsehood, the principle of offensive war will be extirpated.

How far is democracy justified in engaging in war? Godwin warns us against that " love of our country " which is so often advocated by mistaken patriots as a reason for sinking individual judgment in the mass insanity of warfare.

Society is an ideal existence, and not on its own account entitled to the smallest regard. The wealth, prosperity and glory of the whole are unintelligible chimeras. Set no value on anything but in proportion as you are convinced of its tendency to make individual men happy and virtuous. Benefit by every practicable mode man wherever he exists, but be not deceived by the specious idea of affording services to a body of men for which no individual man is the better. Society was instituted, not for the sake of glory, not to furnish splendid materials for the page of history, but for the benefit of its members. The love of our country, if we would speak accurately, is another of those specious illusions which have been invented by imposters in order to render the multitude the blind instruments of their crooked designs.

. . . A wise man will not fail to be the votary of liberty and equality. He will be ready to exert himself in their defence wherever they exist. It cannot be a matter of indifference to him when his own liberty and that of other men with whose excellence and capabilities he has the best opportunity of being acquainted are involved in the event of the struggle to be made. But his attachment will be to the cause and not to the country. Wherever there are men who understand the value of political justice and are prepared to assert it, that is his country. Wherever he can most contribute to the diffusion of these principles and the real happiness of mankind, that is his country. Nor does he desire for any country any other benefit than justice.

According to these principles, the types of war a democrat can support, even if we admit that violence is justified on occasion, are closely limited. He cannot fight to conquer new lands or to

maintain old conquests, to vindicate national honour, to preserve the virility of his race, to avenge insults or to prevent
another nation from commencing hostilities. He can only fight
to defend his own liberty and the liberty of other men, and only
in such conditions that justice is not violated between individuals,
which means that in practice Godwin would have condemned
almost any imaginable war between nations.

His dissertation on war ends with a passage on revolutions in
which he shows that " anarchy," by which he means a state of
strife rather than the unregulated harmony which modern
anarchists intend by this term, is the natural result of despotism,
and that, while we should try by peaceful means to bring about
our revolution, in the last resort " anarchy " itself is preferable
to an indefinite continuance of despotism.

Godwin now turns to the technical nature of democratic
government. Government, where still necessary, should be not
complex, but simple in nature, so as to be nearest to the direct
expression of the will of the people.

Not, as we cannot too often repeat, because their opinion is a standard
of truth, but because, however erroneous that opinion may be, we can
do no better. There is no effectual way of improving the institutions
of any people but by enlightening their understandings. He that
endeavours to maintain the authority of any sentiment, not by argument, but by force, may intend a benefit, but really inflicts an extreme
injury.

Therefore, he opposes the idea of a multiplication of authorities with the intention of providing a check upon rash proceedings. Authority should rest only in an assembly that represents
in the broadest possible way the opinions of the people, and rash-
ness should be prevented not by checks upon action but by the
utmost deliberation in decision. Nor should there be division of
powers, for there should be no artificial limit to the province of a
representative assembly, and the delegation of authority should
be reduced to a minimum. " Legislation—that is, the authorita-
tive enunciation of abstract or general propositions—is a function
of equivocal nature " and should be used as rarely as possible.
The true concern of corporate action is administration, and in
this the whole community should participate as far as possible.
The functions delegated to officials should consist only of providing information and attending to concerns of practical detail.

The province of authority should steadily be reduced. Government, even when it may be deemed necessary, can have only two legitimate purposes, the suppression of injustice within the community and the common defence against external aggression. Only the first has any continual claim upon us, and for dealing with it we need only local co-operation. Here Godwin brings forward the theory of decentralisation which has been one of the principal libertarian tenets since his day.

Great centralised states are harmful and unnecessary for the good of mankind. National glory, national pride, national prosperity are of no value to individuals ; they are merely the fictions by which rogues flourish.

The desire to gain a more extensive territory, to conquer or hold in awe our neighbouring states, to surpass them in arts or arms, is a desire founded in prejudice and error. Power is not happiness. Security and peace are more to be desired than a name at which nations tremble. Mankind are brethren. We associate in a particular district or under a particular climate because association is necessary to our internal tranquillity, or to defend us against the wanton attacks of a common enemy. But the rivalship of nations is a creature of the imagination. . . .
Where nations are not brought into avowed hostility, all jealousy between them is an unintelligible chimera. I reside upon a certain spot because that residence is most conducive to my happiness or usefulness. I am interested in the political justice and virtue of my species because they are men—that is, creatures eminently capable of justice and virtue ; and I have perhaps additional reason to interest myself for those who live under the same government as myself, because I am better qualified to understand their claims and more capable of exerting myself on their behalf. But I can certainly have no interest in the infliction of pain upon others, unless so far as they are expressly engaged in acts of injustice. The object of sound policy and morality is to draw men nearer to each other, not to separate them, to unite their interests, not to oppose them.

Individuals cannot have too frequent or unlimited intercourse with each other, but societies of men have no interests to explain and adjust except so far as error and violence may render explanation necessary. This consideration annihilates at once the principal objects of that mysterious and crooked policy which has hitherto occupied the attention of governments.

As nations, in the forms in which they exist, are thus unnecessary for the well-being of individuals, Godwin foresees the emergence of a localised form of administration.

The appearance which mankind in a future state of improvement may be expected to assume is a policy that in different countries will wear a similar form, because we have all the same faculties and the same wants, but a policy the independent branches of which will extend their authority over a small territory, because neighbours are best informed of each other's concerns and are perfectly equal to their adjustment. . . .

Whatever evils are included in the abstract idea of government are all of them extremely aggravated by the extensiveness of its jurisdiction and softened under circumstances of an opposite species. Ambition, which may be no less formidable than a pestilence in the former, has no room to unfold itself in the latter. Sobriety and equity are the obvious characteristics of a limited circle.

Such a society of small local units would in a sense make the world into one great republic in which men could move and discuss freely without the impedient of national barriers, " and the prospects of him who desired to act beneficially upon a great surface of mind would become more animating than ever."

Godwin considers that in such small local societies, or " parishes," the only form of organisation necessary would be to decide on offences against justice and on controversies.

For exceptional emergencies it might be necessary to have recourse to a general assembly, but Godwin is aware of the dangers of such a course, and condemns anything in the nature of a permanent parliament.

His principal objections to national assemblies are, briefly, these :

In the first place the existence of a national assembly introduces the evils of a fictitious unanimity. . . . In reality all matters that are brought before such an assembly are decided by a majority of votes, and the minority, after having exposed with all the power of which they are capable the injustice and folly of the measures adopted, are obliged in a certain sense to assist in carrying them into execution. . . . He that contributes his personal exertions or his property to the support of a cause which he believes to be unjust will quickly lose that accurate discrimination and nice sensibility of moral rectitude which are the principal ornaments of reason.

Secondly, the existence of national councils produces a certain species of real unanimity, unnatural in its character and pernicious in its effects. . . . In numerous assemblies a thousand motives influence our judgments independently of reason and evidence. Every man looks forward to the effects which the opinions he avows will produce on his success. Every man connects himself with some sect or party. The activity of his thought is shackled at every turn by the fear that his associates may disclaim him. . . .

Thirdly, the debates of a national assembly are distorted from their reasonable tenour by the necessity of their being uniformly terminated by a vote. Debate and discussion are in their own nature highly conducive to intellectual improvement, but they lose this salutary character the moment they are subjected to this unfortunate condition.

The prospect of a vote causes the argument to be conducted for immediate and transitory effect, rather than permanent conviction ; it arouses prejudice rather than judgment. Furthermore, " the deciding upon truth by the casting up of numbers " is an " intolerable insult upon all reason and justice."

In the last place, national assemblies will by no means be thought to deserve our direct approbation if we recollect for a moment the absurdity of that fiction by which society is considered, as it has been termed, as a moral individual. . . . The pretence of collective wisdom is the most palpable of all impostures. The acts of the society never rise above the suggestions of this or that individual who is a member of it.

For these reasons, while in the present state of human wisdom it may be necessary to have recourse to national assemblies, they should be employed " as sparingly as the case will admit."

Democracy of this kind, in which government has been reduced to a minimum, gives no place for the evils which have been associated with democracy in the past.

The true reason why the mass of mankind has so often been made the dupe of knaves has been the mysterious and complicated nature of the social system. Once annihilate the quackery of government, and the most home-bred understanding will be prepared to scorn the shallow artifices of the state juggler that would mislead him.

At first it might be necessary for both the local jury and the national assembly to issue commands. But the need for force arises not " out of man's nature, but out of the institutions by which he has already been corrupted." In a society unburdened by tyranny, men would soon progress so far that it would no longer be necessary to force but only to invite them to refrain from acting in a manner prejudicial to their fellows. And eventually we shall reach a society where wisdom can be transmitted without the intervention of any institution, the society of pure anarchy.

With what delight must every well-informed friend of mankind look forward to the auspicious period, the dissolution of political government, of that brute engine which has been the only perennial cause of the vices of mankind, and which, as has abundantly appeared in the progress of the present work, has mischiefs of various sorts incorporated with its substance, and no otherwise to be removed than by its utter annihilation !

6

Having declared that men are virtuous or vicious, just or unjust, subservient or free, according to the opinions they hold, Godwin proceeds to investigate in what manner opinions are affected by political institutions.

He begins by examining the contention that, although political institutions in the past have been bad, because they have oppressed men and made them vicious, yet they may become good in the future by exerting their efforts to make men virtuous. For a number of reasons, he rejects this as incompatible with the nature of political institutions.

The first objection arises from the nature of society, which is not an entity in itself, but merely a multitude of individuals. What pass as the acts of society are really the acts of the men within it, and those who " usurp the name of the whole," however wise they may be individually, are hampered by " the prejudices, the humours, the weakness and the vice of those with whom they act."

Society therefore in its corporate capacity can by no means be busy and intrusive with impunity, since its acts must be expected to be deficient in wisdom.

Secondly, the acts of society are " not less deficient in efficacy than they are in wisdom." Opinions are founded " upon evidence, upon the perceptions of the understanding." But society is obviously no more capable of illuminating the understanding than are the men who compose it, and, in fact, all the great contributions towards improving knowledge have been those of men in their individual and not in their corporate capacities.

The only advantage society may hold over the individual in the influencing of opinion is in its authority. But by commanding a man we do not change his opinions or make him virtuous.

Besides, the administration of laws is an activity prejudicial to sincere human intercourse and to the liberty of the individual. Yet it is only by such means that extensive governments can attempt to make men virtuous. Here smaller circles again have an advantage, for in them

. . . opinion would be all sufficient ; the inspection of every man over the conduct of his neighbours, when unstained with caprice, would constitute a censorship of the most irresistible nature. But the force of this censorship would depend upon its freedom, not following the positive dictates of law but the spontaneous decisions of the understanding.

A third objection to corporate interference for the propagation of virtue is that " truth and virtue are competent to fight their own battles."

All that is to be asked on the part of government in behalf of morality and virtue is a clear stage upon which for them to exert their energies, and perhaps some restraint for the present upon the violent disturbers of the peace of society that the efforts of these principles may be allowed to go uninterrupted to their natural conclusion. Who ever saw an instance in which error unaided by power was victorious over truth ?

Men act in the way that seems most conducive to their interest, and are likely to be influenced by any evidence to this end.

The real history of the changes of character they experience in this respect is this. Truth for a long time spreads itself unobserved. Those who are the first to embrace it are little aware of the extraordinary effects with which it is pregnant. But it goes on to be studied and illustrated. It perpetually increases in clearness and amplitude of evidence. The number of those by whom it is embraced is gradually enlarged.

Thus, though the methods of governments are inefficacious, social improvement is not less possible. But it must be attempted by the propagation of truth.

Let us not vainly endeavour by laws and regulations to anticipate the future dictates of the general mind, but calmly wait till the harvest of opinion is ripe.

For the present, the man who desires social reformation should devote himself to " enquiry, instruction, discussion." Later, when the people have become imbued with a desire for change, his task will alter. It may be that this change will occur peacefully, but it may also be precipitate and accompanied by commotion. In this event the reformer must " actively assist in unfolding the catastrophe " and " by social emanations of wisdom endeavour to guide the understandings of the people at large to the perception of felicity."

A fourth objection is that corporate interference with opinions and manners is not merely useless but also pernicious, because, while impotent to cause favourable changes in society, it is " powerful to prolong " existing and obsolete habits and propensities.

Whenever government assumes to deliver us from the trouble of thinking for ourselves, the only consequences it produces are those of torpor and imbecility. . . . Mind is in this case robbed of its essential character and genuine employment, and along with them must be expected to lose all that which is capable of rendering its operations salutary and admirable. Either mankind will resist the assumptions of authority undertaking to superintend their opinions, and then these assumptions will produce no more than an ineffectual struggle ; or they will submit, and then the effects will be injurious.

The attempt to enforce the truth by means of laws is further invalidated by the fact that laws have a tendency towards rigidity, whereas the rightness of an action is determined by the circumstances in which it is performed.

Right and wrong are the result of certain relations, and those relations are founded in the respective qualities of the beings to whom they belong. Change those qualities, and the relations become altogether different. The treatment that I am bound to bestow upon any one depends upon my capacity and his circumstances. Increase the first, or vary the second, and I am bound to a different treatment. . . . But if there be any truth in these views, nothing can be more adverse to reason or inconsistent with the nature of man than positive regulations tending to continue a certain mode of proceeding when its utility is gone.

Godwin reinforces his condemnation of political intrusion by showing the contrasting natures of mind and government. Mind is " susceptible of perpetual improvement," but government tends " to retain that with which it is conversant forever in the same state."

Godwin concludes that the result of this examination of political interference in opinion

is nothing more than a confirmation, with some difference in the mode of application, of the fundamental principle that government is little capable of affording benefit of the first importance to mankind. It is calculated to induce us to lament, not the apathy and indifference, but the inauspicious activity of government. It incites us to look for the moral improvement of the species, not in the multiplying of regulations, but in their repeal. It teaches us that truth and virtue, like commerce, will then flourish most when least subjected to the mistaken guardianship of authority and laws.

In the following chapters Godwin examines various manifestations of the influence of political institutions upon opinion.

Religious establishment, tests, oaths of fidelity and office, are all condemned on more or less the same general grounds, that they offend sincerity by requiring men to accept certain beliefs for reasons other than the result of their own private judgments, and that the attempt to reconcile what they may believe with what they are required to profess will inevitably tend to make men hypocritical. Moreover, to swear fidelity to any law or administration is wrong, because we have a duty to resist laws or governments when they are unjust, and should not make any promises that will interfere with our " paramount engagement to the cause of justice and the benefit of the human race."

The suppression of erroneous or heretical religious or political opinions is equally to be condemned. The first objection is that virtue does not spring from ignorance, but is the product of knowledge. Therefore free enquiry should be maintained, because it leads to wisdom and knowledge, and thence to benevolence and justice. Secondly, differences of opinion do not in themselves lead to a disturbance of the peace. It is only when one opinion is supported by the force of authority that civil strife ensues.

Arguments alone will not have the power, unassisted by the sense or the recollection of oppression or treachery, to hurry the people into excesses. Excesses are never the offspring of reason, are never the offspring of misrepresentation only, but of power endeavouring to stifle reason and traverse the common sense of mankind.

Thirdly, we are justified in using force only when it is necessary to curtail other force used against the peace of the community. It is not just to counter argument by force, but only by argument.

The attempt to suppress opinions will be seen to be absurd when we realise that it is impossible to suppress private thoughts. Nor, even if men speak their thoughts, is it possible to exercise such supervision that they will always be detected. If such suppression were successful, the men on whom it was practised would be, not virtuous men, but abject and corrupt slaves. Further, it must be remembered that rulers are by no means infallible, and the opinions they attempt to enforce are not necessarily true.

An equally great offence against truth is a law which, under the pretence of forbidding libels, restricts our freedom of open criticism. It follows from what has been said on political and religious heresy that " no punishment can justly be awarded

against any writing or words derogatory to religion or political
government." But there remain libels against private character,
for the suppression of which a more plausible case has been made.
Here again, for the reasons which follow, Godwin contends that
there should be complete freedom.

If we conceal the faults and errors of men, the issue will be
favourable to vice rather than to virtue. Nothing is more
deterrent of vice than the prospect of its exposure, while virtue
can have no greater reward than " the plain, unvarnished proclamation of its excellence." The unrestricted speaking of the
truth would make men fear to be rogues and wish to be virtuous.
Nor, once the restriction on free speech had ended, need we fear
any increase in slanderous accusations ; on the contrary, these
thrive only because the truth is concealed.

A law that forbids us to fulfil this duty to speak our minds is a
law against sincerity. It obscures the nature of virtue and makes
men cunning and cowardly.

Such characters as ours are the mere shadows of men, with a specious
outside perhaps, but destitute of substance and soul. Oh, when shall
we arrive at the land of realities, when men shall be known for what
they are, by energy of thought and intrepidity of action !

The only effective way of correcting falsehood is not by force,
but by truth, which is the most powerful weapon against error.

A further enforcement of opinion by political institution is the
doctrine of constitutions, which arises from an idea that certain
human laws are fundamental and should be made permanent.
This involves a misunderstanding of the natures of law and man.
True laws are not made by man, but inhere in the structure of the
universe. Men can only interpret these laws according to their
understandings, and, if it is granted that the human mind is
always progressing towards perfection, then its understanding of
the natural laws of conduct is bound to change. Therefore it is
wrong to give permanence to any human law.

Where laws are still necessary, none should be regarded as
more important than others, and none should be permanent. We
should have as few laws as possible, and instead of giving uniformity and permanence to administration, we should seek as far
as possible to allow small groups to administer their own affairs
as seems just in the particular circumstances, and to bring about
" the gradual extinction of law." Instead of a centralised state

governed by the sanctions of a rigid constitution, we should aim at a confederacy of " parishes " united in a free and voluntary bond.

A method by which political institutions can interfere dangerously in the development of opinion is by superintending education. Many radicals of Godwin's day supported schemes for national education, and for this reason he made his examination more deliberate. Consistently with his general theories, he condemns national education, for the following reasons :

The injuries that result from a system of national education are, in the first place, that all public establishments include in them the idea of permanence. They endeavour it may be to secure and diffuse whatever of advantageous to society is already known, but they forget that more remains to be known. If they realised the most substantial benefits at the time of their introduction, they must inevitably become less and less useful as they increased in duration. But to describe them as useless is a very feeble expression of their demerits. They actively restrain the flights of mind and fix it in the belief of exploded errors. . . . Real intellectual improvement demands that mind should as speedily as possible be advanced to the height of knowledge already existing among the enlightened members of the community and start from thence in the pursuit of further acquisitions. But public education has always expended its energies in the support of prejudice ; it teaches its pupils not the fortitude that shall bring every proposition to the test of examination, but the art of vindicating such tenets as may chance to be previously established. . . . All this is directly contrary to the true interest of mind. All this must be unlearned before we can begin to be wise.

It is the characteristic of mind to be capable of improvement. An individual surrenders the best attribute of man the moment he resolves to adhere to certain fixed principles for reasons not now present to his mind but which formerly were. . . . The same principle that applies to individuals applies to communities. There is no proposition at present apprehended to be true so valuable as to justify the introduction of an establishment for the purpose of inculcating it on mankind. Refer them to reading, to conversation, to meditation, but teach them neither creeds nor catechisms, neither moral nor political.

Secondly, the idea of national education is founded in an inattention to the nature of mind. Whatever each man does for himself is done well ; whatever his neighbours or his country undertake to do for him is done ill. It is our wisdom to incite men to act for themselves, not to retain them in a state of perpetual pupillage. He that learns because he desires to learn will listen to the instructions he receives and apprehend their meaning. He that teaches because he desires to teach will discharge his occupation with enthusiasm and energy. But the moment political institution undertakes to assign to every man his place, the functions of all will be discharged with supineness and indifference. . . .

Thirdly, the project of a national education ought uniformly to be discouraged on account of its obvious alliance with national government. This is an alliance of a more formidable nature than the old and much contested alliance of church and state. Before we put so powerful a machine under the direction of so ambiguous an agent, it behooves us to consider well what it is that we do. Government will not fail to employ it to strengthen its hands and perpetuate its institutions. If we could even suppose the agents of government not to propose to themselves an object which will be apt to appear in their eyes not merely innocent but meritorious, the evil would not the less happen. Their view as institutors of a system of education will not fail to be analogous to their views in their political capacity : the data upon which their conduct as statesman is vindicated will be the data upon which their instructions are founded. It is not true that our youth ought to be instructed to venerate the constitution, however excellent ; they should be instructed to venerate truth, and the constitution only so far as it corresponded with their independent deductions of truth. Had the scheme of a national education been adopted when despotism was most triumphant, it is not to be believed that it could have forever stifled the voice of truth. But it would have been the most formidable and profound contrivance for that purpose that imagination can suggest. Still, in the countries where liberty chiefly prevails, it is reasonably to be assumed that there are important errors, and a national education has the most direct tendency to perpetuate those errors and to form all minds upon one model.

How accurate were Godwin's premonitions of the results of state interference in education is shown only too clearly in our own day, when education has become the most formidable of the dictator's methods of deceiving and misleading the people into accepting his authority.

The last of the means of influencing opinion which Godwin considers is that of rewarding men by granting salaries and pensions for public offices. He holds that such salaries should be abolished, because service to the community should be performed as a duty and not for a reward, which obscures its nature and its object. If a man chosen for public office has not sufficient means to provide for his own subsistence, it would be better that he should rely on the assistance of neighbours than become the paid servant of a political institution.

Finally, in a chapter " On the Modes of Deciding a Question on the Part of the Community," Godwin condemns both decision by lot and by ballot. Decision by lot is based on superstition, gives an appearance of indifference to important matters, and deliberately avoids the use of reason. Decision by ballot is an offence against sincerity and fortitude, because it regards the performance of our duty as a matter for concealment, and appears to allow us to avoid " the consequences of our own actions."

If then sortition and ballot be institutions pregnant with vice, it follows that all social decisions should be made by open vote ; that wherever we have a function to discharge, we should reflect on the mode in which it ought to be discharged ; and that whatever conduct we are persuaded to adopt, especially in affairs of general concern, should be adopted in the face of the world.

## 7

The section concerning crimes and punishment is an amplification of themes which have arisen in our discussion of Godwin's general arguments.  It has already been granted that the only valid function of government, where it is still deemed necessary, is to restrain the individual who acts in a manner harmful to the well-being of his neighbours.

But this function cannot be regarded as punishment, which Godwin defines as

. . . the voluntary infliction of evil upon a vicious being not merely because the public advantage demands it but because there is apprehended to be a certain fitness and propriety in the nature of things that render suffering, abstractedly from the benefit to result, the suitable concomitant of vice.

Godwin argues that such an attitude arises from a belief in complete free will.  But, if one accepts necessity, a man, like an inanimate object, is operated upon by circumstances which determine his actions, so that he is not responsible for them. " The assassin," says Godwin, " cannot help the murder he commits any more than the dagger."  (This seems to me to carry the belief in necessity to a logical extravagance, but Godwin's contentions are *substantially* true, for men are turned into criminals and given criminal motives by external circumstances—even though there may be some element of choice in their actions—and therefore it is unjust for us to punish them when we can change their actions by bettering their surroundings.)

The principle to be considered in forming our attitude towards punishment is " that the only measure of equity is utility, and whatever is not attended by any beneficial purpose is not just." Therefore, in examining the questions of restraint and punishment, it is important to bear in mind that these can only be admitted to be just in so far as they result in good to some person. This will preclude all idea of punishment in the sense of retribution.

It has already appeared that the " laws of eternal reason," manifested in morality and duty, are the only standards by which our conduct should be judged. These standards cannot be apprehended by the external application of authority, but only by each man exercising his private judgment. The most that can be done by other men is so to enlighten his understanding that he may be enabled to make sound and just decisions.

Coercion has no tendency to enlighten. On the contrary, " the direct tendency of coercion is to set our understanding and our fears, our duty and our weakness at variance with each other." Coercion is not an argument of truth against falsehood, but a contest where vigour and cunning are the determining factors.

Let us consider the effect that coercion produces upon the mind of him against whom it is employed. It cannot begin with convincing ; it is no argument. It begins with producing the sensation of pain and the sentiment of distaste. It begins with violently alienating the mind from the truth with which we wish it to be impressed. It includes in it a tacit confession of imbecility. If he who employs coercion against me could mould me to his purposes by argument, no doubt he would. He pretends to punish me because his argument is important, but he really punishes me because his argument is weak.

Godwin now considers the purposes of coercion. These are four in number, and have all been discussed in an earlier part of this book. The most innocent is the use of coercion for the immediate repression of force. Even here Godwin believes in certain cases moral vigour may have as much effect in emergency as physical force.

Coercion to restrain a criminal for fear he should repeat his act is subject to a number of objections. We cannot be certain that he will attempt to repeat it, and restraint amounts to " punishment upon suspicion."

Why not arm myself with vigilance and energy, instead of locking up every man whom my imagination may bid me fear, that I may spend my days in undisturbed inactivity.

The remaining forms of coercion, those for retribution and for example, have already been shown to be incompatible with justice.

A further proof of the absurdity of coercion is that there is no means of establishing a relationship between delinquency and restraint.

No standard of delinquency ever has been or ever can be discovered. No two crimes were ever alike; and therefore the reducing them explicitly or implicitly to general classes, which the very idea of example implies, is absurd.

We cannot judge a crime by its external form. Its nature is determined by the intention in the mind of the criminal, and intentions are so various that we cannot imagine justice arising out of any set code of laws. Further, it is almost impossible to unravel and judge all the motives and causes that have led to a man's actions. Therefore, as we have not the knowledge of a man's heart that will allow us to consider his actions worthy of retribution, we cannot justly punish him.

It is equally difficult to estimate the chances of a man's repeating his offence or being imitated by others. Therefore we should regard coercion for the purpose of the prevention of crime with the greatest caution.

Moreover, the complexity of the motives that underlie crime makes it all the more ridiculous to punish for example, for if no two crimes are ever completely similar, it is neither just nor effective to punish one man for one crime to prevent another man committing another crime.

Punishment is rendered still more undesirable if we regard the nature of evidence. Circumstantial evidence is based entirely on supposition rather than ascertained truth, and direct evidence is subject to the failings and interests of the witnesses, as well as to the distortions of interpretation. Moreover, trials are held at a time when passions are hot and prejudices rampant, so that the defendant has no fair chance to impress on his judges the innocence of his conduct or the circumstances that led him to offend.

These arguments have given us sufficient reason to deny coercion a place in any sound system of society. But it may be argued that it is necessary, as a temporary measure. This we should accept with reserve, for crime is related to the form of society, and tends to diminish as society becomes more given to the practice of virtue.

There is a state of society, the outline of which has been already sketched, that by the mere simplicity of its structure would infallibly lead to the extermination of offence : a state in which temptation would be almost unknown, truth brought down to the level of all apprehensions, and vice sufficiently checked by the general discountenance and sober condemnation of every spectator. Such are the consequences that would necessarily spring from an abolition of the craft and mystery of governing ; while on the other hand the innumerable murders that are daily committed under the sanction of legal forms are solely to be ascribed to the pernicious notion of an extensive territory ; to the dreams of glory, empire and national greatness, which have hitherto proved the bane of the human species, without producing solid benefit and happiness to a single individual.

A further consequence that may be deduced from the principles that have here been delivered is that coercion of a municipal kind can in no case be the duty of the community. The community is always competent to change its institutions and thus to extirpate offence in a way infinitely more rational and just than that of coercion. If in this sense coercion has been deemed necessary as a temporary expedient, the opinion admits of satisfactory refutation. Coercion can at no time, either permanently or provisionally, make part of any political system that is built upon the principles of reason.

But, though coercion cannot be the duty of the community, it may be the duty of individuals within the community. The individual's first duty is to endeavour to establish an improved society, but he should also remember that his efforts cannot be immediately successful and that he has an obligation in the meantime to promote the welfare of society by resisting acts against justice. Here Godwin rejects the doctrine of complete non-violence. We should use forbearance and patience as far as we can, but we should be prepared to use force when no other method will suffice to combat evil.

This brings us again to the consideration of the state of " anarchy," by which Godwin means that disorder which results from the dissolution of government without the general acceptance of " consistent and digested views of political justice."

Godwin gives a detailed and vivid picture of the evils of " anarchy," ending by pointing out that man's " ungoverned passions will often not stop at equality but incite them to grasp at power." Yet, for all its evils, " anarchy " is more to be desired than despotism.

Anarchy is transitory, but despotism tends towards permanence.

Anarchy awakens mind, diffuses energy and enterprise through the community, though it does not effect this in the best manner, as its fruits, forced into ripeness, must not be expected to have the vigorous stamina of true excellence. But in despotism mind is trampled into an equality of the most odious sort. Everything that promises greatness is destined to fall under the exterminating hand of suspicion and envy.

Moreover, it is always possible that " anarchy " may terminate in the kind of free society which is based on political justice, for

. . . it has something in it that suggests the likeness, a distorted and tremendous likeness, of true liberty. Anarchy has commonly been generated by the hatred of oppression. It is accompanied with a spirit of independence. It disengages men from prejudice and implicit faith, and in a certain degree incites them to an impartial scrutiny into the reason of their actions.

Nevertheless, it can result in true liberty only if it occurs among men likely to adopt readily the principles of justice. For this reason such a condition should be " held at bay " as long as is possible, in favour of the gradual processes of persuasion and education.

Leaving this digression, Godwin returns to his statement that constraint for the purpose of curbing unjust force may be admitted in certain circumstances, but its purpose must be, not punishment, but only such restraint as may be necessary for the protection of the peace of the community.

Some form of seclusion is the only restraint that is permissible, but this should be attended by no penal deprivations or impositions. It is the duty of the restrainer to attempt to reform the recalcitrant, but he should not keep him in seclusion for this purpose alone.

The consideration of coercion leads us to examine the system of law by which coercion is commonly administered. Law, man-made law as distinct from natural law, Godwin considers undesirable. We should act according to justice, whose rules " would be more clearly and effectually taught by an actual intercourse with human society than they can be by catechisms and codes."

If no two crimes are the same, and each case should be judged on its own merits, then the disadvantages of codified law are obvious. A code that would embrace every case must expand continually and become ever more complex. But laws, as they multiply, become more uncertain, and it is impossible for the ordinary man or even the expert to know them thoroughly. By its nature, law cannot be simple, but the rules of justice that are to be comprehended by every man must partake of this quality.

Law, moreover, attempts a prophetic function, and in this prospective form it is one of the most formidable agents for promoting the stagnation of the human mind and impeding its " unceasing perfectibility."

Law also attempts to impose a stultifying uniformity upon mankind by classifying and restricting their actions within rigid channels of behaviour.

In defiance of the great principle of natural philosophy that there are not so much as two atoms of matter of the same form through the whole universe, it endeavours to reduce the actions of men, which are composed of a thousand evanescent elements, to one standard. . . . If on the contrary justice be a result flowing from the contemplation of all the circumstances of each individual case, if the only criterion of justice be general utility, the inevitable consequence is that the more we have of justice, the more we shall have of truth, virtue and happiness.

In place of law, we should substitute the principle of " reason exercising an uncontrolled jurisdiction over the circumstances of the case." A man of wisdom can surely be relied upon to communicate decisions more virtuous than the decisions of law, which represent not so much the wisdom of our ancestors as " the dictate of their passion, of timidity, jealousy, a monopolising spirit and a lust of power that knew no bounds."

It may be objected that such decisions will be governed by the passions of those who administer them. But, even if we admit our imperfections, these can only be removed by the spread of knowledge, while the law tends to make knowledge stagnant and so to keep men from becoming governed by their reason.

Men are weak at present because they have always been told they are weak and must not be trusted with themselves. Take them out of their shackles, bid them enquire, reason and judge, and you will soon find them very different beings. Tell them that they have passions, are occasionally hasty, intemperate and injurious, but they must be trusted with themselves. Tell them that the mountains of parchment in which they have been hitherto entrenched are fit only to impose upon ages of superstition and ignorance, that henceforth we will have no dependence but upon their spontaneous justice ; that if their passions be gigantic, they must rise with gigantic energy to subdue them ; that if their decrees be iniquitous, the iniquity shall be all their own. The effect of this disposition of things will soon be visible ; mind will rise to the level of its situation ; juries and umpires will be penetrated with the magnitude of the trust reposed in them.

It will not be imagined that the results of such a change in procedure would lead to immediate perfection. At first there would be absurd or atrocious decisions. But, provided all transactions were " conducted in an open and explicit manner," the authors of such decisions would find their actions sufficiently condemned by their neighbours to induce them to change their attitudes.

Their understandings would grow enlarged in proportion as they felt the importance of their trust and the unbounded freedom of their investigation. Here then would commence an auspicious order of things, of which no understanding of man at present in existence can foretell the result, the dethronement of implicit faith and the inauguration of unclouded justice.

Finally, Godwin points out that the conclusion of these reasonings is " that law is merely relative to the exercise of political force and must perish when the necessity for that force ceases, if the influences of truth do not still sooner extirpate it from the practice of mankind."

8

In the last section of *Political Justice*, Godwin examines the institution of property. This is the most famous and perhaps the most important part of his book. Certainly it is the most eloquent and capably reasoned. It is the only part which has been republished in England since the eighteenth century, and copies of H. S. Salt's edition of this fragment are still available. Nevertheless, its arguments are so important that I shall reproduce them as completely as is necessary for their proper understanding.

The subject of property is the keystone that completes the fabric of political justice. According as our ideas respecting it are crude or correct, they will enlighten us as to the consequences of a *simple form of society without government*, and remove the prejudices that attach us to complexity. There is nothing that more powerfully tends to distort our *judgment* and *opinions* than erroneous notions concerning the goods of fortune. Finally, the period that shall put an end to the system of *coercion* and *punishment* is intimately connected with the circumstance of property's being placed upon an equitable basis.

After referring briefly to the abuses that " have insinuated themselves into the administration of property," Godwin turns to consider " those general principles by which it has in almost all cases been directed."

The only criterion by which we can consider to whom any substance should belong is that of justice.

To whom does any article of property, suppose a loaf of bread, justly belong ? To him who most wants it, or to whom the possession of it will be most beneficial. . . . Our animal wants have long since been defined, and are stated to consist of food, clothing and shelter. If justice have any meaning, nothing can be more iniquitous than for one man to possess superfluities, while there is a human being in existence that is not adequately supplied with these.

Justice does not stop here. Every man is entitled, so far as the general stock will suffice, not only to the means of being, but of well-being. It is unjust if one man labour to the destruction of his health or his life that another man may abound in luxuries. It is unjust if one man be deprived of leisure to cultivate his rational powers while another man contributes not a single effort to add to the common stock. The faculties of one man are like the faculties of another man. Justice directs that each man, unless perhaps he be employed more beneficially to the public, should contribute to the cultivation of the common harvest, of which each man consumes a share. This reciprocity indeed, as was observed when that subject was the matter of separate consideration, is of the very essence of justice.

Luxury is as unsatisfactory as it is unjust. It is by no means a beneficial condition, and is based rather on the satisfaction of vanity than on any tangible advantages which the rich man enjoys over the man with a modest livelihood. The applause that satisfies the vanity of the rich man is not based on his instrinsic merit but on his wealth, and is thus worthless and harmful.

The first effect of riches is to deprive their possessor of the genuine powers of understanding and render him incapable of discerning absolute truth. They lead him to fix his affections on objects not accommodated to the wants and the structure of the human mind, and of consequence entail upon him disappointment and unhappiness. The greatest of all personal advantages are independence of mind, which makes us feel that our satisfactions are not at the mercy either of men or of fortune, and activity of mind, the cheerfulness that arises from industry perpetually employed about objects of which our judgment acknowledges the intrinsic value.

The unequal distribution of property thus results in the disadvantage of both the rich and the poor. Moreover, because wealth is distributed according to such accidents as birth or superior cunning, the man of ability is often prevented from developing his usefulness from sheer lack of means.

In fact, every ethical principle teaches us the injustice of accumulated property.

He that sets out with acknowledging that other men are of the same nature as himself, and is capable of perceiving the precise place he would hold in the eye of an impartial spectator, must be fully sensible that the money he employs in procuring an object of trifling or no advantage to himself, and which might have been employed in purchasing substantial and indispensable benefit to another, is unjustly employed. . . .

Does any man doubt of the truth of these assertions ? Does any man doubt that when I employ a sum of money small or great in the purchase of an absolute luxury for myself, I am guilty of vice ? It is high time that we should lay aside the very names of justice and virtue, or that we should acknowledge that they do not authorise us to accumulate luxuries upon ourselves while we see others in want of the indispensable means of improvement and happiness.

The benefits of equality of property, or *The Genuine System of Property*, can best be understood if we regard the disadvantages of the existing system. " Its first effect is . . . a sense of dependence," and it spreads among men " a servile and truckling spirit." It is visionary to expect men to become virtuous while they are subjected to the corruption of selling their independence and their conscience " for the vile rewards that oppression has to bestow." Only if we remove " those external impressions by which their evil propensities are cherished," can we induce them to live according to reason.

The true object that should be kept in view is to extirpate all ideas of condescension and superiority, to oblige every man to feel that the kindness he exerts is what he is bound to perform, and the assistance he asks what he has a right to claim.

Its second evil effect is " the perpetual spectacle of injustice it exhibits. This consists partly in luxury and partly in caprice."

Luxury corrupts the mind by diverting its natural propensity to attain excellence or approbation into the acquisition of wealth rather than of virtue. A man is honoured because he is rich ; he is rich by accident of birth " or from a minute and sordid attention to the cares of gain." These circumstances make it difficult for men to apprehend the lessons of reason.

They have been accustomed to the sight of injustice, oppression and iniquity till their feelings are made callous and their understandings incapable of apprehending the nature of true virtue.

Accumulated property corrupts all classes alike.

The poor are kept in ignorance by want of leisure. The rich are furnished indeed with the means of cultivation and literature, but they are paid for being dissipated and indolent.

Thus, the established system of property is the true levelling system with respect to the human species, by as much as the cultivation of intellect and truth is more valuable and more characteristic of man than the gratifications of vanity or appetite. Accumulated property treads the powers of thought in the dust, extinguishes the sparks of genius, and reduces the great mass of mankind to be immersed in sordid cares. . . .

Let us compare the condition of man now with what is possible under an equal system of property.

If superfluity were banished, the necessity for the greater part of the manual industry of mankind would be superseded ; and the rest, being amicably shared among all the active and vigorous members of the community, would be burthensome to none. Every man would have a frugal yet wholesome diet ; every man would go forth to that moderate exercise of his corporal functions that would give hilarity to the spirits ; none would be made torpid with fatigue, but all would have leisure to cultivate the kindly and philanthropical affections of the soul and to let loose his faculties in the search of intellectual improvement. . . .

Genius would not be depressed with false wants and niggardly patronage. It would not exert itself with a sense of neglect and oppression rankling in its bosom. It would be freed from those apprehensions that perpetually recall us to the thought of personal emolument, and of consequence would expatiate freely among sentiments of generosity and public good.

Nor would the moral benefits be less than the intellectual, for in a system of equal property " all the occasions of crime would be cut for ever." Crime arises principally from " one man's possessing in abundance that of which another man is destitute." The proper method of curing this condition is by reason, but the " tendency of the established system is to persuade men that reason is impotent." They see property protected by force, and themselves mistakenly try to rectify the injustice by the use of violence.

The spirit of oppression, the spirit of servility and the spirit of fraud, these are the immediate growth of the established system of property. These are alike hostile to intellectual and moral improvement. The other vices of envy, malice and revenge are their inseparable companions. In a state of society where men lived in the midst of plenty and where all shared alike the bounties of nature these sentiments would inevitably expire. The narrow principle of selfishness would vanish. No man being obliged to guard his little store, or provide with anxiety and pain for his restless wants, each would lose his own individual existence in the thought of the general good. No man would be an enemy to his neighbour, for they would have nothing for which to contend ; and of consequence philanthropy would resume the empire which reason assigns her. Mind would be delivered from her perpetual anxiety about corporal support and free to expatiate in the field of thought which is congenial to her. Each man would assist the enquiries of all.

It must not be forgotten that there are effects arising indirectly from property which are as harmful as its direct evils. These come from the fact that property confers power over other men, and hence appear tyranny and war. Property makes those who hold it despotic, and renders all men ambitious to increase their property and the power it brings.

It is only by means of accumulation that one man obtains an unresisted sway over multitudes of others. It is by means of a certain distribution of income that the present governments of the world are retained in existence. Nothing more easy than to plunge nations so organised into war. But if Europe were at present covered with inhabitants all of them possessing competence and none of them superfluity, what could induce its different countries to engage in hostility ? If you would lead men to war, you must exhibit certain allurements. If you be not enabled by a system, already prevailing and which derives force from prescription, to hire them to your purposes, you must bring over each individual by dint of persuasion. How hopeless a task by such means to excite mankind to murder each other. It is clear then that war in every horrid form is the growth of unequal property. As long as this source of jealousy and corruption shall remain, it is visionary to talk of universal peace. As soon as the source shall be dried up, it will be impossible to exclude the consequence. It is property that forms men into one common mass and makes them fit to be played upon like a brute machine. Were this stumbling block removed, each man would be united to his neighbour in love and mutual kindness a thousand times more than now ; but each man would think and judge for himself.

The advantages of an equal system of property are thus evident, but there remain objections on the ground of impracticability.

It is objected that luxury is beneficial because it creates industry and encourages the fine arts. This has already been answered in part by the contention that luxury is in reality a leading cause of the moral evils of mankind. Godwin adds that a better incentive would be free access to the means of production.

It is territorial monopoly that obliges men unwillingly to see vast tracts of land lying waste, or negligently and imperfectly cultivated, while they are subjected to the miseries of want. If land were perpetually open to him who was willing to cultivate it, it is not to be believed but that it would be cultivated in proportion to the wants of the community, nor by the same reason would there by any effectual check to the increase in population.

A second objection is that the equal distribution of property will encourage slothfulness and " put an end to industry." This objection is based on the idea that men will only work industriously when they are promised personal gain, and that the withdrawal of this incentive will rob humanity of the motive that has hitherto produced all the great advances in the standard of life.

But against the incentive of gain, which may be lost, we must balance freedom from the crippling effects of the monopoly of property. In " a state of equal property," the amount of labour required to produce necessities, being shared among the community, would be so slight that few men would shrink from it. Godwin anticipates Kropotkin and other later political thinkers in an elaborate discussion of the quantity of labour necessary each day if the production of luxuries were suspended. He estimates it at half an hour per day.

Furthermore, the contention that men will become idle if they have not the stimulus of gain results from a superficial observation of human motives. Men really strive for more than their necessary amount of property, not for the gain itself, but for the distinction it bestows in the eyes of their fellows. In an equal society the love of distinction would be satisfied, not in ostentation, but in beneficial activity.

In tranquil leisure it is impossible for any but the sublimest mind to exist without the passion for distinction. This passion, no longer permitted to lose itself in indirect channels and useless wanderings, will seek the noblest course and perpetually fructify the seeds of public good. Mind, though it will perhaps at no time arrive at the termination of its possible discoveries and improvements, will nevertheless advance with a rapidity and firmness of which we are at present unable to conceive the idea.

Godwin is careful, however, to point out that the love of fame is itself a delusion which will eventually become unnecessary. The man who acts for fame " may produce public good, but if he do, it is from indirect and spurious views." We should act only for the good of mankind in general, and should be led by our conception of justice, " a principle that rests upon this single postulatum, that man and man are beings of the same nature and susceptible, under certain limitations, of the same advantages."

A further objection is that an equal system cannot be permanent because there will always be men who take advantage of their neighbours and try to secure privileges for themselves, so that inequalities will rapidly be introduced again.

But if men had come to desire and establish a state of equality, it is unlikely that their intentions would be so weak as to lead to a breaking down of their resolve to succeed. Crime in general arises from the injustice of an unequal society, and the criminal is usually under the impression that he is repaying an injury ; an equal society, on the other hand, would produce no injustice to motivate this desire for personal advantage.

It is a further answer that luxury is not conducive to lasting satisfaction, and that men who live in a condition of equality will rapidly find " infinitely more pleasure from simplicity, frugality and truth than from luxury, empire and fame."

The theory of impermanence is further invalidated if we envisage the action of such a system.

Let us suppose that we are introduced to a community of men who are accustomed to an industry proportioned to the wants of the whole, and to communicate instantly and unconditionally, each men to his neighbour, that for which the former has not and the latter has immediate occasion. Here the first and simplest motive to personal accumulation is instantly cut off. I need not accumulate to protect myself against accidents, sickness or infirmity, for these are claims the validity of which is not regarded as a subject of doubt, and with which every man is accustomed to comply. I can accumulate in a considerable degree nothing but what is perishable, for exchange being unknown, that which I cannot personally consume adds nothing to the sum of my wealth.

A fourth objection to an equal system of property is that it would curtail personal independence by making each man " a passive instrument in the hands of the community."

But Godwin indicates that

we should distinguish two sorts of independence, one of which may be denominated natural and the other moral. Natural independence, a freedom from all constraint except that of reason and argument presented to the understanding, is of the utmost importance to the welfare and improvement of mind. Moral independence on the contrary is always injurious . . . for, as has abundantly appeared in the course of the present enquiry, there is no situation in which I can be placed where it is not incumbent on me to adopt a certain species of conduct in preference to all others, and of consequence where I shall not prove an ill member of society if I act in any other than a particular manner. . . . But if we ought never to act independently of the principles of reason and in no instance to shrink from the candid examination of another, it is nevertheless essential that we should at all times be free to cultivate the individuality and follow the dictates of our own judgment.

In fact, no restrictions on natural independence are necessary for the functioning of an equal society, which can be governed by " inclination and conviction." We must be ever on our guard against turning men into machines, and for this reason Godwin opposes anything more than is absolutely necessary in co-operative labour and living. Men should be simple in their needs and should not be tied to the convenience of others.

Whether by the nature of things co-operation of some sort will always be necessary is a question that we are scarcely competent to decide. At present, to pull down a tree, to cut a canal, to navigate a vessel requires the labour of many. Will it always require the labour of many ? When we look at the complicated machines of human contrivance, various sorts of mills, of weaving engines, of steam engines, are we not astonished at the compendium of labour they produce ? Who shall say where this species of improvement must stop ? . . . Hereafter it is by no means clear that the most extensive operations will not be within the reach of one man ; or, to make use of a familiar instance, that a plough may not be turned into a field and perform its office without the need of superintendence. . . . The conclusion of the progress which has here been sketched is something like a final close to the necessity of manual labour.

(Godwin gained much derision for these speculations, but the progress of modern inventions has vindicated him. When, later, he talked of the possibility of human immortality, he was on much less certain ground.)

There are, however, certain dangers in too extreme individuality. Intercourse with other men and their ideas is necessary, because character is made by external impressions.

All attachments to individuals except in proportion to their merits are plainly unjust. It is therefore desirable that we should be the friends of man rather than of particular men, and that we should pursue the chain of our own reflections with no other interruption than information or philanthropy requires.

Here Godwin commences his famous attack on marriage. Marriage, like any other form of cohabitation, is based on a false assumption that " the inclinations and wishes of two human

beings should coincide through any long period of time." It
results inevitably in " thwarting, bickering and unhappiness."
Marriage partakes of the evil nature of law, in that it endeavours
to perpetuate a choice made at a particular time of a man's or a
woman's life. It is also " the worst of all properties."

Godwin foresees no evil results from the abolition of marriage.

> The intercourse of the sexes will in such a state fall under the same
> system as any other system of friendship. . . . I shall assiduously
> cultivate the intercourse of that woman whose accomplishments shall
> strike me in the most powerful manner. . . . Reasonable men then will
> propagate their species, not because a certain sensible pleasure is
> annexed to this action, but because it is right that the species should be
> propagated, and the manner in which they exercise this function will be
> regulated by the dictates of reason and duty.

The end of marriage will also mean an end of the domination
of children by their parents, and education will become suited to
the natures and needs of the children.

> No creature in human form will be expected to learn anything but
> because he desires it and has some conception of its utility and value ;
> and every man in proportion to his capacity will be ready to furnish
> such general hints and comprehensive views as will suffice for the
> guidance and encouragement of him who studies from a principle of
> desire.

Above all, every man should be taught to maintain his individuality from a wrongful immersion in the collective.

In the " genuine state of society'" restrictions will not exist.
There will not even be a restriction on the accumulation of property. Opinion will be sufficient to ensure that this does not
occur.

Godwin defines a man's just property as that which is
necessary for his use.

> . . . What I have, though the fruit of my own industry, if unnecessary,
> it is an usurpation for me to retain.

There would be little reason for disputes concerning property.
No man would force from another what he did not give willingly,
nor would any man infringe on another's privacy or attempt to
gain from him what might be necessary for his pursuits.
Disputes regarding property are " the offspring of a misshapen
and disproportioned love of ourselves."

The system of equal property does not mean that each man

should make everything he needs. Men skilled in certain operations might spend their time in specialised work and distribute their products among those who needed them, receiving for their own needs from the surplus of their neighbours. A certain division of labour would thus occur, but not the extravagant kind which flourishes in modern industry. This system would not mean the re-introduction of barter and exchange.

The abstract spirit of exchange will perhaps govern ; every man will employ an equal portion of his time in manual labour. But the individual application of exchange is of all practices the most pernicious. The moment I require any other reason for supplying you than the cogency of your claim—the moment, in addition to the dictates of benevolence, I demand a prospect of advantage to myself—there is an end of that political justice and pure society of which we treat. . . . The profession paramount to all others and in which every man will bear his part will be that of man, and in addition perhaps that of cultivator.

. . . . . .

It remains to consider the means by which the equal society would be introduced. Godwin first shows that, whatever may be the immediate effects of the overthrow of present society, if the final result be the triumph of truth and justice and the end of evils that spring from property and government, then we must be willing to accept any period of terror that may intervene.

But such evils are not in reality the necessary accompaniment of the victory of truth. It is incumbent upon those who would convert men to justice to act in accordance with the benignity they would inspire. Their duty is to speak the truth as they see it, complete and undisguised.

Every community of men, as well as every individual, must govern itself according to its ideas of justice. What I should desire is, not by violence to change its institutions, but by reason to change its ideas. I have no business with factions or intrigue, but simply to promulgate the truth and to wait the tranquil process of conviction.

Godwin has an unbounded confidence in the power of truth to make its way once it has been revealed to the world. He does not despair of even the rich and the great becoming convinced of its validity, voluntarily surrendering their wealth and positions, and entering into the equality of the free society. Men are not governed wholly by self-interest, and they may well perceive the worthlessness of luxury and the dangers that are involved in their undue retention of it. A study of history teaches us that there has been an improvement in the moral customs and ideas of man, and it is reasonable to suppose that this improvement will continue, particularly when assisted by the fearless exhibition of truth.

But this progress is not necessarily inevitable, and it can certainly be made more sure and rapid by a teaching of the true principles of political justice.

Whatever be the object towards which mind spontaneously advances, it is of no mean importance to us to have a distinct view of that object. Our advances will thus become accelerated. It is a well-known principle of morality that he who proposes perfection to himself, though he will inevitably fall short of what he pursues, will make a more rapid progress than he who is contented to aim only at what is imperfect. The benefits to be derived in the interval from a view of equalisation as one of the great objects towards which we are tending are exceedingly conspicuous. Such a view will strongly conduce to make us disinterested now. . . . It will impress us with a just apprehension of what it is of which man is capable and in which his perfection consists, and will fix our ambition and activity upon the worthiest objects. Mind cannot arrive at any great and illustrious attainment, however much the nature of mind may carry us towards it, without feeling some presages of its approach ; and it is reasonable to believe that the earlier these presages are introduced and the more distinct they are made, the more auspicious will be the event.

In this mood of calm confidence in the powers of reason, Godwin delivered his message to a receptive world.

PART IV

# Years of Fame
## 1793—1797

I

POLITICAL JUSTICE established Godwin as one of the leading writers of his time. Until then he had been a struggling
journalist, known to comparatively few writers and politicians, and almost completely unknown to the general
public. Up to 1793 the only book published under his name
had been the *Sketches from History*, a work which attracted no
great attention. But with the appearance of *Political Justice* he
attained a celebrity probably more considerable than any
achieved before or since by the success of a single book.

This fame was probably due to its timely publication. The
work of the political associations was at its height. Revolutionary ideas, almost abandoned by the upper and middle classes,
were still spreading among the petty bourgeoisie and the working
class, and were upheld by most of the intellectuals. A great and
intelligent public was hungry for topics of discussion and thought
—and no book could have furnished more controversial points to
satisfy their curiosity and idealism. It was therefore not surprising that, among radical circles, it made a deep impression and
earned wide popularity.

No work in our time gave such a blow to the philosophical mind of
the country as the celebrated *Enquiry concerning Political Justice* [said
Hazlitt a quarter of a century later]. Tom Paine was considered for the
time as a Tom Fool to him, Paley an old woman, Edmund Burke a
flashy sophist. Truth, moral truth, it was supposed, had here taken up
its abode ; and these were the oracles of thought.

Hazlitt also says that at the time of the publication of his
masterpiece Godwin

. . . was in the very zenith of a sultry and unwholesome popularity ; he
blazed as a sun in the firmament of reputation ; no one was more talked

of, more looked up to, more sought after, and wherever liberty, truth, justice was the theme, his name was not far off.

Among the younger writers, in particular, *Political Justice* aroused enthusiastic reactions. Coleridge lauded Godwin in a bad but extravagant sonnet.

> O form'd t'illumine a sunless world forlorn,
>     As o'er the chill and dusky brow of Night,
> In Finland's wintry skies the Mimic Morn
>     Electric pours a stream of rosy light,
>
> Pleas'd I have mark'd OPPRESSION, terror-pale,
>     Since, thro' the windings of her dark machine,
>     Thy steady eye has shot its glances keen—
> And bade th' All-lovely " scenes at distance hail."
>
> Nor will I not thy holy guidance bless,
>     And hymn thee, Godwin ! with an ardent lay ;
>     For that thy voice, in Passion's stormy day,
> When wild I roam'd the bleak Heath of Distress,
>     Bade the bright form of Justice meet my way
> And told me that her name was HAPPINESS.

Coleridge and Southey, who had, as he says, " read and studied and all but worshipped Godwin," evolved a scheme for a community, on Godwinian principles, called a Pantisocracy, which they hoped to establish in America, on the banks of the Susquehannah. They collected money and reached Bristol, where they realised that their funds were insufficient to charter a ship, and, instead of sailing for Utopia, contracted unfortunate marriages. After this, their enthusiasm declined, and Southey became a lifelong enemy of Godwin, but Coleridge eventually became one of his most intimate friends and his warmest defender in adversity. Wordsworth was another ardent Godwinite, and told a young student : " Burn your books of chemistry and read Godwin on necessity."

The older radicals approved of the book with reservations. They regarded it as instructive, but their attitude to its more characteristic ideas is expressed in the words of the *New Annual Register :* " Some of his positions and projects we consider to be fanciful and extravagant."

Horne Tooke, almost alone among Godwin's acquaintances, told him that it was a bad book, and asserted that Godwin and Holcroft had their heads full of plays and novels and then thought themselves philosophers. But Tooke was an exception, and it is very probable that he spoke thus because his notorious vanity was offended by the praise which Godwin had received.

It was not among literary men alone that *Political Justice* aroused great attention. Both the government and the people soon became aware of its character and implications.

Mr Godwin [says De Quincey] advanced against thrones and dominations, powers and principalities, with the air of some Titan slinger or monomachist from Thebes and Troy, saying—" Come hither, ye wretches, that I may give your flesh to the fowls of the air."

The appearance at this time of a book whose arguments delivered a more complete and radical attack on the existing social order than any of its predecessors, could not fail to perturb a government always fearfully on the watch for signs of subversive activity and rendered more nervous by the outbreak of war in the same month as the book was published. *Political Justice* was the subject of at least one anxious discussion in the Cabinet. The idea of taking proceedings against Godwin was only set aside after Pitt had remarked that a book priced at three guineas could be regarded as innocuous because it cost too much for any but the propertied classes to buy. It is reasonable to suppose that Pitt was not yet anxious to commit himself to the doubtful enterprise of persecuting the writer of a work of a theoretical nature. Nevertheless, Godwin was now regarded as a dangerous radical, and as such the Government obviously had him under observation as a possible victim in later general persecutions.

Pitt had, in fact, been misled by the price of the book, which was probably fixed with the very intention of avoiding a prosecution. Its reputation soon reached the more conscious strata of the workers affected by radical teachings, and various means were found to disseminate its contents. In Scotland and Ireland cheap pirated editions were printed, while in the industrial districts, and even in many country towns, artisans and labourers formed clubs, of which there are said to have been some hundreds, for the express purpose of purchasing it and reading it aloud. Some of the political societies printed pamphlets containing those sections which had a more urgent bearing on the social problems of the time.

*Political Justice*, in spite of Godwin's expressed desire for change to be left for peaceful education and persuasion to accomplish, contained in its attack on the philosophical foundations of government an element so subversive that it could not help being a potent contributor to the social unrest of the time. Godwin became regarded by the respectable and the reactionary as one of the most dangerous enemies of society. Yet so challenging and so thorough was his attack that it was many months before any serious reply was written.

Godwin himself regarded his fame with a certain naïve pride. In his journal for 1794 he remarks :

. . . there was not a person almost in town or country who had any acquaintance with modern publications that had not heard of the *Enquiry concerning Political Justice*, or that was not acquainted in a great or small degree with the contents of that work. I was nowhere a stranger. The doctrines of that work (though if any book ever contained the dictates of an independent mind, mine might pretend to do so) coincided in a great degree with the sentiments then prevailing in English society, and I was everywhere received with curiosity and kindness. If temporary fame ever was an object worthy to be coveted by the human mind, I certainly obtained it in a degree that has seldom been exceeded. I was happy to feel that this circumstance did not in the slightest degree interrupt the sobriety of my mind.

Whether or not his mental sobriety was affected, Godwin's fame and comparative prosperity did not change the simplicity with which he lived. Early in 1793 he took a small house in Somers Town where he dwelt in solitude and deliberate austerity. Mary Shelley has left a note giving some idea of his habits at this period :

He rose between seven and eight, and read some classic author before breakfast. From nine till twelve or one he occupied himself with his pen. He found that he could not exceed this measure of labour with any advantage to his own health, or the work in hand. . . . The rest of the morning was spent in reading and seeing his friends. When at home he dined at four, but during his bachelor life he frequently dined out. His dinner at home at this time was simple enough. He had no regular servant ; an old woman came in the morning to clean and arrange his rooms, and if necessary she prepared a mutton chop, which was put in a Dutch oven.

Godwin felt that the adoption of this kind of life was in accordance with the principles he had maintained in his writings.

No man could be more desirous than I was of adopting a practice conformable to my principles, as far as I could do so without affording reasonable ground of offence to any other person. I was anxious not to spend a penny on myself which I did not imagine calculated to render me a more capable servant of the public, and as I was averse to the expenditure of money, so I was not inclined to earn it but in small portions. I considered the disbursement of money for the benefit of others as a very difficult problem, which he who has the possession of it is bound to solve in the best manner he can, but which affords small encouragement to any one to acquire it who has it not. The plan, therefore, I resolved on was leisure—a leisure to be employed in deliberate composition, and in the pursuit of such attainments as afforded me the most promise to render me useful. For years I scarcely did anything at home or abroad without the enquiry being uppermost in my mind whether I could be better employed for general benefit ; and I hope much of this temper has survived, and will attend me to my grave. The frame in which I found myself exalted my spirits, and rendered me more of a talker than I was before or have been since, and than is agreeable to my natural character. Certainly I attended now, and at all times, to everything that was offered in the way of reasoning and argument, with the sincerest desire of embracing the truth and that only.

Of the state of extreme mental activity and personal assertiveness in which he lived during and after writing *Political Justice*, Godwin many years later gave a much more elaborate description in an essay on Diffidence, published in *Thoughts on Man*. What he says has an important bearing on the peculiarly fruitful activity which characterised this period in comparison with those which preceded and followed it.

A new epoch occurred in my character, when I published, and at the time I was writing, my *Enquiry concerning Political Justice*. My mind was wrought up to a certain elevation of tone ; the speculations in which I was engaged, tending to embrace all that was most important to man in society, and the frame to which I had assiduously bent myself, of giving quarter to nothing because it was startling and astounding, gave a new bias to my character. The habit which I thus formed put me more on the alert even in the scenes of ordinary life, and gave me a boldness and an eloquence more than was natural to me. I then reverted to the principle which I stated in the beginning, of being ready to tell my neighbour whatever it might be of advantage to him to know, to show myself the sincere and zealous advocate of absent merit and worth, and to contribute by every means in my power to the improvement of others and to the diffusion of salutary truths through the world. I desired that every hour that I lived should be turned to the best account, and was bent each day to examine whether I had conformed myself to this rule. I held in this course with tolerable constancy for five or six years ; and, even when that constancy abated, it failed not to leave a beneficial effect on my subsequent conduct.

But, in pursuing this scheme of practice, I was acting a part somewhat foreign to my constitution. I was by nature more a speculative than an active character, more inclined to reason within myself upon what I heard and saw, than to declaim concerning it. I loved to sit by unobserved, and to meditate upon the panorama before me. . . .

. . . My lungs, as I have already said, were not of iron ; my manner was not overbearing and despotic ; there was nothing in it to deter him who differed from me from entering the field in turn, and telling the tale of his views and judgments in contradiction of mine. I descended into the arena, and stood on a level with the rest. . . .

All this however had a tendency to subtract from my vocation as a missionary. I was no longer a knight errant, prepared on all occasions by dint of arms to vindicate the cause of every principle that was unjustly handled, and every character that was wrongfully assailed. Meanwhile I returned to the field, occasionally and uncertainly. It required some provocation and incitement to call me out ; but there was the lion, or whatever combative animal may more justly prefigure me, sleeping, and that might be awakened.

There are certain statements in this passage which perhaps do not agree completely with what appeared to his contemporaries and friends to be Godwin's characteristics. But this does not signify any insincerity on Godwin's part, for in his accounts of himself and his actions he seems always scrupulously honest in telling the tale of every event strictly as he saw it, even if the tale turned against himself—as, for instance, in the case of unfavourable criticisms of his books, which he noted down faithfully and exactly. That he should have seen himself in a slightly better light than his friends did is natural. We all regard ourselves as men of forbearance and cannot understand when other people find flaws in our behaviour over incidents for which we do not hold ourselves to blame.

This period was the happy and triumphant heyday of Godwin's life. He had cast aside completely the bonds that hampered his childhood and youth, had divested himself of all opinions forced upon him by anything but his own reasoning, and had assumed and then destroyed the authority of his father. In gaining his own freedom, he had become, more than any other man of his day, the prophet of human freedom, and by his reasoning had built a philosophical plea for individual liberty which as yet the enemies of progress had not attempted to answer. He had reached fame with an almost incredible rapidity, had become one of the leading writers and thinkers of his day, regarded with deference and curiosity by the whole intellectual world. " I had a numerous audience of all classes, of every age, and of either sex. The young and the fair did not feel deterred from consulting my pages."

Admiration for his achievement brought him many friends, and at this time there were few important figures in literary circles with whom he had not some kind of acquaintance. He had gained sufficient material prosperity to remove him from the insecurity of hack writing and the frustration of journalism. He was able to perform at his leisure work that appeared congenial and useful, to live with a moderate comfort and assume an appearance in which sartorial gaiety broke for a while the almost life-long clericalism of his appearance. Amelia Alderson describes him in these circumstances :

We arrived at about one o'clock at the philosopher's house, whom we found with his hair *bien poudré*, and in a pair of new, sharp-toed, red morocco slippers, not to mention his green coat and crimson under-waistcoat.

But the style in which Godwin lived was always simple in comparison with many of his contemporaries. At no time was he extravagant in providing for his own comforts, and the appearance of wasteful living in his later years was due to a number of circumstances for which he was not directly responsible. At this period he certainly lived in general according to his philosophical ideas, and gained his stimuli from high thought rather than from high living. Borne up by a high intellectual activity and moral fervour, his personal life seems to have moved calmly and with relatively little complication of feeling. The external world was not so calm for an apostle of freedom.

2

" Terror was the order of the day," said Godwin himself, looking back in at least slightly calmer times on the period of intense repression that began shortly after the publication of *Political Justice*. It was a period during which no liberal could feel safe from persecution, and when the crazy festival of the ruling class reached its height, death seemed to hang with terrifying imminence over every known radical in the country.

Up to the middle of 1793 the Government had been content with small and sporadic attacks. A few undistinguished individuals had been sent to prison, a few booksellers had been prosecuted for selling Tom Paine's writings, a few small societies had been closed down. But these minor attacks seemed only to assist the radicals, and in the autumn of 1793 the Government, alarmed at the steady growth of revolutionary sentiment, decided to take drastic action in a way that, they hoped, could not fail to attract public attention and act as a major deterrent.

They chose Scotland as the first scene of attack, because the Scots law favoured their chances of gaining satisfactory verdicts and the Scottish jury system was readily corruptible. In October 1793, the radicals of Scotland decided to hold a Convention to discuss shorter parliaments and universal suffrage. Delegates from the London Corresponding Society attended the conference, which lasted for fifteen days of orderly debate, until it was dispersed by the magistrates and five of the leading delegates were arrested. These were tried before a notoriously partisan judge and sentenced to fourteen years' transportation. → Postgate p. 155, 156

Godwin, although he was no supporter of the London Corresponding Society or the Edinburgh Convention, saw clearly that the issue was much wider than the circumstances might indicate. He foresaw that this was the beginning of a general persecution, and took an active interest in the trial and subsequent fate of the five men. On hearing that they were to be treated as common felons and denied the benefits customary for political prisoners, he wrote a letter to *The Morning Chronicle* in which he exposed publicly the infamy of the Cabinet's action. The letter was couched in terms of blunt condemnation, and shows that uncompromising steadiness with which Godwin always maintained his opinions, however unpopular they might be :

You know, sir, that there is not in the Island of Great Britain a more strenuous advocate for peaceableness and forbearance than I am. But I will not be the partaker of their secrets of State. What they dare to perpetrate, I dare to tell. Do they not every day assure us that the great use of punishment is example, to deter others from incurring the like offence ? And yet they delight to inflict severities upon these men in a corner, which they tremble to have exposed to the eyes of the world. I join issue with administration on this point ; I, too, would have the punishment of Messieurs Muir and Palmer serve for an example. Sir, there are examples to imitate and examples to avoid. . . .
. . . a punishment that exceeds all measure and mocks at all justice, that listens to no sentiment but revenge, and plays the volunteer in insolence and cruelty—a punishment the purpose of which is to inflict on such men slavery, degradation of soul, a lingering decay and final

imbecility—can do nothing but exasperate men's minds, and wind up their nerves to decisive action.

This letter was based on the general attitude expressed in *Political Justice* concerning the uselessness of punishment, but it also contained an element of sound expedient sense which the Government would have been wise to accept. However, neither the Cabinet nor Burke, to whom Godwin made a special appeal, took any notice of his arguments and the unfortunate men were duly shipped to Botany Bay—four of them never to return to their native land.

Among them was a close friend of Godwin, Joseph Gerrald. Gerrald was a West Indian landowner, who had lived in America and had returned to England imbued with republican ideas, which led him to associate closely with the various political societies. Mary Shelley says that " his friends were enthusiastically attached to him on account of his brilliant talents, and his nice sense of honour, and an unconquerable ardour in the pursuit of objects which seemed to him the noblest in the world." Gerrald was set free on bail and had every opportunity to escape from the country, but refused to yield to the importunities of his friends, " resolving that his lot should be the same as that of his partners in a cause, which he looked upon as sacred, and considered it as a base desertion to refuse to share their fate."

Godwin had many conversations with Gerrald while he was awaiting trial, and wrote him a letter which reveals the calm spirit with which these enthusiasts for human brotherhood faced the prospect of oppression and punishment :

I cannot recollect the situation in which you are in a few days to be placed without emotions of respect, and I had almost said of envy. For myself I will never adopt any conduct for the express purpose of being put upon my trial, but if I be ever so put, I will consider that day as a day of triumph.

Your trial, if you so please, may be a day such as England, and I believe the whole world, never saw. It may be the means of converting thousands, and, progressively, millions, to the cause of reason and public justice. You have a great stake, your place, your youth, your liberty, and your talents, on a single throw. If you must suffer, do not, I conjure you, suffer without making use of this opportunity of telling a tale upon which the happiness of nations depends. Spare none of the resources of your powerful mind. Is this a day of reserve, a day to be slurred over in neglect—the day that constitutes the very crisis of your fate ? . . .

Above all, let me entreat you to abstain from harsh epithets and bitter invective. Show that you are not terrible but kind, and anxious for the good of all. Truth will lose nothing by this. Truth can never gain by passion, violence and resentment. It is never so strong as in the firm, fixed mind, that yields to the emotions neither of rage nor fear. It is by calm and recollected boldness that we can shake the pillars of the vault of heaven. How great will you appear if you show that all the injustice with which you are treated cannot move you ; that you are too great to be wounded by their arrows ; that you still hold the stead-fast course that becomes the friend of man, and that while you expose their rottenness you harbour no revenge. The public want men of this unaltered spirit, whom no persecution can embitter. The jury, the world will feel your value, if you show yourself such a man ; let no human ferment mix in the sacred work.

Farewell, my whole soul goes with you. You represent us all.

Gerrald acted at his trial with all the philosophical calm which Godwin had recommended, and the courage with which he maintained his faith in the salvation of humanity must have pro-vided an inspiration for those who still continued in fear that each day would bring their own turn to face the persecuting fury of the state.

Moral light [he told his judges] is irresistible by the mind as physical by the eye. All attempts to impede its progress are in vain. It will roll rapidly along, and as well may tyrants imagine that by placing their feet upon the earth they can stop its diurnal motion, as that they shall be able by efforts the most virulent and pertinacious to extinguish the light of reason and philosophy, which happily for mankind is everywhere spreading around us.

It is difficult to imagine words that would demonstrate more clearly the contrast between the brave sincerity of this fine character and the unprincipled cruelty by which the representa-tives of the ruling class sought to allay their own fear. Gerrald was sentenced to fourteen years at Botany Bay. He survived his arrival only a few months. At his death he said to his friends : " I die in the best of causes, and, as you witness, without repin-ing."

The Government soon decided to extend its attacks to England, and this time the persecution came even closer to Godwin. The Government used the activities of the London Corresponding Society as an excuse for its attacks. The Society had decided to defy authority by holding a Convention similar to that which had ended so cruelly in Scotland. A conspiratorial atmosphere seems to have been preserved over the details of this convention, which gave the Government further excuse. On May 12th, Thomas Hardy, the shoemaker who founded the society, was arrested on a charge of high treason. Within a few days ten others, including Horne Tooke and Thelwall, the pamphleteer friend of Coleridge, were in the Tower or Newgate on the same charge.

A special, hand-picked committee of the House of Commons was formed to collect or concoct evidence against the prisoners, and Habeas Corpus was suspended, amid the unavailing protests of Sheridan and Fox. This allowed the Government to hold the prisoners without charge for an indefinite period. On May 16th Pitt reported on behalf of the committee of investigation that the Corresponding Society had formulated a plan " the object of which was to assemble a pretended convention of the people, for the purposes of assuming the character of a general representation of the nation, superseding the representative capacity of the House, and arrogating the legislative capacity of the country at large." For us, who can see the events of that time in their true historical proportions, it is difficult to imagine how anyone could have given credence to so fantastic a charge or have paid any attention to Pitt's assertion that " a conspiracy so formidable had never existed." Yet such was the state of panic among the propertied classes that they readily believed all the lies concocted by the Government and worked themselves into a fury against the reformers.

The prisoners were kept in gaol until October 2nd, when Lord Chief Justice Eyre presented a formidable charge to a grand jury which returned a bill enabling the trial to proceed. At this hearing Holcroft, who was named in the charge, walked into the court and gave himself up to stand with his comrades.

The publication of the charge caused great concern among the radicals. It was obvious that this was intended as the beginning of a widespread suppression of the " Left," and that if a conviction were obtained it would be the prelude to much more extensive arrests and trials, in which every radical knew that his turn would come, sooner or later. It became known that the Government had some hundreds of signed warrants waiting to be used immediately a conviction had been obtained. No doubt Godwin's name was among the first.

At the time Godwin was away in the country. There he

received a letter from Holcroft, who was imprisoned in Newgate, and returned immediately to London. The urgent nature of the situation was evident. The charge was so cleverly constructed and so thoroughly spread through the country by what propaganda agencies existed, that even many men well disposed to the radicals believed at first that the accused had actually been plotting an attempt to overthrow the Government. It was therefore necessary for the charges to be refuted in as thorough a manner as possible.

Godwin set to work immediately. His reply was finished in forty-eight hours, and on October 20th, more than a week before the date of the trials, appeared in the *Morning Chronicle* under the title of *Cursory Strictures on the Charge delivered by Lord Justice Eyre to the Grand Jury*. It was immediately reprinted as a pamphlet and distributed throughout the land.

Eyre's charge was, in spite of its plausible and legalistic verbiage, based on an attempt to prove that, although no single act of the defendants constituted treason, yet their intention might be said to be treasonable, and their actions might in the end lead to treason. A convention to advocate parliamentary reform was not treasonable, but it was probable, Eyre asserted, that it covered some deeper design to enforce such reforms on the Government, and in this case its design might be interpreted as treasonable. He concluded :

If charges of high treason are offered to be maintained on this ground only, perhaps it may be fitting that, in respect of the extraordinary nature, and dangerous extent, and very criminal nature of such a conspiracy, that case, which I state to you as a new and doubtful case, should be put into a judicial course of enquiry, that it may receive a solemn adjudicature whether it will or will not amount to high treason, in order to which the bills must be found to be true bills.

It was not difficult for a man of Godwin's logical capacity to discover the flaws in Eyre's reasoning. After stating Eyre's position, he goes on to contend that the accused must be proved guilty not of a crime against a particular code of morality but a crime against law.

Let it be granted that the crime is, in the eye of reason and discretion, the most enormous that it can enter into the heart of man to conceive, still I have a right to ask, is it a crime against law ? Show me the statute that describes it ; refer me to the precedent by which it is

defined, quote me the adjudged case in which a matter of such unparalleled magnitude is settled.

The arguments of the Lord Chief Justice were based largely on
probabilities which Godwin had no difficulty in demolishing.
Eyre states that there is a danger of " an association not in its
own nature simply unlawful, too easily degenerating, and becoming unlawful in the highest degree." Godwin crushes this with
forceful wit. " An association for Parliamentary Reform may
desert its object and become guilty of High Treason. True ; so
may a card club, a bench of justice, or even a Cabinet Council."

Godwin goes on to indicate the artful way in which the intention of treason is suggested, although there is no fragment of
proof that such intention existed.

But the authors of the present prosecution probably hope that the
mere names of Jacobin and Republican will answer their purposes, and
that a jury of Englishmen will be found who will send every man to the
gallows without examination to whom these appellations shall once have
been attributed.

After a thorough examination of the other contentions, Godwin
concludes by exposing the complete inhumanity and terrorism
of the attempt.

The Chief Justice quits in this instance the character of criminal judge
and civil magistrate, and assumes that of a natural philosopher, or
experimental anatomist. He is willing to dissect the persons that shall
be brought before him, the better to ascertain the truth or falsehood of
his preconceived conjectures. The plain English of his recommendation
is this. Let these men be put on their trial for their lives, let them and
their friends be exposed to all the anxieties incident to so uncertain and
fearful a condition ; let them be exposed to ignominy, to obloquy, to
the partialities, as it may happen, of a prejudiced Judge, and the perverseness of an ignorant jury ; we shall then know how we ought to
conceive of similar cases.

The effect of this publication was instantaneous. As a contemporary account records :

Instead of the guilt and conviction of the accused, nothing was heard
of, in the streets and places of resort, but the flagrancy of the offences of
the charge.

Hazlitt, a critical judge of such matters, described it many years
later as " one of the most acute and seasonable political pamphlets that ever appeared."

The trials commenced on October 28th with that of Thomas

Hardy. The atmosphere was electric throughout London, where great crowds waited outside the court, and even in the country the pervading feeling of anxiety caused men to leave their work and wait for the stage coach to bring the latest news. The radical leaders and intellectuals were apprehensive, and many had already made arrangements to cross the Channel before the general arrests began.

The trial, bitterly contested, lasted for eight days. The feeling of the people was with Thomas Hardy throughout, and when the jury returned a verdict of " Not guilty " there was great rejoicing throughout the country.

The Government now brought Horne Tooke into the dock. After a trial of five days the jury only retired for eight minutes before they returned to announce their verdict of " Not guilty." Again immense rejoicings showed the mood of the people, and the crowd outside the court unharnessed the horses from the coach of Erskine, the defending counsel, and dragged it through the streets in a great demonstration. The Government, nevertheless, made a last effort and brought up Thelwall, who, after a trial of four days, was also acquitted. The rest of the prisoners were released. More important, the great comb-out of celebrated radicals failed to transpire. The radical cause had won a great victory over the Government, but it was transitory and did little to stem the tide of unpopularity which was turning against liberal thought.

As the war with France continued, the mood of the nation became steadily more patriotic and opposed to any ideas that might be associated with France or the French. Moreover, as always happens in a war, many of the radical leaders were themselves tempted into the reactionary camp by the promise of preferment, and until after Waterloo the liberal movement in England went through a long period of gloomy eclipse.

Godwin's part in the acquittal was at first kept a close secret, and for a time his pamphlet was suspected to be the work of one Miles Vaughn, a liberal attorney. Later, however, his authorship became known, and the radicals in general felt a great gratitude towards him for this timely intervention.

The most moving expression of esteem came from Horne Tooke. Godwin records it in his diary :

The great philologist had frequently rallied me in a good-humoured way on the visionary nature of my politics—his own were of a different cast.   It was a favourite notion with him that no happier or more excellent Government had ever existed than that of the English nation in the reigns of George the First and George the Second.   From disparaging my philosophy, he passed by a very natural transition to the setting light, either really or in pretence, by the abilities for which I had some credit.   He often questioned me with affected earnestness as to the truth of the report that I was the author of the *Cursory Strictures on Chief Justice Eyre's Charge to the Grand Jury*, of which pamphlet he always declared the highest admiration, and to which he repeatedly professed that he held himself indebted for his life.   The question was revived at the dinner I have mentioned.   I answered carelessly to his enquiry that I believed I was the author of that pamphlet.   He insisted on a reply in precise terms to his question, and I complied.   He then requested that I would give him my hand.   To do this I was obliged to rise from my chair and go to the end of the table where he sat.   I had no sooner done this than he suddenly conveyed my hand to his lips, vowing that he could do no less by the hand that had given existence to that production. The suddenness of the action filled me with confusion, yet I must confess that when I looked back upon it, this homage thus expressed was more gratifying to me than all the applause I had received from any other quarter.

With the majority of the political radicals, however, gratitude did not last long.  A few of the more independent figures, it is true, remembered the action to Godwin's credit.   William Taylor, of Norwich, who for some reason had suffered Godwin's criticism, wrote many years later to Southey :

It is the one thing I told Mackintosh I could not forgive in him, to forget that Godwin has rendered critical services to the enthusiasts of the good cause by his strictures on Eyre's Charge.   Godwin is sincere, independent and disinterested, more than most men.   What signifies it what he thinks of me ?

This was an oblique reproof of Southey, whose attitude was no better than Mackintosh's.

Hazlitt, writing thirty years afterwards, pointed out the debt owed by the radical cause to Godwin's actions :

This temporary effusion . . . gave a turn to the trials for high treason in the year 1794, and possibly saved the lives of twelve innocent individuals, marked out as political victims to the Moloch of Legitimacy, which then skulked behind a British throne, and had not yet dared to stalk forth (as it has done since) from its lurking-place, in the face of day, to brave the opinion of the world.   If it had then glutted its maw with its intended prey (the sharpness of Mr Godwin's pen cut the legal cords with which it was attempted to bind them) it might have done so sooner, and with more lasting effect.

But men like Taylor and Hazlitt were detached from the intrigues which have an unfortunate prominence in political movements. They could retain impartiality of judgment, and give a man credit for what seemed to them laudable characteristics or achievements, even when criticising features of which they disapproved. The political mind, however, is governed principally by expediency. A man is regarded with approval so long as he is willing to further the interests of politician or party, but whenever he takes a critical attitude which is likely to influence popular feeling against the political movement, then he must be condemned by any possible method. No political group is ever willing to accept or tolerate a standard of judgment other than its own, and if any conception of truth stand outside the party line, it must be ignored and its upholder condemned.

Godwin was soon to learn this in practice. So long as he showed solidarity with his fellow radicals in danger they treated him with praise and approval. But when he began again to point out the faults of their political associations, they turned against him with renewed bitterness, and those, like Thelwall, who owed him the greatest debt, seemed by this very fact to be prompted to become his most violent antagonists. It is an ironical and a disgraceful fact that the greatest English radical philosopher should have been deserted and attacked by the left-wing politicians even before the reactionaries began to vilify him, and there is no doubt that the peculiar venom with which the anti-liberal attacks were directed against Godwin in particular was due more than anything to the fact that the radical demagogues had turned against him already and thus made him the more vulnerable to the Government hacks. By this shameful desertion of a man who had defended them when his action might very well have been a " hanging matter," the radicals caused a breach in the whole liberal movement which made it easy for its enemies to immobilise it for many decades.

The immediate cause of the breach between Godwin and the politicians was the pamphlet which he published in 1795 on the Bills introduced by Grenville and Pitt for restraining " the right of meeting and of speaking in public in matters of present politics." Godwin published the pamphlet anonymously as " A Lover of Order," because he did not wish to prejudice the efficacy of his arguments by any extravagance that might be attached to his

name, and he wrote it with studied moderation, in order to show
that the proposals of the Government offended against the
ordinary standards of common sense and the accepted criteria of
political decency. But he never concealed from his friends and
associates that he was the real author, and the text contained
many recognisably Godwinian arguments.

The passages to which the radical demagogues objected were
those which expressed disquiet at the consequences of the French
Revolution and condemned the methods of the London Corresponding Society, advocating instead Godwin's own method of
revolution by education and the gradual spread of truth.

These were merely re-statements of what had already been
said in *Political Justice*, and there was no reason to accuse Godwin
of duplicity for repeating views which everybody knew he had
held for many years, and which had been tolerated when he had
made himself useful to the political groups.

Moreover, if Godwin reproved the London Corresponding
Society for what appeared to him the faults of its actions, he was
much more censorious in his attacks on the Government and its
methods. In one passage he paints a vivid picture of the kind of
tyrant state which might arise out of such legislation. It is a
picture that could well be used to portray the condition of the
totalitarian nations of the modern world :

It will perhaps be thought too trite if we were to dwell, in this place,
upon the ill consequences to result from instituting a national militia of
spies and informers. What kind of a man is a spy ? He is a man that
insinuates himself into your confidence in order to betray you. He
pretends to be uncommonly vehement and intemperate, that he may
excite you to be the same. He watches your unguarded moments, he
plies you with wine, that he may excite you to speak without restraint.
He undertakes to remember words, and he has an invincible bias in his
mind, inducing him to construe them in a particular way, and insensibly
to change them for words more definite and injurious. His very income
depends upon the frequency of his tales, and he is paid in proportion as
the tales that he brings, whether true or false, tend to the destruction of
the persons to whom they relate.

Miserable beyond compare must be the state of that country, where
such men as this are to be found in every town, in every street, in every
village, and in every house. " Evil communications corrupt good
manners." It is impossible that I should continue to associate with
knaves, without losing something of the unsullied lustre of my virtue.
Two virtues are most important in civil society : frankness, that I
should practice no duplicity, that I should play no part under a mask ;

and mutual trust and confidence. Now, what confidence can there be, when men are surrounded with spies and informers ? When, from the frequency of the phenomenon, I am unable certainly to tell, whether my friend or my brother be not a man, whose trade is accusation, and who will one day cause me to be transported or hanged ? In a country where the existence of spies and informers is frequent, the whole nation must of necessity be made up of two classes of hypocrites : hypocrites who hold out a false appearance, the better to ensnare ; and hypocrites, who hold out a false appearance, that they may not be ensnared.

Moreover, Godwin's denunciation of Pitt and Grenville was complete and uncompromising.

What sort of hearts are these men endued with ? What sort of understandings ? They scatter about punishments upon every occasion, and the punishment of the slightest offence is death. They know no principles of comparison, they are dead to every feeling of the heart, they pronounce with total indifference the punishment of death upon multitudes yet unborn ; in the spirit of King Richard in the play, " I will not dine, until his head be brought me ! "
Well may these men be the enemies of science, well may they declare every philosopher who investigates the nature of man or society subject to the pain of high treason ; well may they emulate the irruptions of the Goths and Vandals, who spread barbarism and intellectual darkness over the whole face of the earth ! They know no touch of civilisation ; they were never humanised by science or art ; they come forth in the pride of ignorance ; laugh at the scruples of human kindness, and trample upon all the barriers by which civil society can alone be preserved.

The exponents of political agitation were careful to ignore such passages in their condemnation of Godwin's pamphlet, and among the results of the incident was a split in the London Corresponding Society between a section led by Thelwall, which advocated political action, and one led by Francis Place which supported the Godwinian idea of changing society by means of education. The Thelwall faction was the more considerable, and the Society became, for the remainder of its brief life, one of the strongest centres of feeling against Godwin.

Thelwall, however, remained a Godwinian in at least one point —his contempt of gratitude, for he was one of the men who had been saved from the scaffold by Godwin's intervention in the preceding year. He attacked Godwin both in his public lectures and in his periodical, *The Tribune*, and a correspondence ensued in which Thelwall conducted himself with violence and Godwin with an admirable forbearance.

This incident, which must have cost Godwin considerable pain, represents both the end of his active intervention in current politics, and the beginning of that decline in his popularity which a few years later made him the most hated man of his day. His descent into the political arena had been beneficial in its effects, but the fact that he still contrived to retain his independence of judgment and refused to submerge his opinions in the partisan mass brought about an inevitable clash with organised political movements, which proved to him in practice what he had already stated theoretically in *Political Justice*—that political associations are of doubtful value in their achievements, and that " truth despises the assistance of marshalled numbers."

### 3

One of the least justified sneers thrown at Godwin was that he was too visionary. In fact, he was always aware of the need of translating his ideals into concrete form, and was himself conscious that a book like *Political Justice* did not allow him to relate his teachings sufficiently closely to the daily life of the community. He was always emphatic in his opinion of the need for the philosopher to have a balanced and accurate view of the world around him, and to be able to see his ideals in terms of practical achievement :

The wise and virtuous man ought to see things as they are, and judge of the actual constitution of his country with the same impartiality as if he had simply read of it in the remotest page of history.

It was in order to portray " things as they are " in a more concrete form, a form more readily understandable by the majority, that he descended from the philosopher's rostrum and took the humbler pen of the novelist. The result was his second masterpiece, and one of the best novels of its age, *Caleb Williams*. In its day it had an even greater fame than *Political Justice*, and raised Godwin to the highest rank among imaginative writers.

Caleb Williams [he tells us] made his first appearance in the world in the same month in which the sanguinary plot broke out against the liberties of Englishmen, which was happily terminated by the acquittal of its first intended victims in the close of that year.

It is, indeed, a book that vibrates with the restless spirit of its time, and is born of the same flow of enthusiasm that produced *Political Justice*—Godwin himself says that it " may, perhaps, be considered as affording no inadequate image of the fervour of my spirit ; it was the offspring of that temper of mind in which the composition of my *Political Justice* left me."

He has left an elaborate account of the manner in which he conceived and constructed the plot of *Caleb Williams*. It was written, like most of the novels of the period, for publication in three volumes. Godwin planned first of all the third volume, in which he envisaged a pursuit maintained with violent action, " the fugitive in perpetual apprehension of being overwhelmed with the worst calamities, and the pursuer, by his ingenuity and resources, keeping his victim in a state of the most fearful alarm." He then proceeded, in the second volume, to construct a situation that would account for the relentless pursuit ; this he based on the discovery by the fugitive of a murder committed by the pursuer, which leads the latter " incessantly to alarm and harass his victim, with an inexhaustible resolution never to allow him the least interval of peace and security." In the first volume he delineated the circumstances of the murder and the character of the murderer in such a way as to make possible the events of the second and third volumes. It will be seen that the first idea that sprang to Godwin's mind was the individual victim of society, which, as we shall observe later, became the central and perennial theme of all his novels.

Having constructed the plot, Godwin went on to a systematic reading of accounts of murders, pursuits and escapes, in order to gain the necessary circumstantial details. He then sat down to write the novel as methodically and as painstakingly as he had constructed *Political Justice*.

His task was not entirely without misgivings and interruptions. There were times when he lacked complete confidence in his work, and he submitted his manuscript at various stages to a number of his friends. Most of them were reassuring, like Mrs Inchbald, who wrote enthusiastically on the first volume :

God bless you !
That was the sentence I exclaimed when I had read about half a page.
Nobody is so pleased when they find anything new as I am. I found your style different from what I have ever yet met. You come to the point (the story) at once, another excellence. . . . I have to add to your praise that of a most *minute*, and yet most *concise* method of delineating human sensations. . . .

On reading the completed book her enthusiasm was even more extravagantly expressed :

Your first volume is far inferior to the two last. Your second is sublimely horrible—captivatingly frightful.

Your third is all a great genius can do to delight a great genius, and I never felt myself so conscious of, or so proud of giving proofs of a good understanding, as in pronouncing this to be a capital work.

It is my opinion that fine ladies, milliners, mantua-makers, and boarding-school girls will love to tremble over it, and that men of taste and judgment will admire the superior talents, the *incessant* energy of mind you have evinced.

Mrs Inchbald's opinions were somewhat nearer to those of the world than the gloomy prognostications of the faithful Marshal, who took it upon himself to condemn the novel with all the roundness that Godwinian sincerity demanded. When the first volume was almost finished, he asked leave to read the manuscript ; he returned it with an honest but tactless note :

If you have the smallest regard for your own reputation or interest, you will immediately put the enclosed papers in the fire. I was strongly tempted to have done this friendly office for you, but that I recollected I had placed myself under a promise to return them.

Godwin was so much affected by this practice of his own teachings of frankness that he was unable to write with ease for three days. He had a heated *démêlé* with Marshal, but in a day or two the latter wrote a further note in which he maintained and enlarged his criticisms :

The incidents are ill chosen ; the characters unnatural, distorted ; the phraseology intended to mark the humorous ones inappropriate ; the style uncouth ; everything upon stilts ; the whole uninteresting ; written as a man would make a chair or a table that had never handled a tool. I got through it, but it was as I get over a piece of ploughed-up ground, with labour and toil. By the way, judging from the work in question, one might suppose some minds not to be unlike a piece of ground. Having produced a rich crop, it must lie fallow for a season, that it may gain sufficient vigour for a new crop. You were speaking for a motto for this work—the best motto in my opinion would be a *Hic jacet ;* for depend upon it, the world will suppose you to be exhausted ; or rather what a few only think at present, will become a general opinion, that the Hercules you have fathered is not of your begetting.

Marshall's prophesies went unfulfilled. *Caleb Williams* was accepted both by the reading public and by the critics as one of the great novels of the age, and men like Hazlitt retained throughout their lives an admiration for which it is now difficult to find a complete justification. For there is at least a degree of truth in Marshal's assertions. *Caleb Williams*, in spite of its virtues, has also a number of manifest faults.

The story is improbable, and the characterisation is often crude, in comparison with an exceptional contemporary novel like *Pride and Prejudice*. The writing, though vigorous throughout, is occasionally heavy and rhetorical. The first volume, with its long description of the circumstances that preceded the persecution of the innocent Caleb Williams, gives a tedious and limping start. Nevertheless, the story is eventually worked up in a crescendo of incident, and, in spite of the various defects, the general effect is impressive in its gloomy presentation of the injustice of man to man.

Much of the defectiveness of story and characterisation is due to the didactic nature of the book, and to the inevitable limitations of a social allegory. Godwin, indeed, did not attempt to hide the tendencious nature of the novel. It was intended to maintain and spread the teaching of *Political Justice*, and to display to an even larger circle of readers the evils inflicted on man by the existence of authority and exploitation. His preface is explicit on this point :

What is now presented to the public is no refined and abstract speculation ; it is a study and delineation of things passing in the moral world. It is but of late that the inestimable importance of political principles has been adequately apprehended. It is now known to philosophers that the spirit and character of the government intrudes itself into every rank of society. But this is a truth highly worthy to be communicated to persons whom books of philosophy and science are never likely to reach. Accordingly, it was proposed in the invention of the following work to comprehend, as far as the progressive nature of a single story would allow, a general review of the modes of domestic and unrecorded despotism, by which man becomes the destroyer.

The result was not merely an impressive indictment of an authoritarian and class-divided society, but also a vigorous novel which was signally distinguished from most contemporary works of its nature by directness of narrative and lucidity of style. As a discerning modern critic, H. N. Brailsford, has said, it is " the one great work of fiction in our language which owes its existence to the fruitful union of the revolutionary and the romantic movements.   It spoke to its own day as Hugo's *Les Misérables* and Tolstoy's *Resurrection* spoke to later generations."

The principal theme of *Caleb Williams*, a theme which was repeated in all of Godwin's later novels, is that of the crushing of the individual by the forces of organised society.   In each of his novels we find in the central character the victim, often of physical coercion from his immediate neighbours and always of the legal and moral conventions of the society around him.   His life is a flight in which he always seeks a state of peace where he will escape the evils that prey upon men wherever " positive institution " rules in place of the natural law.   He is the symbol of man frustrated by force and prejudice, and in his fate is portrayed that of mankind while it continues to live without reason. In this esoteric manner, when he knew that any direct writing on political principles would have gone unheeded and might have resulted in personal misfortune, Godwin still contrived to speak his beliefs.   His ideas may have grown less vigorous in expression as age and anxiety sapped his energy and self-confidence, but at least he never turned away into the apostacy of so many of his friends and contemporaries.   Always, to the extent of his ability, he strove " to do my part to free the human mind from slavery," and the least of his works is redeemed by a steadfast and unflinching attempt to show the truth as he saw it.

The plot of *Caleb Williams* is in itself simple in form, and the strength of the book is built up mostly in the detail with which Godwin depicts the injustices of human society.

A feud arises between two country gentlemen, Tyrrel, a coarse bully, and Falkland, a cultured man who has imbibed all the " poison of chivalry."   Tyrrel humiliates Falkland in a quarrel, and is murdered by his rival who allows two innocent yeoman to be hanged in his place.   Caleb Williams, Falkland's secretary, chances upon his secret and is kept silent by the threats of his master.   Eventually, he tries to escape from his service, but is caught and sent to prison on a capital charge of stealing jewellery which had been secreted among his effects.   After several attempts he escapes and joins a gang of thieves, whose nobility of action is used admirably to accentuate the corruption of law-abiding society.   He then flees to London, where he is detected, and brought to trial, but his master, fearful of exposure, does not appear, and he is set free.   His freedom, however, is illusory, for wherever he goes the agents of his enemy follow, stimulating the prejudices of the people among whom he lives, so that he becomes an outcast from their society. Eventually Williams is persecuted to the end of his endurance and resolves to expose his master. He and Falkland are brought face to face, and in a dramatic scene in which Caleb speaks with a sincerity that moves all the beholders, Falkland, a dying man, confesses and praises the rectitude of his accuser.

Into this story Godwin contrives to work all the principal ideas of *Political Justice*, and to expose all the major injustices of his day. He describes eloquently the tyranny by which landowners were at the time destroying the peasantry. His indictment of the prison system is made more formidable by his personal indignation at the sufferings which many of the radicals underwent while he was writing *Caleb Williams*. From these partial tyrannies he demonstrates the general tyranny by which the great in wealth and position enslave the minds and dwarf the lives of their weaker neighbours. The positive institutions of society are means to uphold this tyranny. Coercion and punishment are shown in their full folly and injustice. The doctrine of necessity is invoked to explain the waywardness of criminals, and the benevolence of a society of equal and free men is shown as the antidote to social evils. But it is also emphasised that such a condition can be attained not by force, as the admirable thieves attempted, but by the power of education and example. Godwin was thorough in his efforts to convey the teachings of *Political Justice* to the novel-reading public.

*Caleb Williams* was immediately successful, and added greatly to Godwin's influence. Within three years it had been published in America, France and Germany, and shortly afterwards it was dramatised by George Colman and produced under the title of *The Iron Chest*, one of the most popular plays of the period. The praise showered on it by Hazlitt thirty years after its publication demonstrates the impression it made on the more powerful minds of the age.

Mr Godwin is an inventor in the regions of romance, as well as a skilful and hardy explorer of those of moral truth. *Caleb Williams* and *St Leon* are two of the most splendid and impressive works of the imagination that have appeared in our times. It is not merely that these novels are very well for a philosopher to have produced—they are admirable and complete in themselves, and would not lead you to suppose that the author, who is entirely at home in human character and dramatic situation, had ever dabbled in logic or metaphysics. The first of these particularly, is a masterpiece, both as to invention and execution. . . .

We conceive no one ever began *Caleb Williams* that did not read it through ; no one that ever read it could possibly forget it, or speak of it after any length of time but with an impression as if the events and feelings had been personal to himself. . . .

A later generation, that of De Quincey, produced a reaction and Godwin's novels were frequently dismissed as worthless. Today the controversy has almost died away because few people read any of Godwin's novels, even *Caleb Williams*, either to praise or to condemn.

In reality, this book is neither so good as Hazlitt nor so bad as De Quincey thought. It is a story which, in spite of its improbability and clumsiness, still holds and stimulates the mind until the final tragedy. It is an allegory which depicts effectively the flight of the individual from the hostile forces of a mass society—an aspect not so obvious to Hazlitt as it is to the modern reader with his intensive experience of the effects of positive institution. It gives some interesting reflections of the age from which it sprang, and exposes some of the great injustices of that age in a manner which undoubtedly touched the consciences of many of its readers. Finally, if it is not the best novel of its age, it is *among* the best. It may not be so subtle as the novels of Jane Austen or so colourful as those of Scott, but it has a greatness of vision and a strength of indignation which make it a giant among the majority of the novels of Godwin's day, the writings of the Hannah Mores and the Inchbalds.

Godwin was never a litterateur primarily. His literary pretensions were always secondary to his desire to propagate moral ideas, and the virtues of his style—which in its classic dignity compares favourably with that of the acknowledged stylists of his day—sprang mostly from a need to give clear and logical expression to his ideas. We shall be just to Godwin's own aims only if we judge his works according to their success in portraying a moral vision of the nature of man and of human society. Judged by this criterion, *Caleb Williams* was a successful novel. Its literary virtues, which in balance are not negligible, only add to this success.

4

After the publication of *Caleb Williams*, Godwin's literary labours became for a time less energetic. The fame of his books had brought him into contact with many new friends, and he spent much time in a succession of social gatherings in which he played, to a decreasing extent, the part of the " oracle," as Hazlitt called him. During 1795 he carried out revisions of *Political Justice* and *Caleb Williams*, second editions of which appeared early in the following year, but it was not until the early months of 1797 that a new work was published. This was *The Enquirer*, a book of essays on educational, social and literary subjects.

The essays, Godwin tells us, " are principally the result of conversations, some of them held many years ago, though the Essays have all been composed for the present occasion." He points out that they are based on " experiment and actual observation," rather than on the method of reasoning from a few original premises, which was used in *Political Justice*. He is particularly anxious to approach his readers without any show of arrogance.

From what has been said the humble pretensions of the contents of the present volume are sufficiently obvious. They are presented to the contemplative reader, not as *dicta*, but as the materials of thinking. They are committed to his mercy. In themselves they are trivial ; the hints of enquiry rather than actual enquiries : but hereafter perhaps they may be taken under other men's protection, and cherished to maturity. The utmost that was here proposed, was to give, if possible, a certain perspicuity and consistency to each detached member of enquiry. Truth was the object principally regarded, and the author endeavoured to banish from his mind every modification of prepossession and prejudice.

This humility may have been due in a degree to the increasing unpopularity of Godwin's ideas, both among reactionaries and radicals. On the other hand, Godwin was of so steadfast a nature, and had so recently displayed his fearlessness of persecution when his enemies were more dangerous, if less numerous, that he is unlikely to have feigned humility on these grounds. The more satisfactory explanation is that Godwin's ideas had undergone considerable changes since the writing of *Political Justice*, and that, in particular, he had become less confident of the powers of pure reason. It was therefore natural that he should be less confident of the powers of his individual reason, and so assume a humility in expressing his ideas as sincere as the assurance with which he had expounded the theories of *Political Justice*.

This change in his attitude is further shown by his defining clearly, for the first time, his attitude towards the French Revolution, even to the extent of bringing it into a somewhat irrelevant place in the preface.

> While the principles of Gallic republicanism were yet in their infancy, the friends of innovation were somewhat too imperious in their tone. Their minds were in a state of exaltation and ferment. They were too impatient and impetuous. There was something in their sternness that savoured of barbarism. The barbarism of our adversaries was no adequate excuse for this. The equable and independent mind should not be diverted from its bias by the errors of the enemy with whom it may have to contend.
>
> The author confesses that he did not escape the contagion. Those who range themselves on the same party, have now moderated their intemperance, and he has accompanied them also in their present stage. With as ardent a passion for innovation as ever, he feels himself more patient and tranquil. He is desirous of assisting others, if possible, in perfecting the melioration of their temper. . . . He ardently desires that those who shall be active in promoting the cause of reform, may be found amiable in their personal manners, and even attached to the cultivation of miscellaneous enquiries. He believes that this will afford the best security for our preserving kindness and universal philanthropy, in the midst of the operations of our justice.

*The Enquirer* is, in a sense, the sequel to *Political Justice*, in that it elaborates certain points already raised in the earlier book. But there are important differences, both in approach and in content. The essays are less formal and rigidly constructed. The prose is fluid and conversational, and the classic style is broken down into a more intimate utterance. The argument is not held so closely in the web of logic, and example is given as high a place as reason. But the most important change is the alteration in emphasis on the two great Godwinian principles of Education and Reason. In *Political Justice* the revolution in society is envisaged as deriving from the use of men's reasoning powers and the elevation of Reason into the natural law by which human relationships shall be governed. Education appears, but its rôle is secondary ; it is merely a means towards attaining the ascendancy of reason in men's minds, and the space given to discussing it is very small. This is all in keeping with the general mood of assurance and optimism. Godwin's view of social change had then a certain immediacy, for he believed that men's minds would be open to the persuasion of reason, and that if the truth were shown to them with sufficient assiduity they would be converted into living according to the natural laws apprehended by their understandings. He did not then realise how strongly the false ideas which have been implanted in childhood will stay in the minds of adult and even intelligent men and women. In the three or four years that followed the appearance of *Political Justice*, however, he had good cause to discover that men were not so open to argument and reasoning as he had imagined. The accumulation of prejudices and false conceptions prevented them from recognising or accepting the truth when it was presented to them.

Godwin saw that the task of establishing a conception of life based on justice was to be much longer and more formidable than he had foreseen. It would proceed, not by a rapid conversion of humanity, but by small and often imperceptible changes spread over a long period. If the dominion of falsehood were to be overthrown, the attack must begin not when men were mature and set in their ideas, but in childhood, before the deforming prejudices had taken root in the mind. To bring up a generation of children whose minds would be receptive to truth and capable of reason, who would be prepared to live according to the laws of natural justice, was perhaps even more important than to attempt to implant reason in the brains of their unwilling elders. Therefore Godwin turned his attention more closely to education, and *The Enquirer* is largely a treatise on this subject ; the whole of the first and more important half is devoted to it, while the miscellaneous essays of the latter part bear many references to education in a more general sense. This, of course, represents no fundamental change of attitude, for a faith in education is the one constant factor that runs through Godwin's life.

Taken as a whole, Godwin's writings and his practice of teaching convey a conception of education based on the development of individual understanding and intended as a preparation of children for the creation and enjoyment of a society where men would live by the natural laws of justice and truth. In this manner it was certainly in advance of any contemporary or previous educational system. The theories of Rousseau and Helvétius were built on a pretence of freedom and equality which, as Godwin pointed out, had its roots in coercion, its ultimate sanction in force, and therefore could not produce a mind free from the flaws imposed by prejudice. Godwin, however, based his system on a real freedom, supported by no hidden coercion ; he realised that the purpose of education was not to impose knowledge on a child from without, but to bring out the qualities latent in his mind, which would make him turn naturally towards wisdom and benevolence. He had cast away with his religious beliefs the dogma of original sin. He believed that the child at birth was innocent and capable only of good, and that tendencies to evil were not inherent but imposed by bad environment and inefficient education. Therefore he conceived education as a process strictly in accordance with a definition of the word itself, a process of leading out the natural good and strengthening it against the hostile forces which would attack it in a corrupt society. Education, he realised eventually, is the basis of freedom ; but the proposition is equally true in the reverse direction—freedom is the basis of education. The realisation of this reciprocal relationship is what makes Godwin's writings on education, and particularly *The Enquirer*, so important even today, perhaps more than ever today when education is being used to teach men submission rather than to teach them wisdom.

" The true object of education," says Godwin at the beginning of *The Enquirer*, " like that of every other moral process, is the generation of happiness." By this he means in the first place the happiness of the individual. But as " in society the interests of individuals are intertwisted with each other, and cannot be separated," it is also necessary " to train him to be useful, that is, virtuous. . . ."

To make a man virtuous we must make him wise. . . . He who would be eminently useful, must be eminently instructed.

But,

Wisdom is not only directly a means to virtue ; it is also directly a means to happiness. The man of enlightened understanding and persevering ardour has many sources of enjoyment which the ignorant man cannot reach.

It is impossible to say in what way the capacities of children may differ at birth. But, whatever these capacities may be, it is the work of the teacher to awaken the mind of his pupil, and to infuse it with the desire for knowledge and attainment.

Education should begin early, for, " the more inexperienced and immature is the mind of the infant, the greater its pliability," and bad habits of thought are acquired earlier than is commonly supposed. But the object of early education is not to impart particular knowledge, but to awaken the mind :

It is of less importance, generally speaking, that a child should acquire this or that species of knowledge, than that, through a medium of instruction, he should acquire habits of intellectual activity. . . . The preceptor in this respect is like the incloser of uncultivated land ; his first crops are not valued for their intrinsic excellence ; they are sown that the land may be brought into order. . . . In a word, the first lesson of a judicious education is, Learn to think, to discriminate, to remember, and to enquire.

After awakening and exercising the mind, it is the function of the educator to furnish knowledge and to encourage any talents which he may perceive to be latent in his pupil, for " talents are the instruments of usefulness " and in their development lies the hope of a good society.

Godwin asserts that, so far as their mental capacities are concerned, men are virtually equal at birth, and that genius " is not born with us, but generated subsequent to birth." He states that, given " all the motives that have excited another man, and all the external advantages he has had to boast, . . . I shall arrive at an excellence equal to his." This extreme egalitarianism was an heritage from his French masters, and in later years he qualified it by an admission that men were born with certain tendencies and that therefore, instead of all men being capable, given the favourable circumstances, of acquiring all things, each man was capable of fulfilling himself in a certain vocation. Even in *The Enquirer* he is careful to indicate that genius is not likely to be produced by education alone, for " thousands of impressions are made on us, for one that is designedly produced," and genius arises from the combined effects of all a child's impressions.

Yet, although he admits that, up to the present, education

does not appear to have produced genius, he does not despair of a day when, by experiment and observation, men will be able by their sagacity to induce what previously appears to have been produced by chance.

In spite of these speculations, the ideas in *The Enquirer* are by no means fantastic recipes for the production of genius. They contain sound ideas of educational method, which are universally valuable for the development of those attributes undoubtedly latent in every normal child.

Godwin's first suggestion is the development of an early taste for reading :

Books gratify and excite our curiosity in innumerable ways. They force us to reflect. They hurry us from point to point. They present direct ideas of various kinds, and they suggest indirect ones. In a well-written book we are presented with the maturest reflections, or the happiest flights, of a mind of uncommon excellence. It is impossible that we can be much accustomed to such companions, without attaining some resemblance of them.

Reading should begin while the mind is flexible, for then a man will gain more improvement than if he commences when his mind has become fixed and stiff in its operation.

In discussing the methods of imparting knowledge, he attacks the customary relationship of children to their instructors, which seems to him little better than slavery, and concludes that instruction must be given in a manner that will cause the least interference with the liberty of the pupil. A child should not be forced to learn. He should be induced to learn by the exhibition of some motive that will make him desire knowledge.

The true object of juvenile education, is to provide, against the age of five and twenty, a mind well regulated, active, and prepared to learn. Whatever will inspire habits of industry and observation, will sufficiently answer this purpose. Is it not possible to find something that will fulfil these conditions, the benefit of which a child shall understand, and the acquisition of which he may be taught to desire ? Study with desire is real activity : without desire it is but the semblance and mockery of activity. Let us not, in the eagerness of our haste to educate, forget all the ends of education.

Therefore the basis of educational method should be changed completely :

According to the received modes of education, the master goes first and the pupil follows. According to the method here recommended, it is probable that the pupil would go first, and the master follow. If I learn nothing but what I desire to learn, what should hinder me from being my own preceptor ?

This plan [Godwin claims with some justice] is calculated entirely to change the face of education. The whole formidable apparatus which has hitherto attended it, is swept away. Strictly speaking, no such characters are left upon the scene as either preceptor or pupil. The boy, like the man, studies, because he desires it. He proceeds upon a plan of his own invention, or which, by adopting, he has made his own. Every thing bespeaks independence and equality. The man, as well as the boy, would be glad in cases of difficulty to consult a person more informed than himself. That the boy is accustomed almost always to consult the man, and not the man the boy, is to be regarded rather as an accident, than any thing essential.

In displacing the teacher from his position of authority and superiority, in making the desire of the pupil, rather than the will of the teacher, the motive element in education, Godwin makes a truly revolutionary departure in educational method, superseding not only the thoughtless " cramming " practised by the old-fashioned schoolmasters of his day, but also the " advanced " ideas of his predecessors, like Rousseau, who still regarded the pupil's mind as matter to be moulded by the action of his teacher, rather than as an organism to grow according to its own natural tendencies. It speaks highly for the quality of Godwin's vision and his understanding of the child's mental development, that today, a hundred and fifty years afterwards, educationalists in general are beginning to adopt what he laid down as a fundamental theory of teaching.

He claims a number of advantages for his new attitude towards education :

First, liberty. Three fourths of the slavery and restraint that are now imposed upon young persons would be annihilated at a stroke.

Secondly, the judgment would be strengthened by continual exercise. . . . No one would learn without a reason, satisfactory to himself, why he learned ; and it would perhaps be well, if he were frequently prompted to assign his reasons. . . .

Thirdly, to study for ourselves is the true method of acquiring habits of activity. The horse that goes round in a mill, and the boy that is anticipated and led by the hand in all his acquirements, are not active. . . . Activity is a mental quality. If therefore you would generate habits of activity, turn the boy loose in fields of science. Let him explore the path for himself. . . .

Lastly, it is the tendency of this system to produce in the young, when they are grown up to the stature of men, a love of literature.

This, he claims, is in contrast with the established modes of education, which tend to produce in the majority an attitude of dislike for literature because of the tyranny by which it has been imposed on them in childhood.

It is worth recording that, where attempts have been made in modern times to educate children in the revolutionary manner advocated by Godwin, by placing the emphasis on the desire of the child instead of the will of the teacher, the advantages claimed by him have in fact tended to accrue.

In a number of succeeding essays Godwin treats of some of the problems which face teachers and parents in their relationship to children. Firstly, he indicates the disadvantages of family life, with its tendency to cause the child to grow up in an environment of authority. Harshness in the treatment of children can produce great evils. He sees as clearly as the psychologists of today that unhappiness in childhood is the cause of much of the mental illness of adult people and of mankind as a whole :

> The most fundamental of all the principles of morality is the consideration and deference that man owes to man ; nor is the helplessness of childhood by any means unentitled to the benefit of this principle. The neglect of it among mankind at large, is the principal source of all the injustice, the revenge, the bloodshed and the wars, that have so long stained the face of nature. It is hostile to every generous and expansive sentiment of our dignity ; it is incompatible with the delicious transports of self-complacence.

Harshness defeats its own end, for, instead of bringing " the delinquent to a sense of his error," its result is " to fill him with indignation against your despotism, to inspire him with a deep sense of the indignity to which he is subjected, and to perpetuate in his mind a detestation of the lesson that occasions his pain."

Godwin suggests that one of the most important causes of this harshness is to be found in the undue familiarity which is the consequence of family " cohabitation." Even if some form of family life is found necessary, those who participate in it should be made aware of the danger of acquiring a contempt for the rights of individual members, and particularly of children.

He goes on to indicate the superior value of an equal basis of discussion between parent or teacher and the child. At the same time he condemns the pretence of equality, which is used as a mask for authority. This merely rouses a sense of injustice in the child, and therefore, if the exercise of authority is found to be necessary, we should " take care that it be not exercised with asperity, and that we do not add an insulting familiarity or unnecessary contention, to the indispensable assertion of superiority."

Above all, we should not use deception in the treatment of children :

It teaches our children the practice of similar arts, and, as they have been overreached by their superiors, to endeavour to overreach them in return.

It is on this ground that Godwin makes his most severe criticism of Rousseau, whose system of education he describes as " a series of tricks, a puppet-show exhibition, of which the master holds the wires, and the scholar is never to suspect in what manner they are moved."

If parents and teachers should themselves avoid deception, they should also take care not to give the children in their care any reason to practise this undesirable quality.

If we would have our children frank and sincere in their behaviour, we must take care that frankness and sincerity shall not be a source of evil to them. If there be any justice in the reasonings of a preceding essay, punishment would find no share in a truly excellent system of education ; even angry looks and words of rebuke would be wholly excluded. But upon every system it cannot fail to appear in the highest degree impolitic and mischievous, that young persons should have reason given them to repent of their sincerity.

Godwin deprecates the ideas of those who wish to make a child prematurely manly or to keep him continually childish :

The man should, by incessant degrees, be grafted upon the youth ; the process should perhaps commence from the period of birth. There is no age at which something manly, considerate and firm, will not be found graceful. . . .
For this purpose, it is not necessary that we should check the sallies of youth. Nothing is of worse effect in our treatment either of the young or the old, than a continual anxiety, and an ever eager interference with their conduct. Every human being should be permitted, not only from a principle of benevolence, but because without this there can be no true improvement or excellence, to act from himself.

He reverts to the basic necessity to gain the confidence of the pupil and to establish a sympathetic and personal relationship with him before a process of education can begin satisfactorily.

Then, in an excellent essay *Of Choice in Reading*, he attacks the practice of allowing children to read only those books which have been selected and approved by their teachers or parents.  This, he shows, makes them only more anxious to read the forbidden books, and throws them open to vicious modes of thought by making them deceitful and furtive in their actions.  No book is capable of harming a mind in which vice is not already present, or unless its vicious content has been given a spurious value by the prohibitions with which it is surrounded.  Thus, while the preceptor is justified in recommending the pupil to read books which he considers valuable for his educational development, the pupil should also be allowed freely to read all the books which attract him and may lead him to discover for himself new paths of thought.

Finally, there is a vigorous passage *On Early Indications of Character*, in which Godwin shows that the excesses of youth are often indications of energy and genius in manhood, and condemns the action of parents and teachers who blacken a child's character for these early follies :

There is nothing more contrary to true justice and enlightened morality, than the unsparing harshness with which the old frequently censure the extravagances of the young.  Enamoured of black forebodings, and gorged with misanthropy, they pour out their ill-omened prophesyings with unpitying cruelty.  The sober, the dull, the obedient, lads that have no will and no understanding of their own, are the only themes of their eulogium.  They know no touch of candour and liberal justice.  They make no allowance for the mutability of youth, and have no generous presentiment of their future recollection and wisdom.  They never forgive a single offence.  They judge of characters from one accidental failing, and will not deign to turn their attention to those great and admirable qualities, by which this one failing, it may be, is amply redeemed. They may be compared to that tyrant of antiquity who, intending to convey a symbolical lesson upon the principles of despotism, passed through a field of corn, and struck off every ear that had the audacity to rear its head above the dull and insipid level of its fellows.

With this broadside against the parents and pedagogues of his day, Godwin terminates the first part of *The Enquirer*.  It represents the most remarkable and advanced treatise on education that had appeared by the end of the eighteenth century, and, with its emphasis on freedom as the basis of an education in which the pupil, rather than the teacher, is the central figure, it anticipates the best in modern educational theory, and is actually still in advance of educational practice in a world that demands

from its people obedience rather than the full and free development of their personal potentialities.

The second part of *The Enquirer* consists of a series of twelve
essays on miscellaneous subjects of a social or literary nature.
Most of them elaborate themes already introduced in *Political
Justice*, and, although their method of presentation and development is often excellent, they do not in general introduce any
approach with which readers of *Political Justice* are not already
familiar.   Nevertheless, as examples of the social essay which
became popular at this time, they are well worth reading and
are, in my opinion, as good as anything Hazlitt wrote in this
style.   Some, indeed, are quite memorable examples of the
romantic essay.

*Of Riches and Poverty* elaborates the theme that " he that is born
to poverty, may be said, under another name, to be born a slave."
If work were done in a scientific and equal manner, the amount
of labour for each man would be much less than the poor have
to contribute today :

The genuine wealth of man is leisure, when it meets with a disposition
to improve it.   All other riches are of petty and inconsiderable value.
Is there not a state of society practicable, in which leisure shall be
made the inheritance of every one of its members ?

The succeeding essays, *Of Avarice and Profusion* and *Of Beggars*,
build up, with a formidable power of argument, the case against
a society which contains the extremes of poverty and wealth, and
in which the prosperity of the rich is based on the misery of their
less fortunate fellows.

In a similar manner, the essay *Of Servants*, by discussing the
apparently respectable topic of how children can acquire bad
habits of thought and action from too frequent contact with
servants, works up to a great indictment of a society which forces
men to accept menial employment, whose consequences are loss
of moral rectitude and degradation of character.

Perhaps the most entertaining essay is *Trades and Professions*,
which analyses the effects of participation in shopkeeping, law,
medicine and the church, the army and the sea.   Godwin spares
no criticism, and lays about him without mercy when he comes
to describe the characters typical of men in these walks of life.
The tradesman he calls " this supple, fawning, cringing creature,
this systematic, cold-hearted liar, this being, every moment of

whose existence is centred on the sordid consideration of petty gains. . . ." Of the lawyer he says : "Nothing so much conduces to his happiness, as that his neighbours should be perpetually engaged in broils and contentions. Innumerable are the disputes that would soon terminate in an amicable adjustment, were it not for the lawyer who, like an evil genius, broods over the mischief and hatches it into a suit." Of the physician : " Pain, sickness and anguish are his harvest. He rejoices to hear that they have fallen upon any of his acquaintance. He looks blank and disconsolate, when all men are at their ease." The clergyman " will be timid in enquiry, prejudiced in opinion, cold, formal, the slave of what other men may think of him, rude, dictatorial, impatient of contradiction, harsh in his censures, and illiberal in his judgments. Every man may remark in him study rendered abortive, artificial manners, infantine prejudices, and a sort of arrogant infallibility." Like all generalisations, these statements are not universally true, and among Godwin's own acquaintances, such as the clergyman Fawcet, the lawyer Curran, the surgeon Carlisle, and some of the publishers who treated him with comparative generosity, Godwin knew men who did not fit into these descriptions. Nevertheless, there was a measure of truth in all of them, and the pointedness of the description of the clergyman's characteristics so angered Dr Parr that he ceased to be Godwin's friend and later became his enemy.

The least successful essay is that *Of English Style*. Godwin's sense of literary discrimination developed late, in his forties, largely through the influence of Lamb and Coleridge. At the time when he wrote *The Enquirer* he had little appreciation and, indeed, little knowledge of English literature before the eighteenth century, except for Shakespeare. His reading had been most copious in the classical texts and various philosophical and political works of the eighteenth century, and his knowledge of the English writers whom he considered in this essay was at the time somewhat superficial. Otherwise he could hardly have adopted the method of viewing English style as a progression in which none of the products of the past equalled in quality those of his own day. This essay roused Hazlitt's just anger, and was by far the least successful product of Godwin's most fruitful period.

But, apart from this unfortunate lapse, the writing and thought in *The Enquirer* show Godwin at his freshest and most vigorous, and the book deserves a higher place than it enjoys among the representative works of its age. But it is not merely an example of good writing. The vision and understanding with which Godwin handles the theme of education give it a practical relevance which will continue until the truths expressed have become accepted by all who attempt the guidance of children.

5

The writing of *The Enquirer* was roughly parallel in time with the most important personal event in Godwin's life, his relationship with Mary Wollstonecraft. Mary Wollstonecraft's character and life have made so great an appeal to biographers that the principal events of her career are relatively well known. It is therefore unnecessary for me to describe her life except in so far as it influenced that of Godwin. This does not imply any reflection on the qualities or importance of a woman who in no circumstances could appear other than noble, and who was probably the greatest personal influence in Godwin's life.

As we have already seen, they met first in 1791, and were not greatly pleased with each other. They met again once or twice in the following year, but without any better feeling, and in 1792 Mary departed to Paris, where she lived precariously through the Terror and formed her relationship with the American adventurer, Imlay.

They did not meet again until January, 1796. By this time, Mary's natural pride had been humbled by her unhappy experience with Imlay, and Godwin had perhaps become less arrogant through the danger in which his opinions had recently placed him. He says, in the moving Memoir which he wrote after her death, that Mary returned to England " softened and improved, . . . fraught with imagination and sensibility." Godwin himself had forgotten his annoyance with her conversational exuberance and stylistic awkwardness, and was much impressed by her *Letters from Norway*.

Except for this absence of hostility, and for Godwin's " sympathy in her anguish," this first meeting has " no particular effect," but during their ensuing encounters a mutual feeling seems to have grown up, and, when Mary took a lodging in Cumming Street, Pentonville, not far from Godwin's home, their relationship began to grow intimate.

The partiality we conceived for each other was in that mode, which I have always regarded as the purest and most refined style of love. It grew with equal advances in the mind of each. It would have been impossible for the most minute observer to have said who was before, and who was after. One sex did not take the priority which long-established custom has awarded it, nor the other overstep that delicacy which is so severely imposed. I am not conscious that either party can assume to have been the agent or the patient, the toil-spreader or the prey, in the affair. When, in the course of things, the disclosure came, there was nothing, in a manner, for either party to disclose to the other. . . .

In July, 1796, Godwin went for nearly a month into Norfolk. " The temporary separation had its effect on the mind of both parties. It gave a space for the maturing of inclination." The two friends found an increased pleasure in meeting again. " It was, however, three weeks longer before the sentiment which trembled upon the tongue, burst from the lips of either. . . . It was friendship melting into love."

Mary rested her head upon the shoulder of her lover, hoping to find a heart with which she might safely treasure her world of affection ; fearing to commit a mistake, yet, in spite of her melancholy experience, fraught with that generous confidence, which, in a great soul, is never extinguished.

" I had never loved till now," he asserted for himself, but then, perhaps recalling Amelia Alderson and Mrs Reveley, qualified this by adding " or, at least, had never nourished a passion to the same growth, or met with an object so consummately worthy."

The two lovers now began to live together, but in such a manner as not to fall into the evils of continual cohabitation which both of them, in accordance with the principles of *Political Justice*, regarded with disapprobation. Godwin took rooms twenty houses away from his previous dwelling, which had been chosen as their joint abode.

It was my practice to repair to the apartment I have mentioned as soon as I rose, and frequently not to make my appearance in the Polygon, till the hour of dinner.

Sometimes he even slept at the apartment, and frequently took his meals there. He and Mary often went visiting separately, both before and after their marriage.

We agreed in condemning the notion, prevalent in many situations in life, that a man and his wife cannot visit in mixed society, but in company with each other ; and we rather sought occasions of deviating

from, than of complying with this rule.  By these means, though, for
the most part, we spent the latter half of each day in one another's
society, yet we were in no danger of satiety.  We seemed to combine,
in a considerable degree, the novelty and lively sensation of a visit, with
the more delicious and heart-felt pleasures of domestic life.

They seem to have lived from the beginning in an easy and
contented manner, tolerantly, and in comparative peace.  They
were, perhaps, as well suited as any couple could have been.
Mary was thirty-seven, three years younger than Godwin, and
the varied experiences of her life had made her mature and
balanced in character.  She was strong and courageous in her
attitude to the world, yet, in spite of the masculine vigour with
which she had defended the rights of women, she remained, as
Godwin put it, " lovely in her person, and in the best and most
engaging sense, feminine in her manners."

She was quick to take offence at what she took to be injustice,
and, in the early days, a little impatient with Godwin's bachelor
selfishness and the inefficiency in practical affairs which had
resulted from Marshal's taking off his hands such matters as
might interfere with his facility of writing.  One of the little
notes she wrote to him in their early days illustrates this kind of
difference :

Mary will tell you about the state of the sink, &c.  Do you know you
plague me—a little—by not speaking more determinately to the land-
lord. . . .
I wish you would desire Mr Marshal to call on me.  Mr Johnson or
somebody has always taken the disagreeable business of settling with
tradespeople off my hands.  I am perhaps as unfit as yourself to do it,
and my time appears to me as valuable as that of other persons accustomed to employ themselves.  Things of this kind are easily settled with
money I know ; but I am tormented by the want of money, and feel,
to say the truth, as if I was not treated with respect, owing to your desire
not to be disturbed.

A few days later Mary seems to have shown some anger and
reproached Godwin with negligence, for we find him writing :

I am pained by the recollection of our conversation last night.  The
sole principle of conduct of which I am conscious in my behaviour to
you, has been in everything to study your happiness.  I found a wounded
heart, and as that heart cast itself on me, it was my ambition to heal it.
Do not let me be wholly disappointed. . . .

In a short time Godwin adapted himself, and became more
considerate, and Mary more tolerant.  Godwin it is certain, had

found a greater happiness than he had enjoyed before or was ever to experience again after Mary's death. Mary found that Godwin developed a kindness and gentleness which perhaps she had not dared to expect, and her attachment grew strong as their association ripened.

There seems never to have been any question of one becoming subordinate to the other in an intellectual sense. In argument, whether at home or in company, Mary held her own and Hazlitt tells of one occasion when " she seemed to me to turn off Godwin's objections to something she advanced with quite a playful, easy air." At times the intellectual battles do not appear to have been altogether good-humoured, and occasionally Mary's attitude seems to have given Godwin some offence, for in one of her notes she says :

I believe I ought to beg your pardon for talking at you last night, though it was in sheer simplicity of heart, and I have been asking myself why it so happened. Faith and troth, it was because there was nobody else worth attacking, or who could converse. . . .

In personality they were widely different. Godwin was logical and methodical in thought, an intellectual in the purest sense of the term. Mary was impulsive and emotional, guided by intuition and endowed with a live imagination. Yet this very divergence was conducive rather than inimical to mutual harmony and happiness. Instead of clashing, they gave what was in their natures to widen each other's capacities. Mary's thought was made more methodical by the influence of Godwin's reasoning. Godwin was made to realise that the reason is not the sole means of apprehension. Mary found a needed peace in this relationship. Godwin's nature benefited from it, for he became more human and kindly and, in every way, a more developed man.

He realised fully the extent of his debt, and at the end of his *Memoir* there occurs a remarkable passage in which he describes their relationship. The description, so far as one can tell from outside witnesses and from the internal evidence of Godwin's novels, is accurate, and it has that tone of humble sincerity which characterises the whole of this book. I quote from the second edition, in which the references are more explicit :

Mary and myself perhaps each carried farther than to its common extent the characteristic of the sexes to which we belonged. I have bee stimulated, as long as I can remember, by the love of intellectual distinction, but, as long as I can remember, I have been discouraged, when casting the sum of my intellectual value, by finding that I did not possess, in the degree of some other persons, an intuitive sense of the pleasures of the imagination. Perhaps I feel them as vividly as most men ; but it is often rather by an attentive consideration, than an instantaneous survey. They have been liable to fail of their effect in the first experiment ; and my scepticism has often led me anxiously to call in the approved decisions of taste, as a guide to my judgment, or a countenance to my enthusiasm. One of the leading passions of my mind has been an anxious desire not to be deceived. This has led me to view the topics of my reflection on all sides, and to examine and re-examine without end the questions that interest me. Endless disquisition however is not always the parent of certainty.

What I wanted in this respect, Mary possessed in a degree superior to any other person I ever knew. Her feelings had a character of peculiar strength and decision ; and the discovery of them, whether in matters of taste or of moral virtue, she found herself unable to control. She had viewed the objects of nature with a lively sense and an ardent admiration, and had developed their beauties. Her education had been fortunately free from the prejudices of system and bigotry, and her sensitive and generous spirit was left to the spontaneous exercise of its own decisions. The warmth of her heart defended her from artificial rules of judgment ; and it is therefore surprising what a degree of soundness pervaded her sentiments. In the strict sense of the term, she had reasoned comparatively little ; and she was therefore little subject to diffidence and scepticism. Yet a mind more candid in perceiving and retracting error, when it was pointed out to her, perhaps never existed. This arose naturally out of the directness of her sentiments, and her fearless and unstudied veracity.

A companion like this excites and animates the mind. From such an one we imbibe, what perhaps I principally wanted, the habit of minutely attending to first impressions, and justly appreciating them. Her taste awakened mine ; her sensibility determined me to a careful development of my feelings. She delighted to open her heart to the beauties of nature ; and her propensity in this respect led me to a more intimate contemplation of them. My scepticism in judging, yielded to the coincidence of another's judgment, and especially when the judgment of that other was such, that the more I made experiment of it, the more was I convinced of its rectitude.

The short period of Godwin's life with Mary certainly led to a change of his attitude in many points. In particular it led him to regard the domestic affections very differently. The kind of domesticity he enjoyed with Mary Wollstonecraft was so superior to the family life that had marred his childhood that it atoned for the latter's deficiencies, and in Godwin's mind cleared the family of what he had once regarded as its inherent faults. A year after

Mary's death he was actually to write a novel, one of whose declared objects was the vindication of domestic happiness against such detractors as the author of *Political Justice* !

A circumstance which might well have made difficulties in an ordinary marriage was the presence of Fanny, Mary's daughter by Imlay.  But Godwin was naturally attached to children and regarded their proper upbringing and education as an essential part of the reclaiming of mankind to virtue and freedom.  Moreover, his own theories forbade discrimination between people because of their relationship or otherwise to himself.  Fanny existed, and had been brought into his care.  She needed education, care and love, and Godwin considered it his duty to give her these as freely as he would have done to his own child.  He accepted her with an affection which was returned by Fanny, and from that time she was brought up as his own child, both in name and in the treatment she received from him.

The relationship between Mary and Godwin was at first kept a secret even from many of their intimate friends.  This was partly because :

Mary had an extreme aversion to be made the topic of vulgar discussion ;  and, if there be any weakness in this, the dreadful trials through which she had recently passed, may well plead in its excuse.

Mary Shelley assigns another motive for this secrecy :

My father narrowly circumscribed both his receipts and disbursements.  The maintenance of a family had never been contemplated, and could not at once be provided for.  My mother, accustomed to a life of struggle and poverty, was so beloved by her friends that several, and Mr Johnson in particular, had stood between her and any of the annoyances and mortifications of debt.  But this must cease when she married.

Very soon, however, their plans were forcibly changed by Mary's pregnancy.  She then decided that it was expedient for them to marry :

She was unwilling, and perhaps with reason, to incur that exclusion from the society of many valuable and excellent individuals, which custom awards in cases of this sort.

Godwin seems to have felt scruples, but willingly relinquished them, and on March 29th, 1797, they were married secretly at Old St Pancras, the trustworthy Marshal being the only friend present.

Godwin announced the marriage early in April.  There is no

doubt that he felt uneasiness at what the world would think of
the apparent divergence between the views on marriage expressed
in *Political Justice* and his own practice when the situation faced
him. In a letter to one friend, Thomas Wedgwood, from whom
he had solicited a loan of fifty pounds without revealing that it
was to meet his expenses in setting up a joint home, he took pains
to justify himself at some length :

Some persons have found an inconsistency between my practice in
this instance and my doctrines. But I cannot see it. The doctrine of
my *Political Justice* is, that an attachment in some degree permanent,
between two persons of opposite sexes is right, but that marriage, as
practiced in European countries, is wrong. I still adhere to that opinion.
Nothing but a regard for the happiness of the individual, which I had
no right to injure, could have induced me to submit to an institution
which I wish to see abolished, and which I would recommend to my
fellow-men never to practice, but with the greatest caution. Having
done what I thought necessary for the peace and respectability of the
individual, I hold myself no otherwise bound than I was before the
ceremony took place.

The letter ends with a postscript, " We do not entirely
cohabit," in which he tries to show that the author of *Political
Justice* at least acted in the deed if not in the letter according to
the principles he had laid down.

With other friends he treated the matter in a casual or a
jocular manner. To Holcroft he sent a note merely announcing
that he was married, but not to whom. To Mary Hays, the
friend at whose house he had met Mary Wollstonecraft again
after her return from France, he wrote :

My fair neighbour desires me to announce to you a piece of news,
which it is consonant to the regard that she and I entertain for you, you
should rather learn from us than from any other quarter. She bids me
remind you of the earnest way in which you pressed me to prevail upon
her to change her name, and she directs me to add, that it has happened
to me, like many other disputants, to be entrapped in my own toils ; in
short, that we found that there was no way so obvious for her to drop
the name of Imlay, as to assume the name of Godwin. Mrs Godwin—
who the devil is that ?—will be glad to see you at No. 29, Polygon,
Somers Town, whenever you are inclined to favour her with a call.

The reception of the news was mixed. Godwin's family and
most of his close friends were pleased. Holcroft wrote :

From my very heart and soul I give you joy. I think you the most
extraordinary married pair in existence. May your happiness be as pure
as I firmly persuade myself it must be.

Mrs Reveley wept, according to Mary Shelley, because she " feared to lose a kind and constant friend," but soon discovered that " instead of losing one she had secured two friends, unequalled, perhaps, in the world for genius, single-heartedness and nobleness of disposition, and a cordial intercourse subsisted between them." Old Mrs Godwin wrote an affectionate and characteristic letter, in which she hoped that Godwin's changed attitude towards marriage would lead to an acceptance of the Gospels.

You are certainly transformed in a moral sense, why is it impossable in a spiritual sense, which last will make you shine with the radiance of the sun for ever. . . .

Among a great number of their acquaintances, however, as well as some of their pretended friends, the marriage was received with disfavour. This was because the more conventional of these people had chosen to reconcile their moralistic views and their desire for Mary's intelligent company, by the pretence that she was married to Imlay, in spite of her frequent and candid explanations of her true position.

Observe the consequence of this [says Godwin, with justified indignation]. While she was, and constantly professed to be, an unmarried mother, she was fit society for the squeamish and the formal. The moment she acknowledged herself a wife, and that by a marriage perhaps unexceptionable, the case was altered. Mary and myself, ignorant as we were of these elevated refinements, supposed that our marriage would place her upon a surer footing in the calendar of polished society, than ever. But it forced these people to see the truth, and to confess their belief of what they had carefully been told ; and this they could not forgive.

The two people whose defection was most painful were Mrs Inchbald and Mrs Siddons. Mrs Inchbald was perhaps the more pardonable, for she seems to have felt more strongly for Godwin than she would have admitted, and, again according to Mary Shelley, she, like Mrs Reveley, wept when she heard of the marriage. Mrs Siddons seems to have been moved by little more than an anxiety that her good name as an actress should not be sullied by associating with such public examples of immorality.

For the rest, " it was only the supporters and the subjects of the unprincipled manners of a court " who withdrew. The majority of their valued friends remained, and their short married life was not marred by any real isolation.

Marriage made no important difference to their lives. They continued to act independently. Godwin kept his own rooms for study, and they still went out separately and spent large portions of the day apart. Godwin worked on his revisions of *Political Justice* and *Caleb Williams ;* Mary started a novel, to be called *The Wrongs of Women,* and worked on a series of *Letters on the Management of Infants.*

In June of 1797 Godwin toured the Midlands with Basil Montagu, a young disciple who later joined his detractors and so earned Coleridge's contempt. Godwin described the journey in a series of letters to Mary, which, taken together, form one of the most pleasant pieces of his writing and give the indelible impression of a warm-hearted, affectionate and humorous man, far different from the cold-hearted monster of intellect his enemies delighted to portray.

The letters abound in affectionate references :

And now, my dear love, what do you think of me ? [asks Godwin]. Do you not find solitude infinitely superior to the company of a husband ? Will you give me leave to return to you again when I have finished my pilgrimage and discharged the penance of absence ? Take care of yourself, my love, and take care of William. Do not you be drowned, whatever I am. I remember at every moment all the accidents to which your condition subjects you, and wish I knew of some sympathy that could inform me from moment to moment how you do, and what you feel.

I am not fatigued with solitude [Mary replies] yet I have not relished my solitary dinner. A husband is a convenient part of the furniture of a house, unless he be a clumsy fixture. I wish you, from my soul, to be rivetted in my heart, but I do not desire to have you always at my elbow, although at this moment I should not care if you were.

You cannot imagine how happy your letters made me [writes Godwin]. No creature expresses, because no creature feels, the tender affections so perfectly as you do ; and, after all one's philosophy, it must be confessed that the knowledge that there is some one that takes an interest in one's happiness, something like that which each man feels in his own, is extremely gratifying. We love, as it were, to multiply the consciousness of our existence, even at the hazard of what Montagu described so pathetically one night upon the New Road, of opening new avenues for pain and misery to attack us.

He was learning steadily that the intellect could never make a watertight world of its own where the less rational feelings and emotions would not enter and make their ravages.

The journey was prolonged beyond the projected period,

and by the end of the week a note of grievance appears in the letter which Mary sent round to Godwin's rooms on the morning of his return. She seems to have been annoyed with the bachelor selfishness which still characterised his actions :

One of the pleasures you tell me that you promised yourself from your journey was the effect your absence might produce on me. Certainly at first my affection was increased, or rather was more alive. But now it is just the contrary. Your later letters might have been addressed to anybody, and will serve to remind you where you have been, though they resemble nothing less than mementoes of affection. . . . .
In short, your being so late tonight, and the chance of your not coming, shows so little consideration, that unless you suppose me to be a stick or a stone, you must have forgot to think, as well as to feel, since you have been on the wing. I am afraid to add what I feel.

Godwin appears to have learnt from Mary's distress on this occasion, for he acted towards her from that time onward with studied consideration, and, although outside reference to their relationship is comparatively slight, it contains no hint of strife. " No one was ever more happy in marriage than Mrs Godwin," said Mrs Fenwick, one of their intimate friends. Godwin, it is certain, was a happier man in that summer of 1797 than at any other time in his life.

The source of his happiness was to last no longer than the summer itself. Towards the end of August, Mary's pregnancy drew to a close, and on Wednesday, the 30th of that month, she went to bed, and during the night gave birth, not to the expected William, but to a girl, Mary. The pregnancy had apparently been completely healthy, but after the child was born complications set in through the adhesion of the placenta. For more than a week the illness persisted, Mary wavered between life and death, and Godwin lived in the extremes of hope and despair. He has left an account of the details of this terrible week which is all the more moving because it is written with dignity and restraint. On Sunday morning, September 10th, she died. In the last moments of consciousness she said of Godwin, " He is the kindest, best man in the world."

Godwin was broken-hearted. A relationship that seemed to promise a lifetime of happiness was ended so soon, and it seemed that he could never be happy again. His grief was great and sincere.

" Who ever endured more anguish than Mr Godwin endures ? " wrote Mrs Fenwick to Everina Wollstonecraft. To Holcroft, Godwin himself wrote :

I firmly believe that there does not exist her equal in the world. I know from experience we were formed to make each other happy. I have not the least expectation that I can now ever know happiness again.

To Mrs Cotton, an old friend whom Mary had wished to be her nurse, he wrote some six weeks afterwards a letter which showed that he was also troubled as to what he could do for the children she had left.

I am still here, in the same situation in which you last saw me, surrounded by the children, and all the well-known objects, which, though they all talk to me of melancholy, are still dear to me. I love to tread the edge of intellectual danger, and just to keep within the line which every moral and intellectual consideration forbids me to overstep, and in this indulgence and this vigilance I place my present luxury.
The poor children ! I am myself totally unfitted to educate them. The scepticism which perhaps sometimes leads me right in matters of speculation, is torment to me when I would attempt to direct the infant mind. I am the most unfit person for this office ; she was the best qualified in the world. What a change. The loss of the children is less remediless than mine. You can understand the difference.

At this period Godwin was evidently trying to dramatise his grief, which had perhaps become less genuinely all-absorbing. But it is certain that he continued to feel a genuine love and sorrow for Mary, and the pages of his *Memoir* impress one with the utmost sincerity in the feelings he expresses with such restraint. He never forgot Mary, or ceased to talk of her. To the end of his life her portrait by Opie hung over the table where he worked, and his writing contained many pious references to her memory.

" This light was lent to me for a very short period, and is now extinguished for ever," he wrote at the end of his *Memoir*. But its reflection still persisted throughout his life, and, even in the depth of the adversities that were to follow him in after years, he was, as Coleridge said to Southey, " in heart and manner . . . all the better for having been the husband of Mary Wollstonecraft."

PART V

# Years of Calumny

## 1798–1801

### I

THE death of Mary Wollstonecraft formed the major crisis of Godwin's life, a crisis all the more severe in that it coincided with an external change of fortunes which altered his situation from success and fame to frustration and undeserved neglect. As H. N. Brailsford has said :

The year 1797 marks the culmination of Godwin's career, and it would have been well for his fame if it had been its end. . . . With the death of Mary Wollstonecraft, ended all that was happy and stimulating in Godwin's career. It was for him the year of private disaster, and from it dated also the triumph of the reaction in England.

Yet the reversal of Godwin's fortunes took some time to reach its fullest magnitude, and it was several years before he accepted the fact that his message was unwelcome in a hostile world whose praise had turned to execration. The end of his open social proselytising came in 1801, with the publication of a trenchant reply to his attackers. But in a sense he never ceased to preach his doctrines of political justice, for in his novels he maintained a veiled advocacy of the ideals of equality and brotherhood ; in 1820 he produced an enormous but belated reply to Dr Malthus who had attempted to destroy the foundations of *Political Justice* by a theory of the growth of populations in a higher ratio than the increase of food supplies ; and towards the end of his life he produced two books of essays, *Thoughts on Man* and *The Genius of Christianity Unveiled*, in which he returned with scarcely diminished ardour to the themes that had brought him so much fame and infamy forty years before.

Nevertheless, all Godwin's most important work was completed by the end of 1798, and the remaining years of his life have an interest that is principally biographical. The story is one of a steady and courageous adherence to basic principles, accompanied by an application to irksome intellectual toil in order to provide for a growing circle of dependants.

The world was unwilling to listen to counsels of reason, so Godwin became silent, but his silence never betokened an acquiescence in the error that he saw growing up around him. Where his reason told him that he had erred in the past he frankly admitted his mistakes and altered his teachings, but towards those opponents who attacked the fundamental principles on which his teachings had been based, he maintained an unflinching constancy of opinion. He never renounced what his reason still told him was true, and never allowed himself to be led, like so many contemporaries, into a rationalised justification of an apostasy that was the payment for a knighthood or a fellowship. He stood by his considered opinions, and accepted the consequences.

These difficult years contain some unlovely passages, when circumstances led Godwin to become immersed in the crude business of commercial gain for the maintenance of his dependants. He made mistakes in the arrangement of his life, which had frustrating consequences and at times brought out his less creditable traits. But the inconsistencies with his original doctrines have been much exaggerated, and it is possible, without unduly ingenious reasoning, to find justifications in the circumstances for most of his actions. On the whole, his later years were characterised by courageous perseverance in the face of difficulties that must often have made his struggle seem hopeless. It is perhaps a melancholy story, yet it has passages of achievement, and it contains a series of compensating friendships which show that Godwin's intellectual powers, if they were rejected by the majority, were still admired by many men of genius and discrimination.

2

Godwin's difficulties began immediately after Mary's death. He was left with two young children. His financial position was insecure—he was already in debt to Wedgwood and others, and he had little immediate prospect of earning any large quantity of money. He felt too dispirited to write fluently, and already his reputation was becoming so unpopular that it was doubtful whether any book from his pen would be very profitable.

To care for the children he employed as housekeeper a young woman named Louisa Jones, a friend of his sister Harriet. The loneliness that settled on him after Mary's death was, in part at least, diminished by daily visits to his friends. This, indeed, was another period of intense social intercourse, and, during the next year or so, his relationship with Coleridge matured into friendship, and he met for the first time Charles Lamb, William Hazlitt and Henry Crabb Robinson, all of whom have left in their writings copious records of the impressions his company made upon them.

At first he spent his time arranging for publication the manuscripts which Mary left, and compiling the *Memoir* from which I have quoted in the preceding chapter. This work gave him a certain comfort, and its result was one of the best and certainly the most sensitive of his books. The reception which it gained, however, was in general hostile, and gave Godwin a foretaste of what he was to expect from the literary world in the years to come. His candour offended even those who were inclined to be least censorious, and Southey, who should have known better but who was always ready to find a fault in anything that Godwin did, declared that he had shown " a want of all feeling in stripping his dead wife naked."

In the next year, 1798, Godwin's spirits rose sufficiently to allow him to embark on a wide programme of reading, including the Latin poets, the old English dramatists and the classic French authors. He also planned a number of imposing literary works, of which the most important were never written. His notes of two of them, however, remain, and are worth recording, partly as examples of the development of his thought and of his honest admission of past mistakes, and partly to show the manner in which his powers of analytical thought might have been used had not the necessity of providing for a family led him to return to the hack writing from which he had once thought himself free.

The first of these projects was a book to be entitled *First Principles of Morals*.

The principal purpose of this work is to correct certain errors in the earlier part of *Political Justice*. The part to which I allude is essentially defective, in the circumstance of not yielding a proper attention to the empire of feeling. The voluntary actions of men are under the direction of their feelings : nothing can have a tendency to produce this species of action, except so far as it is connected with ideas of future pleasure or pain to ourselves or others. Reason, accurately speaking, has not the smallest degree of power to put any one limb or articulation of our bodies into motion. Its province, in a practical view, is wholly confined to adjusting the comparison between different objects of desire, and investigating the most successful mode of attaining those objects. It proceeds upon the assumption of their desirableness or the contrary, and neither accelerates nor retards the vehemence of their pursuit, but merely regulates its direction, and points the road by which we shall proceed to our goal.

Again, every man will, by a necessity of nature, be influenced by motives peculiar to him as an individual. As every man will know more of his kindred and intimates than strangers, so he will inevitably think of them oftener, feel for them more acutely, and be more anxious about their welfare. This propensity is as general as the propensity we feel to prefer the consideration of our own welfare to that of any other human being. Kept within due bounds, it is scarcely an object of moral censure. The benefits we can confer upon the world are few, at the same time that they are in their nature, either petty in their moment or questionable in their results. The benefits we can confer upon those with whom we are closely connected are of great magnitude, or continual occurrence. It is impossible that we should be continually thinking of the whole world, or not confer a smile or a kindness but as we are prompted to it by an abstract principle of philanthropy. The series of actions of a virtuous man will be the spontaneous result of a disposition naturally kind and well-attempered. The spring of motion within him will certainly not be a sentiment of general utility. But it seems equally certain that utility, though not the source, will be the regulator, of his actions ; and that however ardent be his parental, domestic, or friendly exertions, he will from time to time examine into their coincidence with the greatest sum of happiness in his power to produce. It seems difficult to conceive how the man who does not make this the beacon of his conduct can be styled a virtuous man. Every mode of conduct that detracts from the general stock of happiness is vicious. No action can be otherwise virtuous than exactly in the degree in which it contributes to that stock.

I am also desirous of retracting the opinions I have given favourable to Helvétius' doctrine of the equality of intellectual beings as they are born into the world, and of subscribing to the received opinion, that, though education is a most powerful instrument, yet there exist differences of the highest importance between human beings from the period of their birth.

I am the more anxious to bring forward these alterations and modifications, because it would give me occasion to show that none of the conclusions for the sake of which the book on *Political Justice* was written are affected by them. I am fully of opinion that the sentiments of that book are intimately connected with the best interests of mankind, and am filled with grief when I reflect on the possibility that any extravagances or oversights of mine should bring into disrepute the great truths I have endeavoured to propagate. But thus my mind is constituted. I have, perhaps, never been without the possession of important views and forcible reasonings ; but they have ever been mixed with absurd and precipitate judgments, of which subsequent consideration has made me profoundly ashamed.

Unfortunately, this work was never published. Godwin's tentative ideas show that he realised the main faults of *Political Justice*. A modification of the rigid dependence on the human reason and of the strict insistence on the natural equality of men could only have strengthened his philosophical and psychological contentions without detracting from the force of the social arguments he maintained. It is not difficult to see in these changes of attitude the influence of the more tender emotions which had characterised the happy period of his life with Mary Wollstonecraft. His logic was perhaps no longer so sure and uncompromising as it had been in the past, but his knowledge of life and his intuitive realisation of the functioning of the human mind had become much more mature and accurate.

These changed opinions were not included in the third and last English edition of *Political Justice*, which was published in this year. Godwin's critics have attached a great and undue importance to his revisions of this book. Coleridge deplored them. Hazlitt said, in 1830, that "Mr Godwin, out of complaisance to the public, qualified, and in some degree neutralised, his own doctrines." De Quincey, writing some years after Godwin's death, uttered a violent denunciation :

The second edition, as regards principles, is not a re-cast, but absolutely a travesty of the first ; nay, it is all but a palinode. In this collapse of a tense excitement I myself find the true reason for the utter extinction of the *Political Justice*, and of its author considered as a philosopher.

De Quincey's statement is so ridiculous that it would hardly be worth exhuming if it had not become the beginning of a myth which has survived among people who have never read Godwin, and which represents him as bending before popular indignation and making a thorough recantation of his revolutionary social teachings. Nothing could be more untrue. Contrary to De Quincey's lie, the later editions of *Political Justice* contained no

MARY WOLLSTONECRAFT
*From the portrait by John Opie*

[*Facing page* 150

single alteration in the basic principles, and no deletion of any importance in the social conclusions to be drawn from them. Godwin modified the language, inserted a number of unimportant qualifying clauses, and here and there expanded his arguments in order to counter unforeseen but important criticisms which had arisen after the book was published. The general effect of these alterations was to diminish the vigour of the writing and to introduce at times a tediousness which lessened the impact of the ideas. But I do not think there is any reason to agree even with Hazlitt, however much more we may respect his integrity than that of De Quincey, in his statement that Godwin had in any degree " neutralised his own doctrines." The principal social criticisms remained, uncompromising and unanswerable, and I am convinced that the only alterations arose from Godwin's own feeling of their justification rather than, as Hazlitt suggests, " out of complaisance to the public."

The second book which Godwin had in mind during 1798 was one to be entitled *Two Dissertations on the Reasons and Tendency of Religious Opinion.*

The object of this book is to sweep away the whole fiction of an intelligent former of the world, and a future state ; to call men off from those incoherent and contradictory dreams that so occupy their thoughts, and vainly agitate their hopes and fears, and to lead them to apply their whole energy to practicable objects and genuine realities. The first Dissertation would be applied (1) to show that the origin of worlds is a subject out of the competence of the human understanding ; (2) to invalidate the doctrine of final causes ; and (3) to demonstrate the absurdity and impossibility of every system of Theism that has ever been proposed. The second Dissertation would treat of the injurious and enfeebling effects of religious belief in general, and of prayer in particular. The consideration would be wholly confined to the most liberal systems of Theism, without entering into superfluous declamation upon the pretences of imposters and fanatics.

This book, also, was not written at the time, and it is probable that Godwin himself decided that, in the state of public opinion, a work of this nature would do more harm to an already bruised reputation. Nevertheless, he continued to regard religion with a considerable and natural interest.

3

By the early part of 1798, Godwin's domestic arrangements

were still in an unsatisfactory condition, and he began to consider the idea of re-marriage, if only to provide a more settled
background for the children and to relieve him of the domestic
details which tended to crowd out the more important demands
of his literary profession.  Also, he was still lonely, and the continued round of social evenings left a desire for more stable companionship.  In his phlegmatic and somewhat cold way, he
began to look for a woman who would be a suitable wife.

That he should have started to seek a successor to Mary Wollstonecraft so soon after her death, did not mean that his love for
her had not been intense, or that his grief had not been genuine.
His short life with her had been his happiest year ; he did not
hope to be so happy again.  But in his sorrow he remained the
philosopher, and no doubt it seemed to him for the general good
that he should take a wife who would look after Mary's children
and take her place in his house, if not in his mind, so that he
would be able to devote his time to writing books for the benefit
of humanity—the books his circumstances were never to allow
him to complete.

Although Godwin seems to have been somewhat calculating in
his pursuit of a wife, he had fairly high requirements of intelligence and personality.  It appears, for instance, that Louisa
Jones, his housekeeper and the nurse of his children, would have
been willing to take Mary Wollstonecraft's place, but Godwin
did not reciprocate her desires.  Like a previous choice of his
sister Harriet, she appeared too negative to be a desirable wife
for a distinguished author.

In the spring of 1798, however, he went on a trip to Bath, and
there encountered a lady who seemed to suit his requirements.
She was Harriet Lee, who, with her sister Sophia, ran a girl's
school and wrote novels, plays and poems.  Godwin met the
sisters on four occasions during his visit, made up his mind
quickly as to the desirability of Harriet, and set about with more
energy than subtlety to achieve his end.  The main result of his
efforts was a series of some of the most dispassionate love letters
that can ever have been written.

Godwin's first letter was one of bold reconnaissance :

When I last had the pleasure of seeing you, you said you supposed you
should hear of me.  What was your meaning in this, I do not think
proper to set myself to guess, lest I should find that you meant nothing,

or what in my estimate might amount to nothing.  In saying therefore, that you *supposed* you should hear *of* me, I am determined to understand that you *expected* to hear *from* me. . . .  There are so few persons in the world that have excited that degree of interest in my mind which you have excited, that I am loth to have the catalogue of such persons diminished, and that distance should place a barrier between them and me, scarcely less complete than that of death.  Indulge me with the knowledge that I have some place in your recollection.  Suffer me to suppose, in any future production that you may give to the world, that while you are writing it, you will sometimes remember me in the number of your intended readers.  Allow me to believe that I have the probability of seeing you in no long time here in the metropolis.

He extends a bold invitation to his own home, and hastens to add :

I do not perceive that there could be any impropriety in it.  A sister of the Miss Joneses, with whom I resided at Bath, lives at my house upon the footing of an acquaintance, and is so obliging as to superintend my family, and take care of my children. . . .  I should imagine, therefore, that you might accept the invitation without sinning against the etiquette that you love.

When two months had passed without a reply, and Godwin learnt that Harriet Lee had been in London without attempting to get in touch with him, he began to feel that he had behaved without tact, and wrote a querulous letter of apology and inquiry. Harriet Lee read it critically, and wrote in the margin her shrewd comments :

The tone of this letter appears to me to betray vanity disappointed by the scantiness of the homage it has received, rather than mortified by any apprehension of discouragement.  If any offence was given by the former letter this is calculated to renew and increase it ; for it is equally presuming without being more explicit. . . .

Nevertheless, she was not entirely hostile to Godwin's suit, for she agreed to meet him when he re-visited Bath in June, and at the " conference " expressed her " regard and esteem," without giving any definite decision of refusal or acceptance of Godwin's proposal.

There followed a series of long letters in which Godwin summoned all his reasoning powers to propel the lady into acceptance, by dilating on the value of marriage and by demolishing her objections to this particular union.  His encomiums reveal how thorough had been the change in his attitude towards the domestic virtues :

F 2

. . . I have said to you once before, do not go out of life without ever having known what life is. Celibacy contracts and palsies the mind, and shuts us out from the most valuable topics of experience. He who wastes his existence in this state may have been a spectator of the scene of things, but has never been an actor, and is just such a spectator as a man would be who did not understand a word of the language in which the concerns of man are transacted. The sentiments of mutual and equal affection, and of parental love, and these only, are competent to unlock the heart and expand its sentiments—they are the Promethean fire, with which, if we have never been touched, we have scarcely attained the semblance of what we are capable to be. When I look at you, when I converse with you, it is more, much more the image of what you might be, and are fitted to be, that charms me, than the contemplation of what you are. I regard you as possessing the materials to make that most illustrious and happiest of all characters, when its duties are faithfully discharged—a wife—a mother. But if you are eminently and peculiarly qualified for these offices, it is the more to be regretted, and shall I add ? the more to be censured in you, if you peremptorily and ultimately decline them.

The two principal doubts which prevented Harriet Lee from consenting immediately were, whether she should marry a man of such a revolutionary reputation, and whether she should marry an agnostic. On neither side of the negotiation does the dominant factor appear to have been love. Harriet's first concern was her good name, and Godwin's his comfort and the care of his family.

To the first objection Godwin replied in terms which, at best, indicate a certain blindness to the real nature of his position in the world at this time :

What will the world say ? In the first place, I am not sure that you do not labour under some mistake in this case. I must be permitted to say on this occasion, that among those who personally know me, the respect and love I have obtained is, I believe, fully equal to any reputation I may be supposed to have gained for talents. I believe no person who has so far run counter to the prejudices and sentiments of the world has ever been less a subject of obloquy. I know that many whose opinions on politics and government are directly the reverse of mine, yet honour me with their esteem. I cannot, therefore, be of opinion that your forming a connection with me would be regarded as by any means discreditable to you.

Unfortunately, it was Godwin, and not Harriet Lee, who was mistaken as to his reputation by the middle of 1798.

To Harriet's religious objections he answered with great eloquence and persistence. He went so far as to quote St Paul in his own favour on the subject of marriage, but on his main religious position he was firm, and his repudiation of Miss Lee's narrow views was energetic and, at the end, bitter :

I know that your heart—the bias and leaning of your heart—is on my side. But you have found the secret of suppressing the feelings of your heart, and subjecting them to the mystery and dogmas of your creed. . . . This is the very quintessence of bigotry, to overturn the boundaries of virtue and vice, to try men, not by what we see of their conduct and know of their feelings, but by their adherence to, or rejection of, a speculative opinion. You have a certain Shibboleth, a God and a future state, which if any man deny, you assert he can have no firm and stable integrity. And, which is most curious, you say to him, " If you have only the sentiment of virtue, if you only do good from a love of rectitude and benevolence, and do not feel yourself principally led to it by a foreign, an arbitrary and a mercenary motive, I can have no opinion of you." I am happy to know that these errors of yours have no necessary connection with either Deism or Christianity.

Godwin's arguments, in his letters and at a meeting in London, appear rather to have deterred than convinced Harriet Lee, who replied with a firm rejection, in which she repudiated some of his accusations :

. . . all the powers of my understanding, and the better feelings of my heart concurred in the resolution I declared before we parted ; every subsequent reflection has but confirmed it. With me our difference of opinion is not a mere theoretical question. I never did, never can feel it as such, and it is only astonishing that you should do so. It announces to me a certain difference in—I had almost said a *want* in—the heart, of a thousand times more consequence than all the various shades of intellect or opinion. My resolution then remains exactly and firmly what it was : it gives me great pain to have disturbed the quiet of your mind, but I cannot remedy the evil without losing the rectitude of my own. . . .

If, in our conversations, I have ever appeared in any moment undecided, it was only at those when it occurred to me that truth and genuine feeling were so strongly on my side, that while you were collecting arguments to enlighten my mind, I felt persuaded of the possibility of a change in your own. And why should I not ? A doctrine so necessary to the heart, so consonant to the reason as that of a just and all-powerful Deity will I hope one day find its way to both.

Godwin wrote one or two angry letters, but Miss Lee was unmoved, and in August he gave up his efforts. With his characteristic forbearance, he does not appear to have borne her any lasting resentment for his humiliation, and after a time they resumed a friendly correspondence. According to Mary Shelley,

" to the end of his life he always spoke of her with esteem and regard."

After this disappointment, Godwin seems to have become reconciled, for the time being, to the idea of continuing his inconvenient household arrangements. The arrival of John Arnot, a Scottish disciple who later disappeared in the remoter parts of Europe, relieved him of the amorous inclinations of Louisa Jones who still, however, continued to act as his housekeeper, and for a while there seems to have been no woman who appeared to him at once desirable and attainable.

In July, 1799, however, an unexpected event set him on a second pursuit. In that month Reveley died suddenly from the breaking of a blood vessel in the brain. Mrs Reveley locked herself in a room at the top of the house, and remained there for a week " in a state bordering on frenzy."

Godwin heard of the incident on the same day. According to Mary Shelley, " he became thoughtful and entirely silent—he already revolved the future in his mind. Maria Reveley had been a favourite pupil, a dear friend, a woman whose beauty and manners he ardently admired."

Godwin decided quickly. His doctrine of perfect sincerity taught him to disregard established etiquette, and less than a month after Reveley's death he commenced an epistolatory wooing as vigorous as that of Harriet Lee. This was a less dispassionate correspondence, for Godwin appears to have felt a genuine and considerable affection for Maria.

His first approaches met with little success. Maria Reveley refused to see him and his wooing had to be conducted through Mrs Fenwick. Very soon a tone of thwarted exasperation appeared in Godwin's writing, and it seems, if we read closely into the background, that Mrs Reveley, who had been glad to enjoy Godwin's regard when his fame was at its zenith, was by no means anxious to reciprocate the love of a man whose reputation was stained by popular abuse.

The game for which we play [wrote the impatient wooer] the stake that may eventually be lost is my happiness and perhaps your own.

You have it in your power to give me new life, a new interest in existence, to raise me from the grave in which my heart lies buried . . .

How singularly perverse and painful is my fate. When all obstacles interposed between us, when I had a wife, when you had a husband, you said you loved me, for years loved me ! Could you for years be deceived ? Now that calamity on the one hand, and no unpropitious fortune on the other, have removed these obstacles, it seems your thoughts are changed, you have entered into new thoughts and reasonings. . . .

Maria still refused to see Godwin, and expressed her uncertainty of the fitness of their marriage, because of Godwin's greater intelligence. Godwin was astonished, flattered, filled with false confidence and wrote a long and closely reasoned letter which he obviously hoped would bear down all her objections and bring about a decisive termination of the negotiations in his own favour. The letter is interesting for the evidence it gives of Godwin's changed attitude towards the relationship of the sexes :

And so you would really demand in a partner an understanding too little comprehensive to see into many things, and a heart, for these are wholly or nearly inseparable, of too little sensibility to feel many things ? Surely to state such a requisition is sufficiently to display the misapprehension on which it is founded. I should have thought experience would have shown you how little is to be hoped from characters of this kind. Make one generous experiment upon a man of a different sort. Can you fail to be aware that the man of real powers will infallibly, at least when he loves, be affectionate, attentive, familiar and totally incapable of all questions of competition or ideas of superiority ; while the man of meaner or middling understanding may almost always be expected to be jealous of rivalship, obstinate, self-willed and puffed up with the imaginary superiority he ascribes to himself ? Can you fail to be aware of the inferences which you ought to draw from the respective characters of the two sexes ? We are different in our structure ; we are perhaps still more different in our education. Woman stands in need of the courage of man to defend her, of his constancy to inspire her with firmness, and, at present at least, of his science and information to furnish to her resources of amusement, and materials for studying. Women richly repay us for all that we can bring into the common stock, by the softness of their natures, the delicacy of their sentiments, and that peculiar and instantaneous sensibility by which they are qualified to guide our tastes and to correct our scepticism. . . .

You cannot form so despicable an opinion of me as to suppose that I can view you with no eyes but those of a lover. You saw the contrary for years ; and, believe me, I know what I say ; I can conquer myself again and again, as often as the conquest shall be necessary. There is nothing upon earth that I desire so ardently, so fervently, so much with every sentiment and every pulse of my heart, as to call you mine. But dispose of that point as you please, I am too vigorous and robust of soul ever to be made the suicide of my body or the suicide of my mind. No objection to our intercourse can therefore arise from that point. . . .

It is, however, more than probable that in all I have said respecting our intercourse, I have been fighting a shadow. In one of your first intimations to me since your widowhood, you said you could not see me, or any unmarried man, *for some time :* that did not sound as if our intercourse was to be closed for ever. I think, however, you pay too little attention to my feelings. Two months of etiquette have now nearly elapsed, and no elucidation of this *some time* has yet reached my ears. You ought perhaps to have known that respecting persons in whom I feel myself interested, uncertainty fills my soul with tumults and tortures my fancy with a thousand painful and monstrous images.

Godwin's elaborate reasoning was unsuccessful, and he does not appear to have persisted in his unwelcome attentions. No doubt he expected that time would melt her resistance, and that then the impression he hoped he had made on her affections would have its effect. But when at last he saw her in December it was in the company of John Gisborne, whom she eventually married in secret. Godwin was as much mortified by this insincerity as by the loss of her hand. Gisborne, according to the contemporary reports, more than lived up to Maria Reveley's requirements of masculine stupidity.

### 4

When Godwin was so concerned to re-establish marital life, it was only to be expected that domestic felicity should form one of the principal themes of the book on which he was engaged in this period. This work was *St Leon*, his second novel, which appeared in 1799, between the two courtships we have described.

*St Leon* is a fantastic and improbable novel which deals with the sufferings of a man who has been given the alchemical secrets of the philosopher's stone and the *elixir vitæ*, conveying boundless wealth and eternal youth, conferring an almost equally boundless power of good and evil, but also involving the endless hostility of the normal world and the destruction of personal relationships and domestic happiness until the recipient of these unparalleled gifts is left lonely and hunted in his golden immortality.

Godwin was careful to indicate that the story should not be regarded for its literal significance, and the allegorical nature of the book is obvious, although it is by no means so simple as has been imagined by some of the commentators, such as Kegan Paul, who asserted that " the aim of the tale is to show that boundless wealth, freedom from disease, weakness and death, are as nothing in the scale against domestic affection and 'the charities of private life.' "

It is true that one of the avowed objects of the novel is to correct what had been said in *Political Justice* against the virtues of married life. On this Godwin is explicit in his introduction :

Some readers of my graver productions will perhaps, in perusing these little volumes, accuse me of inconsistency ; the affections and charities of private life being everywhere in this publication the topic of the warmest eulogium, while in the *Enquiry Concerning Political Justice* they seemed to be treated with no great degree of indulgence and favour. In answer to this objection, all I think it necessary to say on the present occasion is, that, for more than four years, I have been anxious for opportunity and leisure to modify some of the early chapters of that work in conformity to the sentiments inculcated in this. Not that I see cause to make any change respecting the principle of justice, or anything else fundamental in the system there delivered ; but that I apprehend domestic and private affections inseparable from the nature of man, and from what may be styled the culture of the heart, and am fully persuaded that they are not incompatible with a profound and active sense of justice in the mind of him that cherishes them.

Moreover, to the praise of domestic happiness and an elaborate tribute to Mary Wollstonecraft, portrayed as Marguerite, the wife of St Leon, so large a portion of the early part of the book is devoted, before the most active part of the story is commenced, that the balance is destroyed. The picture of Mary shows clearly the sincerity of Godwin's love and sorrow, and also the torturing guilt he seems to have felt towards her, a kind of guilt often experienced by men whose wives die in bearing their children.

Nevertheless, domestic affections and Godwin's feelings towards Mary Wollstonecraft are not the only or even, in my opinion, the main themes of the allegory. It seems probable that Godwin, who later wrote a book on *The Lives of the Necromancers*, was aware of the occult significance of gold in the writings of the hermetic philosophers. Gold signifies wisdom, the philosopher's stone the means of attaining wisdom. If Godwin had this knowledge, it is reasonable to see in *St Leon* the allegorical teaching that a man who attains wisdom and wishes to use it for the general good, must expect and be willing to forego the ordinary comforts of life, and the benefits of domestic affection and even friendship in the course of his efforts. Every man's hand will be against him, and men will turn aside in misunderstanding and hostility from the benefits he seeks to bestow on them. It is easy to find the parallel between the persecutions which Godwin was already beginning to endure in return for telling men how they could live in happiness, and those which were inflicted on St Leon for attempting to use his knowledge and wealth to benefit stricken humanity. *St Leon*, like *Caleb Williams*, is first of all concerned with Godwin's perpetual and real dream of the conflict between society and the conscious individual.

Apart from these more general themes, many of the familiar Godwinian arguments are illustrated in *St Leon*. The inquisition is a demonstration of the evils of the interference of positive institutions or state establishments for the regulation of opinion and the supposed establishment of virtue. The inquisitors themselves are examples of men of integrity who mistakenly mix virtue with vice by attempting to achieve good ends by evil means. The terrifying figure of Bethlem Gabor, the most impressive character in the book, is symbolic of the evil passions which are aroused in men, in reaction against the injustices of the society that oppresses and robs them.

*St Leon* achieved a fair success and saved Godwin from immediate financial disaster by bringing him four hundred pounds. It was hailed by Hazlitt as one of " the most splendid and impressive works of the imagination that have appeared in our times," and for many years it was one of the standard works of the Romantic movement, admired extravagantly by Shelley, Byron and Keats.

It is inferior to *Caleb Williams*, more tediously loaded with heavy rhetoric, less swift in the succession of its dramatic incidents, and less concrete in its portrayal of the evils of human life. At times the imagery and language rise to a richness more exuberant than anything else in Godwin's work, but in general the style is uneven and less direct than that of the earlier novels. Nevertheless, it is better than most novels of its period or than anything Godwin wrote afterwards, and still maintains a certain fascination for whoever is patient enough to read through the tedious introductory chapters.

5

We have already made a number of references to the reaction against Godwin and his ideas which was in full swing at the time of the publication of *St Leon*. It appears to have begun some two years before, while Mary Wollstonecraft was still alive, for in the *Thoughts Occasioned by the Perusal of Dr Parr's Spital Sermon*, Godwin tells us :

Down to the middle of the year 1797, the champions of the French Revolution in England appeared to retain their position and I remained unattacked. . . . After having for four years heard little else than the voice of commendation, I was at length attacked from every side, and in a style which defied all moderation and decency. No vehicle was too mean, no language too coarse and insulting, by which to convey the venom of my adversaries. The abuse was so often repeated, that at length the bystanders, and perhaps the parties themselves, began to believe what they had so vehemently asserted. The cry spread like a general infection, and I have been told that not even a petty novel for boarding-school misses now ventures to aspire to favour, unless it contain some expressions of dislike and abhorrence to the new philosophy, and its chief (or shall I say its most voluminous ?) English adherent.

The attack was pursued on many sides and several planes, from the malicious but relatively intelligent sneers of Southey, Scott and D'Israeli, to the vicious and puerile jests of the *Anti-Jacobin Review*, the bad verse of Charles Lloyd, himself an apostate, the bad novels of Mrs Hannah More, and the idiocies of many score of country parsons and university dons who aspired to poetic honours. For the lower class of these attackers no jest or lie was too despicable, and Mary Wollstonecraft had been dead a very short time before her name was dragged through the mire by these unprincipled hacks.

No quarter was given by the Government critics [says Hazlitt], the authorised censors of the press, to those who followed the dictates of independence, who listened to the voice of the tempter Fancy. Instead of gathering fruits and flowers, immortal fruits and aramanthine flowers, they soon found themselves beset not only by a host of prejudices, but assailed with all the engines of power : by nicknames, by lies, by all the arts of malice, interest and hypocrisy, without the possibility of their defending themselves " from the pelting of the pitiless storm," that poured down upon them from the strongholds of corruption and authority.

The reader who is interested in such relics will find a great number if he searches through the pages of the *Anti-Jacobin Review* between 1798 and 1801. As an example I will content myself with quoting three stanzas from an anonymous poem, entitled " The Vision of Liberty," printed by that *Review* in August, 1801, which attacked all the great radical leaders and intellectuals in turn :

Then saw I mounted on a braying ass
William and Mary, sooth, a couple jolly :
Who married, note ye how it came to pass
Although each held that marriage was but folly—
And she of curses would discharge a volley
If the ass stumbled, leaping pales or ditches—
Her husband, sans-culottes, was melancholy,
For Mary, verily, would wear the breeches—
God help poor silly men from such usurping b——s.

Whilom this dame the Rights of Women writ,
That is the title to her book she places,
Exhorting bashful womanhood to quit,
All foolish modesty, and coy grimaces ;
And name their backsides as it were their faces ;
Such licence loose-tongued liberty adores,
Which adds to female speech exceeding graces ;
Lucky the maid that on her volume pores,
A scripture, archly framed, for propagating w——s.

William has penn'd a wagon-load of stuff,
And Mary's life at last he needs must write,
Thinking her whoredoms were not known enough,
Till fairly printed off in black and white,—
With wondrous glee and pride, this simple wight
Her brothel feats of wantonness sets down,
Being her spouse, he tells, with huge delight
How oft she cuckolded the silly clown,
And lent, O lovely piece ! herself to half the town.

Godwin stood up to this torrent of abuse with fortitude and dignity. Hazlitt was thinking of him when he said :

The philosophers, the dry abstract reasoners, submitted to this reverse pretty well, and armed themselves with patience " as with triple steel," to bear discomfiture, persecution and disgrace.

But, although he was, or appeared to be, little affected by the more vulgar forms of abuse, Godwin was certainly perturbed when, in a year or two, he began to experience the attacks of men whose intelligence he respected, some of whom had once shared his ideas and had even appeared to be his friends.

The first of these was James Mackintosh, who had once been one of the most enthusiastic opponents of Burke and, as we have seen, was an intimate and sympathetic friend of Godwin during the writing of *Political Justice*. Mackintosh does not appear ever to have been a man of very strong political convictions, and when his personal interests and his doubts led him in the same direc-

tion, he did not require a great deal of persuasion to induce him
to become as enthusiastic an apologist for the reaction as he had
been for the revolution.

His changeover earned him great unpopularity.    Coleridge
hated him because he was an apostate—ironically Coleridge was
hated by Hazlitt for the same reason.    Lamb was moved by his
indignation to write an epigram which remains one of the best
of his not-very-good poems :

> Though thou'rt like Judas, an apostate black,
> In the resemblance one thing thou dost lack ;
> When he had gotten his ill-purchas'd pelf,
> He went away, and wisely hanged himself ;
> This thou may do at last, yet much I doubt,
> If thou hast any Bowels to gush out.

Mackintosh's public declaration of his apostasy took the form
of a series of lectures *On the Law of Nature and Nations*, which he
delivered in Lincoln's Inn between January and June, 1799.
His avowed intention was " publicly and unequivocally to abhor,
abjure and forever renounce the French Revolution, with all its
sanguinary history, its abominable principles and for ever
execrable leaders."    Mackintosh did not neglect to include
among his victims all the progressive writers of his time, and his
references, although not specific, undoubtedly pointed to Godwin.
The lectures appear to have had the single virtue of great
dexterity, for Hazlitt, a hostile witness, says :

> Those of us who attended day after day, and were accustomed to have
> all our previous notions confounded and struck out of our hands by
> some metaphysical legerdemain, were at last at some loss to know
> whether *two and two made four*, till we had heard the lecturer's opinion on
> that head.

Godwin was mortified by this gratuitous and unexpected attack
from a man whom he had always regarded with respect and
trust.

> Poor Godwin, [says Hazlitt,] who had come, in the *bonhomie* and
> candour of his nature, to hear what new light had broken in upon his
> old friend, was obliged to quit the field, and slank away after an exulting
> taunt thrown out at " such fanciful chimeras as a golden mountain or a
> perfect man."

Godwin wrote a letter of protest to Mackintosh.   It has not
survived.   Mackintosh's reply was conciliatory    he was evi-

dently desirous of retaining Godwin's good will even when he saw fit to attack his opinions with venom. He explained his attack away as far as he could, and, for the rest, admitted that his strictures should have been directed, not against Godwin, but only against his ideas.

There seems to have been some sincerity in Mackintosh's protestations, for in later years he went out of his way to seek Godwin's friendship, and assisted him in a number of ways, through favourable criticism in the *Edinburgh Review*, and financial assistance during monetary crises.

Mackintosh's attack was followed, in the next year, by a broadside from another former friend, Dr Parr, who had been estranged owing to Godwin's strictures on the clergy in *The Enquirer* and had taken Mackintosh's part over the Lincoln's Inn Lectures. On April 15th, 1800, Dr Parr preached the annual Spital Sermon before the Lord Mayor, and chose the opportunity to make a full attack on Godwin and his philosophy. Parr's own position was somewhat obscure, for, in spite of ranging himself beside the reactionaries in attacking Godwin, he seems to have remained a radical in other matters, continued to regard Pitt as an inordinate rascal, and eventually quarrelled with Mackintosh because the latter entered the service of the Government. The most likely interpretation of his action seems to be not so much that he was an apostate as that he was moved by personal spleen against Godwin. This makes it all the more despicable in him to have attacked an old friend at a time when he most needed public support against those who were enemies of all progressive men.

Godwin was disturbed by this event, and wrote to Parr a very polite and tentative letter, in which he referred to Parr's sermon and said :

I am sorry for this. Since Mackintosh's Lectures it has become a sort of fashion with a large party to join in the cry against me. It is the part, I conceive, of original genius, to give the tone to others, rather than join a pack, after it has already become loud and numerous. . . . I am entitled to conclude that you have altered your mind respecting me. In that case I should be glad you would answer to your own satisfaction, what crimes I am chargeable with now in 1800, of which I had not been guilty in 1794, when with so much kindness and zeal you sought my acquaintance.

Parr, unlike Mackintosh, replied with acrimony accusing

Godwin of impiety, immodesty, corruption of the young, and all the various crimes which have been alleged perenially against original thinkers since the trial of Socrates.

An opponent who deserved more serious attention was Dr Malthus, whose *Essay on Population*, published in 1789, attempted to confute Godwin's theories on sociological grounds. Malthus's theory was that, without the hindrances caused by the present social system, people would breed indiscriminately and the result would be an increase in population at a much greater ratio than any possible increase in the production of food on the earth. Therefore to interfere with the present processes of limitation by the application of universal benevolence was in fact contrary to the interests of humanity. These ideas were seized upon by the reactionaries to justify their ignoring completely the claims of the poor to a better form of life. Godwin considered them of great importance, and it was not until 1820 that he wrote his considered reply. Meanwhile, it was left to Hazlitt to deal with the question much more effectively in his essays on Malthus. Today, when in civilised countries the tendency of population is to fall rather than to rise in proportion to the available amenities, the whole controversy seems academic, and it is obvious that Malthus based his ideas not only, as Hazlitt asserted, on inexact figures, but also on a miscalculation of the complex psychological and social factors involved in the changes in populations.

Godwin felt that, however much he could afford to ignore the vulgar abuse of hack versifiers and petty novel writers, he must make some kind of reply to such critics as Mackintosh, Parr and Malthus. In 1801, therefore, he wrote and published a long pamphlet to answer his opponents, under the title of *Thoughts Occasioned by the Perusal of Dr Parr's Spital Sermon, being a Reply to the Attacks of Dr Parr, Mr Mackintosh, the Author of An Essay on Population, and others*.

This pamphlet is an example of Godwin's writing at its best, vigorous in expression, clear in thought, and sincere in argument. It was the last really good piece of writing he produced for many years, during which the reaction was doing its work against him not in the tangible and answerable forms of abuse and argument, but with the far more insidious method of an oblivion which made his living as a writer precarious and forced him to continual hack writing unworthy of his talents.

He begins his *Thoughts* by tracing the strange course of his literary reputation, the unexpected and gratifying praise which for four years after the publication of *Political Justice* had showered on him from every side, and the equally unexpected, but much less pleasant stream of contradiction which began to flow at the end of these four years and which soon engulfed his reputation in the utmost obloquy. He surveys the strange change in the opinions of those who had once been so ardent supporters of the French Revolution—even more ardent than himself—and who had regarded with satisfaction the spread of Jacobin opinions, yet when these same opinions had become uninfluential, suddenly discovered them to be dangerous.

They were deserting a cause which they regarded as lost, and attacked it in order to prove their conversion. Godwin is charitable to their weakness :

It is not in the nature of man to like to stand alone in his sentiments or his creed. We ought not to be too much surprised, when we perceive our neighbours watching the seasons, and floating with the tide. Nor is this fickleness by which they are influenced, altogether an affair of design. It is seldom that we are persuaded to adopt opinions, or be persuaded to abandon them, by the mere force of arguments. The change is generally produced silently, and unperceived except in its ultimate result, by him who suffers it. . . . The human intellect is a sort of barometer, directed in its variations by the atmosphere which surrounds it. Add to this, that the opinion which has its principle in passion, includes in its essence the cause of its destruction. " Hope deferred makes the heart sick."

But, while Godwin is willing to be tolerant to the changes of men's opinions, he is unprepared to allow their attacks to go unanswered :

But this I must say, that they act against all nature and reason when instead of modestly confessing their frailty and the transformation of their sentiments, they rail at me because I have not equally changed. If I had expressed a certain degree of displeasure at their conduct, I should have had a very forcible excuse. But I was not prepared with a word of reproach : I would have been silent, if they would have permitted me to be so.

Yet Godwin did not allow anger to affect the nature of his answer, which is restrained, reasonable and dignified, and in no point sinks to the level of abuse or personal acrimony. This pamphlet, more than anything else he wrote, demonstrates the candour and uprightness of Godwin's character.

In his reply to Dr Parr, whom he considers the most formidable of his opponents, he makes a frank recantation of his attacks on the domestic affections :

I ought not only in ordinary circumstances to provide for my wife and children, my brothers and relations before I provide for strangers, but it would be well that my doing so should arise from the operation of those private and domestic affections by which through all ages of the world the conduct of mankind has been excited and directed.

But the admission of the value of the private affections does not alter the main tenour of Godwin's arguments. Although the actions of men need not necessarily be governed by pure reason, the criteria for these actions will remain the laws of justice and truth :

The person who has been well instructed and accomplished in the great schools of human experience has passions and affections like other men. But he is aware that all these affections tend to excess, and must be taught each to know its order and its sphere. He therefore continually holds in mind the principles by which their boundaries are fixed.

Godwin contends that Parr's arguments arose from misunderstanding and that the quarrel is largely one of definitions. Mackintosh's statements show the deadening influence of a conversion to conservatism. He regards Malthus with respect, but denies that his arguments are valid, because prudence is an effective check on population and is likely to become general in a just and virtuous society :

What the heart of men is able to conceive, the hand of man is strong enough to perform. For myself I firmly believe that days of greater virtue and more ample justice will descend upon the earth.

6

In the days of Godwin's persecution one of his great consolations was that many of his friends remained and that others were added in the place of those who deserted him, some of them attracted by the stoical resignation with which he bore himself in adversity. Of these the greatest was Samuel Taylor Coleridge, whom Godwin later described as the fourth of his principal oral instructors.

Coleridge, on his first encounter with Godwin, had very little respect for him as a man, in spite of the admiration with which, for a short time, he regarded his ideas. He asserted in 1794 that

Holcroft was a much more able man, whom he liked " a thousand times better " than Godwin. In 1795 he wrote to Grosvenor Bedford : " Godwin, as a man, is very contemptible," and recounted with delight to Southey how Godwin was crushed by Porson's rudeness. In 1796 he took Thelwall's part in the controversy over Godwin's pamphlet, and remarked to him :

I was once and only once in company with Godwin. He appeared to me to possess neither the strength of intellect that discovers truth, nor the powers of imagination that decorate falsehood ; he talked sophisms in jejune language.

In the same correspondence he announced his intention of writing a book to confute Godwin by comparing his system unfavourably with Christianity, but, although he mentioned the idea to Southey as well, the book does not appear ever to have been written. Later he said, again to Thelwall : " It is not his atheism that has prejudiced me against Godwin, but Godwin who has, perhaps, prejudiced me against atheism."

It is difficult to trace the exact course of Coleridge's ideas on Godwin for some years after this, but there is little doubt that for a long time they remained unfavourable, and that the change was very gradual.

By the end of 1799, however, a cordial friendship appears to have replaced the old enmity, although Coleridge still regarded Godwin with a rather patronising amusement. In that year he and his family dined with Godwin on Christmas Day, and Coleridge wrote to Southey, suiting his style to Southey's notorious contempt of Godwin :

Tomorrow Sara and I dine at Mister Gobwin's, as Hartley calls him, who gave the philosopher such a rap on the shins with a ninepin that Gobwin in huge pain *lectured* Sara on his boisterousness. I was not at home. *Est modis in rebus.* Moshes is somewhat too rough and noisy, but the cadaverous silence of Godwin's children is to me quite catacombish, and thinking of Mary Wollstonecraft, I was oppressed by the day, Davy and I dined there.

During the following year Coleridge began to see Godwin more frequently, and developed a considerable respect for his powers and an affection for his character. Godwin reciprocated these feelings, and Lamb says that Godwin was " above all men, mortified," when Coleridge departed to the Lakes in the early summer of 1800. A voluminous correspondence commenced, in which Coleridge wrote some of his most interesting prose and showed a growing esteem for Godwin's qualities as a man and a writer. In March we find him writing of evenings of drinking and discussion. In May his regard is outspoken :

" . . . as I am not behind you in affectionate esteem, so I would not be thought to lag in those outward and visible signs that both show and vivify the inward and spiritual grace. Believe me, you recur to my thoughts frequently, and never without pleasure, never without making out of the past a little day dream for the future."

The influence wielded by Coleridge over Godwin's opinions is shown more explicitly in an extract from Godwin's journal for the year 1800 :

In my forty-fourth year I ceased to regard the name of Atheist with the same complacency I had done for several preceding years, at the same time retaining the utmost repugnance of understanding for the idea of an intelligent Creator and Governor of the universe, which strikes my mind as the most irrational and ridiculous anthropomorphism. My theism, if such I may be permitted to call it, consists in a reverent and soothing contemplation of all that is beautiful, grand or mysterious in the system of the universe, and in a certain conscious intercourse and correspondence with the principles of these attributes, without attempting the idle task of developing and defining it—into this train of thinking I was first led by the conversations of S. T. Coleridge.

It is doubtful whether Coleridge would have agreed to this kind of broad pantheism as a definition of his own beliefs—certainly it has little relationship to the Christian orthodoxy of his later years. Nor does it represent so great a departure from Godwin's earlier ideas—the note in 1785 attacking organised religion affirms a similar faith, and Godwin's conception of a system of natural law and of criteria of justice and truth inherent in the structure of the universe, which occur in *Political Justice*, are of a religious nature. As Mr Frank Lea has pointed out in *Shelley and the Romantic Revolution*, there is little difference between the idea of Reason postulated by Godwin and the pantheistic God of Spinoza. However, it appears that, if Coleridge did not transmit any new idea to Godwin in the matter of religion, he certainly helped him to clarify his previously vague ideas on the nature of the universe. Coleridge was also largely responsible for the broadening of Godwin's literary tastes at this time to include an appreciation of the old English authors.

In September Godwin went to visit Curran in Ireland, and wrote to Coleridge a long description of his impressions. Coleridge replied with an eloquent description of the Lakes and suggestion that Godwin should join him.

I question if there be a room in England which commands a view of mountains, and lakes, and woods and vales, superior to that in which I am now sitting. I say this, because it is destined for your study, if you come. You are kind enough to say that you feel yourself more natural and unreserved with me than with others. I suppose that this in great measure arises from my own ebullient unreservedness. Something, too, I will hope may be attributed to the circumstances that my affections are interested deeply in my opinions.

. . . I wish you would come and look out for a house for yourself here. You know, " I wish " is privileged to have something silly to follow it.

Shortly afterwards Coleridge wrote with unmerited enthusiasm on the ill-fated tragedy, *Antonio*, which Godwin wrote during 1800 and produced with disastrous results :

Your tragedy to be exhibited at Christmas ! I have indeed merely read your letter, so it is not strange that my heart still continues beating out of time. Indeed, indeed, Godwin, such a stream of hope and fear rushed in on me, when I read the sentence, as you would not permit yourself to feel. If there be anything yet undreamed of in our philosophy ; if it be, or if it be possible, that thought can impel thought out of the visual limit of a man's own skull and heart ; if the clusters of ideas, which constitute our identity, do ever connect and unite with a greater whole ; if feelings could ever propagate themselves without the servile ministrations of undulating air or reflected light—I seem to feel within myself a strength and a power of desire that might dart a modifying, commanding impulse on a whole theatre. What does this mean ? Alas ! that sober sense should know no other to construe all this, except by the tame phrase, I wish you success. . . .

Later in the same letter Coleridge describes Godwin as " a *bold* moral thinker," and suggests that he should write " a book on the power of the words, and the processes by which the human feelings form affinities with them."

Godwin evidently replied by suggesting that in the state of public opinion against him at that time it was useless to embark on philosophical work, for Coleridge wrote a month later to express his confidence in Godwin and his future, and to make some shrewd observations on Godwin's character and abilities.

Now for something which I would fain believe is still more important, namely, the property of your philosophical speculations. Your second objection, derived from the present *ebb* of opinion, will be best answered by the fact that Mackintosh and his followers have the *flow*. This is greatly in your favour, for mankind are at present gross reasoners. They reason in a perpetual antithesis ; Mackintosh is an oracle, and Godwin therefore a fool. Now it is morally impossible that Mackintosh and the sophists of his school can retain this opinion. You may well exclaim with Job, " O that my adversary would write a book ! " When he publishes, it will be all over with him, and then the minds of men will incline strongly to those who would point out in intellectual perceptions a source of moral progressiveness. Every man in his heart is in favour of your general principles. A party of dough-baked democrats of fortune were weary of being dissevered from their fellow rich men. They want to say something in defence of turning round. Mackintosh puts that something into their mouths, and for a while they will admire and be-praise him. In a little while these men will have fallen back into the ranks from which they had stepped out, and life is too melancholy a thing for men in general for the doctrine of unprogressiveness to remain popular. Men cannot long retain their faith in the Heaven *above* the blue sky, but a Heaven they will have, and he who reasons best on the side of that universal wish will be the most popular philosopher. As to your first objection, that you are no logician, let me say that your habits are analytic, but that you have not read enough of Travels, Voyages, and Biography, especially of men's lives of themselves, and you have too soon submitted your notions to other men's censures in conversation. A man should nurse his opinions in privacy and self-fondness for a long time, and seek for sympathy and love, not for detection or censure. Dismiss, my dear fellow, your theory of Collision of Ideas, and take up that of Mutual Propulsions.

Coleridge warned Godwin not to be optimistic concerning his tragedy *Antonio*, and commiserated with him when it failed, but was tactless enough to encourage him to continue in this unfortunate medium, by suggesting a play from a theme in Tavernier's *Travels into Persia*, a suggestion which Godwin worked on with alacrity.

Coleridge took Godwin's part enthusiastically against his enemies, and expressed great satisfaction with the *Thoughts on Dr Parr's Spital Sermon :*

I read it with unmingled delight and admiration with the exception of that one hateful paragraph, for the insertion of which I can account only on a superstitious hypothesis that, when all the gods and goddesses gave you each a good gift, Nemesis counterbalanced them all with the destiny, that, in whatever you published, there should be some outrageously *imprudent* suicidal passage. But you have had enough of this. With the exception of this passage, I can never remember to have read a pamphlet with warmer feelings of sympathy and respect. . . .

That these opinions were written in complete sincerity is demonstrated by a note which Coleridge wrote in his own copy of the pamphlet, now in the British Museum :

I remember few passages in ancient or modern authors that contain more just philosophy in appropriate, chaste or beautiful diction than the fine following pages.  They reflect equal honour on Godwin's head and heart.  Though I did it in the zenith of his reputation, yet I feel remorse ever to have only spoken unkindly of such a man.

The correspondence between the two men became less frequent after Godwin's second marriage, but their mutual esteem continued, in spite of an occasional misunderstanding.   Ten years after, when Southey delivered a harsh attack on one of Godwin's books, Coleridge sent Godwin a letter in which he castigated Godwin's detractors, excused Southey as best he could, and reiterated his own feelings :

Ere I had yet read or seen your works, I, at Southey's recommendation, wrote a sonnet in praise of the author.  When I had read them, religious bigotry, the but half-understanding of your principles, and the *not* half-understanding my own, combined to render me a warm and boisterous anti-Godwinist.  But my warfare was open ;  my unfelt and harmless blows aimed at an abstraction I had christened with your name ; and you at that time, if not in the world's favour, were among the captains and chief men in its admiration.  I became your acquaintance when more years had brought somewhat more temper and tolerance ; but I distinctly remember that the first turn in my mind towards you, the first movements of a juster appreciation of your merits, was occasioned by my disgust at the altered tone and language of many whom I had long known as your admirers and disciples. . . .

A few days later, Henry Crabb Robinson was in the company of Coleridge and Hazlitt, and noted in his diary that

Coleridge spoke feelingly of Godwin and the unjust treatment he has met with. . . . Coleridge spoke with severity of those who were once the extravagant admirers of Godwin and afterwards, when his fame declined, became his most angry opponents. . . . Coleridge said there was more in Godwin after all than he was once willing to admit, though not so much as his enthusiasts fancied. . . .

After 1812 the correspondence between Coleridge and Godwin came to an end, and they saw each other less frequently.   Nevertheless, in 1825 their relationship was sufficiently in Hazlitt's mind for him to devote a large part of his essay on Coleridge in *The Spirit of the Age* to a comparison between him and Godwin.

Coleridge came off second best on most of the points of comparison.

## 7

Lamb had begun by sharing Coleridge's antipathy towards Godwin. In 1796 he said to Coleridge, " Why sleep the *Watchman's* answers to that Godwin ? ", and his attitude does not seem to have changed materially until he and Godwin became acquainted in 1798.

During that year the *Anti-Jacobin Review* had produced a cartoon of leading radicals, by Gillray, in which Coleridge, Southey and Godwin were portrayed as asses, Lamb as a toad and Charles Lloyd as a frog. Shortly afterwards Lamb and Godwin dined on the same evening at Coleridge's. According to Southey's account :

Lamb got warmed with whatever was on the table, became disputatious, and said things to Godwin which made him quietly say, " Pray, Mr Lamb, are you Toad or Frog ? " Mrs Coleridge will remember the scene, which made her sufficiently discomfortable. But the next morning S.T.C. called on Lamb, and found Godwin breakfasting with him, from which time their intimacy began.

The indication which Lamb himself gave of his attitude towards Godwin is contained in a letter to their common acquaintance, Thomas Manning :

Godwin I am a good deal pleased with. He is a very well-behaved, decent man ; nothing very brilliant about him or imposing as you may suppose ; quite another guess sort of a gentleman from what your Anti-Jacobin Christians imagine him. I was well pleased to find he has neither horns nor claws ; quite a tame creature, I assure you : a middle-sized man, both in stature and in understanding ; whereas, from his noisy fame, you would expect to find a Briareus Centimanus, or a Tityus tall enough to pull Jupiter from his heavens.
I begin to think you atheists not quite so tall a species !

At the time of Godwin's visit to Ireland Lamb passed on the news to Coleridge and remarked : " Before he went I passed much time with him, and he has showed me particular attentions. N.B. A thing I much like."

A little later Lamb played a leading role in the tragic farce that attended the production of Godwin's melodramatic tragedy, *Antonio*. This was certainly the worst piece of writing Godwin ever produced, but by a curious perverseness he considered it the best, and set great hopes on it, both for a renewal of his finances and a bettering of his fame.   He spent a vast amount of time and trouble in writing and revision, and called on all his friends, including Lamb, Coleridge, Holcroft and Sheridan, for criticisms and suggestions.   At last the play was finished, and through the influence of Sheridan it was produced at Drury Lane on December 13th, 1800, against the better judgment of Kemble.   Everything was done to ensure its success.   Lamb wrote a prologue and an epilogue which were quite as bad as the play itself, Kemble and Mrs. Siddons took the leading parts, and Godwin's authorship was concealed for fear of popular prejudice, John Tobin accepting the nominal responsibility.

The play was a complete failure and Lamb, who sat with Godwin and Marshal in one of the boxes, has left a vivid account of the event in his *Essays of Elia*.   Godwin preserved a philosophic resignation, and continued to regard *Antonio* as an unjustly condemned masterpiece.   But his feelings on that decisive evening must have been those of great disappointment and almost of desperation, for he needed money to maintain his family and was already in debt.   In a further letter to Manning, Lamb spoke of him with great feeling :

Manning, all these things came over my mind ; all the gratulations that would have thickened on him, and even some have glanced aside upon his humble friend ; the vanity, and the fame, the profits (the Professor is £500 ideal money out of pocket by this failure, besides £200 he would have got for the copyright, and the Professor is never much beforehand with the world ; what he gets is all by the sweat of his brow and dint of brain, for the Professor, though a sure man, is also a slow) ; and now to muse upon thy altered physiognomy, thy pale and squalid appearance (a kind of *blue sickness* about the eyelids) and thy crest fallen, and thy proud demand of £200 from thy bookseller changed to an uncertainty of his taking it at all, or giving the full £50.   The Professor has won my heart by this *his* mournful catastrophe.   You remember Marshall, who dined with him at my house ; I met him in the lobby immediately after the damnation of the Professor's play, and he looked to me like an angel ; his face was lengthened and all over perspiration. I never saw such a care-fraught visage ; I could have hugged him, I loved him so intensely.   " From every pore of him a perfume fell."   I have seen that man in many situations, and, from my soul, I think that a more god-like honest soul exists not in this world.   The Professor's poor nerves trembling with the recent shock, he hurried him away to my house to supper, and there we comforted him as well as we could.   He came to consult me about a change of catastrophe ; but alas ! the piece was condemned long before that crisis. I at first humoured him with a specious proposition, but have since joined his true friends in advising him to give it up. He did it with a pang, and is to print it as *his*.

As Lamb forecast, Godwin, unsatisfied with the public rejection of a work he considered his masterpiece, insisted on publishing it under his own name. The effect was only to give his enemies some justification for renewing their attacks, and no substantial profits accrued to ease his financial distress.

When, at Coleridge's advice, Godwin set about planning a second play, *Abbas*, Lamb was aghast :

Hath not Bethlehem College a fair action for non-residents against such professors ? [he wrote to Manning]. Are poets so *few* in *this age*, that He must write poetry ? *Is morals* a subject so exhausted, that he must quit that line ? Is the metaphysics well (without a bottom) drained dry ?

If I can guess at the wicked pride of the Professor's heart, I would take a shrewd wager that he disdains ever again to dip his pen in *Prose*. Adieu, ye splendid theories ! Lawsuits, where I am counsel for Archbishop Fenelon *versus* my own mother, in the famous fire cause !

Later, however, when Godwin had accepted the failure of the play on the theme of Abbas, and was starting to write a third play on a theme adapted from the life of Richard Savage, Lamb gave him some encouragement and wrote him two long letters of information and advice.

But Lamb's friendship was not confined to literary matters. Godwin's principles never led him to adopt any asceticism in his life, although he eschewed extravagant living, and he always practised an unstinted hospitality towards any of his friends who chanced to visit him. Lamb appears to have availed himself freely of this genial entertainment, for on one occasion he tells Manning : " Last Sunday was a fortnight, as I was *coming to town* from the Professor's, inspired with new rum, I tumbled down and broke my nose. I drink nothing stronger than malt liquors." And Southey, ever ready for a malicious tale of Godwin, retails the story of how the philosopher fell asleep one evening after dinner, as was his habit, and Lamb and Fell, in great delight, proceeded to pick his pockets and carry off his spirits and snuff.

Lamb and Godwin continued close friends for the next thirty years, and, after a quarrel in their old age, were finally brought together again shortly before Lamb's death.

## 8

As has already been indicated in the preceding chapters, Godwin was greatly troubled during the years 1800 and 1801 by the decline of his literary earnings through the great unpopularity into which he and his works had fallen. *Antonio* was an attempt to break into the profitable circle of successful playwrights, and its failure meant much more to Godwin than a mere failure to gain popular approval. He was brought once again into contact with imminent poverty. In his days of hack writing he had experienced it, but then he had been responsible only for his own well-being. Now he had to consider the future of his two children, and the upkeep of someone to look after them and keep house for him. His old friend Holcroft, at that time in Germany, had the insight to realise the condition of Godwin's household, when he wrote :

> I cannot relieve you ; that is—do not think the phrase too strong—that is my misery : yet I wish you would tell me what is the state of your money affairs ? I am in great anxiety. I form a thousand pictures of hovering distress of the dear children, the house you have to support, and the thoughts that are perhaps silently corroding your heart. Do not subtract from the truth in compassion to my feelings, strong as they are for myself and others, they always end in enquiring if there be any effectual remedy ?

Financial insecurity had, indeed, become a dominant factor in Godwin's life, and was to remain for the next thirty years the cause of an anxiety that crippled his literary activities and soured his personal life. Yet, almost miraculously, Godwin contrived to live and maintain his family during these perilous years. But the very methods by which he was forced to live were precarious and caused further anxiety, as well as, in the end, producing a certain insensitivity in his character after so much experience of the slights which fall upon a man who is greatly dependent on the generosity and patience of his friends.

Already, in 1797, Godwin had begun his career of borrowing, and in the lean years of 1800 and 1801 we find the beginnings of that melancholy series of letters to and from various creditors which continued as a regular feature of his life for many years.

Yet, in spite of his practical difficulties, Godwin was still thinking deeply on many subjects, as his notes attest, and on none of these subjects more deeply than on himself. There remains a fragment of self-analysis, written in 1800 or 1801, which shows a surprising accuracy in the observation of his own character, and bears an interesting comparison with the estimates of his friends and contemporaries, particularly Hazlitt. I quote in full the significant sections of this document :

A timorous advocate, both of men and opinions, on individual occasions—afraid to advance opinions lest I should be unable to support them—always beginning with a kind of skirmishing war. This owing to frequent miscarriage, and experience of my own inaccuracy.

Too sceptical, too rational, to be uniformly zealous. Nervous of frame, mutable of opinion, yet in some things courageous and inflexible.

So fond of disinterestedness and generosity that everything in which these are not has always been insipid to me—inextinguishably loving admiration and fame, yet scarcely in any case envious. Habitually disposed to do justice to the merits of others ; never depreciating an excellence I felt, and eager for the discovery of excellence, yet in some cases too languid an assertor of it—ever addicted to reflection and reasoning, frequently to ardour.

I am extremely modest. What is modesty ? First, I am tormented about the opinions others may entertain of me ; fearful of intruding myself, and of co-operating to my own humiliation. For this reason I have been, in a certain sense, unfortunate through life, making few acquaintances, losing them *in limine*, and by my fear producing the thing I fear. I am bold and adventurous in opinions, not in life ; it is impossible that a man with my diffidence and embarrassment should be. This, and perhaps only this, renders me often cold, uninviting and unconciliating in society. Past doubt, if I were less solicitous for the kindness of others, I should have oftener obtained it.

I am anxious to avoid giving pain, yet, when I have undesignedly given it, I am sometimes drawn on, from the painful sensation that the having done what we did not intend occasions, to give more.

My nervous character—to give it a name, if not accurate, well understood—often deprives me of self-possession, when I would repel injury or correct what I disapprove. Experience of this renders me, in the first case, a frightened fool, and in the last, a passionate ass ; in both my heart palpitates and my fibres tremble ; the spring of mental action is suspended ; I cannot deliberate or take new ground ; and all my sensations are pain and aversion—aversion to the party, impatience to myself. This refers merely to active scenes, not to colloquial disquisition ; in the latter my temper is one of the soundest and most commendable I ever knew.

Perhaps one of the sources of my love of admiration and fame has been my timidity and embarrassment. I am unfit to be alone in a crowd, in a circle of strangers, in an inn, almost in a shop. I hate universally to speak to the man that is not previously desirous to hear me. I carry feelers before me, and am often hindered from giving an opinion, by the man who spoke before giving one wholly adverse to mine.

I am subject to sensations of fainting, particularly at the sight of wounds, bodily infliction and pain : perhaps this may have some connection with my intellectual character.

I am feeble of tact, and occasionally liable to the grossest mistakes respecting theory, taste and character ; the latter experience corrects the former consideration ; but this defect has made me too liable to have my judgment modified by the judgment of others ; not instantaneously perhaps, but by successive impulses. I am extremely irresolute in matters apparently trivial, which occasionally leads to inactivity, or subjects me to the being guided by others.

I have a singular want of foresight on some occasions as to the effect what I shall say will have on the person to whom it is addressed. I therefore often appear rude, though no man can be freer from rudeness of intention, and often get a character for harshness that my heart disowns.

I can scarcely ever begin a conversation where I have no preconceived subject to talk of ; in these cases I have recourse to topics the most trite and barren, and my memory often refuses to furnish even these. I have met a man in the street who was liable to the same infirmity ; we have stood looking at each other for the space of a minute, each listening for what the other would say, and have parted without either uttering a word.

There are many persons that have gone out of life without enjoying it—that is not my case. I have enjoyed most of the pleasures it affords. I know that at death there is an end of all, but I have not lived in vain for myself ; I hope not for others.

There is an evenness of temper in me that greatly contributes to my cheerfulness and happiness ; whatever sources of pleasure I encounter, I bring a great part of the entertainment along with me ; I spread upon them the hue of my own mind and am satisfied. Yet I am subject to long fits of dissatisfaction and discouragement ; this also seems to be constitutional. At all times agreeable company has an omnipotent effect upon me, and raises me from the worst tone of mind to the best.

No domestic connection is fit for me but that of a person who should habitually study my gratification and happiness ; in that case I should certainly not yield the palm of affectionate attentions to my companion. . . .

These notes show a considerable psychological insight, which Godwin appears to have gained from the observation of his mental processes, and they display a considerable honesty in self-criticism. As explanations of his external conduct they are extremely valuable, and should be remembered in the consideration of his subsequent actions.

This seems to have been regarded by Godwin as a period of

climacteric importance in his life, for almost at the same time as he wrote this self-analysis, he produced the curious fragment of autobiography from which we have quoted frequently in an earlier part of the book. Indeed, as events were shortly to demonstrate, it was the major turning point.

## PART VI

# Years of Patience

## 1801–1836

I

To Godwin, in the years shortly after Mary Wollstonecraft's death, marriage seemed the solution to all his ills. If he could find a capable wife who would take away the major part of the upbringing of his children, he felt he would be free to write and somehow to extricate himself from the financial difficulties into which he had fallen.

His rejection by Harriet Lee and Maria Reveley did not make him abandon the idea of marriage. He merely postponed the issue because he knew no other women who seemed to him eligible.

Then, one evening in May, 1801, as he was sitting outside his window in the Polygon, a handsome widow addressed him from the neighbouring balcony with the phrase, " Is it possible that I behold the immortal Godwin ? " He accepted the gross flattery with great satisfaction, and the relationship, fostered by a common desire for wedlock, grew apace.

The lady was Mrs Mary Jane Clairmont. Of her past little is known, but a single note by Godwin leads us to suppose that she had been used to a leisured and easy life, for he speaks of her health having declined during the first years of her marriage " for want of those relaxations and excursions to sea-bathings and watering-places, which are the usual lot of women in the class of life in which she was born." The stories retailed about her immoral past were probably produced by the malice her own foolish conduct aroused in those she encountered. Of Mr Clairmont nothing is known, but an appearance of probability is given to his existence by the presence of two children in Mrs Clairmont's household, a son, Charles, then at school, and a daughter, Jane, slightly older than Fanny Imlay.

Mrs Clairmont is reported to have been energetic, clever and good-looking. She was a good cook, and had sufficient knowledge of French and ability in English composition to make saleable translations, besides having a good handwriting and being a capable amanuensis. Her admiration for Godwin appears to have been genuine and considerable. These were her good qualities, which were the more evident during Godwin's courtship, and it is not really surprising that he regarded her as a desirable wife. Her bad qualities began to become evident after their marriage.

The courtship was short and decisive. Lamb describes it ironically in a letter to their common friend Rickman :

I know of no more news from here, except that the Professor is *Courting*. The lady is a widow with green spectacles and one child, and the Professor is grown quite juvenile. He bows when he is spoke to, and smiles without occasion, and wriggles as fantastically as Malvolio, and has more affection than a canary bird pluming his feathers, when he thinks some one is looking at him. He lays down his spectacles, as if in scorn, and takes 'em up again in necessity, and winks that she mayn't see he gets sleepy about Eleven o'clock. You never saw such a philosophic coxcomb, nor anyone play the Romeo so unnaturally.

It was an almost undocumented courtship. The comments in Godwin's diary are brief and uninformative, and only one letter survives, written when Godwin went with his publisher, Sir Richard Phillips, to view Chaucer's home at Woodstock. It is an unusual lover's letter, consisting for the most part of criticisms of Phillips and descriptions of Woodstock. Only in the last paragraph does he become personal.

My dear love, take care of yourself. Manage and economize your temper. It is at bottom most excellent : do not let it be soured and spoiled. It is capable of being recovered to its primæval goodness, and even raised to something better. Do not however get rid of all your faults. I love some of them. I love what is human, what gives softness, and an agreeable air of frailty and pliability to the whole. Farewell a thousand times. I shall be at home on Monday evening : are not you sorry ? Kiss Fanny and Mary. Help them to remember me, and to love me. Farewell.

Godwin would have been wiser had he paid more attention to Mrs Clairmont's faults. But he was bent on marriage, and his proposal was accepted as readily as it was made.

In November he tried to visit Paris, but his radical reputation was still strong enough to gain him a refusal of his request for a passport.

On December 21st, he was married to Mrs Clairmont at Shoreditch Church, evidently chosen because Godwin did not wish to revive the painful memories of Mary Wollstonecraft by re-marrying in the local church of St Pancras. But the second marriage resembled the first in at least two details. It was kept a secret from all Godwin's friends, and the faithful Marshal was the only witness besides the parish clerk. In his diary Godwin wrote, with unemotional brevity,

" M.　Shoreditch Church, &c., with C. and M. : Dine at Snaresbrook : sleep."

After marriage Mary Jane Godwin began to show in an increasing degree the faults which at first had appeared almost charming to Godwin. Her bad qualities rapidly became preponderant, and, on the whole, her advent into Godwin's household was productive of far more unhappiness than of comfort and pleasure. Godwin soon learnt that marriage is after all an institution of a somewhat equivocal nature.

Mary Jane Godwin showed herself devoid of all the Godwinian virtues of universal benevolence, impartial justice and perfect sincerity. She was jealous and possessive to a degree, and although these qualities may have sprung from praiseworthy personal affections, their result was lamentable and went to prove Godwin's contention that the private affections must be disciplined by the reason according to the criterion of justice.

Contrary to Godwin's own practice of impartial and equal kindness to all children under his care, she showed a marked preference for her own. Mary reacted with spirited resentment, but the quiet Fanny with resignation and an increasing melancholy. Godwin did what he could to counteract the unfair treatment, but was powerless to stop it completely.

Mrs Godwin also displayed a strongly possessive attitude towards Godwin, and an implacable hostility towards his friends, particularly the most devoted, including Coleridge, Curran, Lamb and Marshal. It must be said in extenuation that her position was not altogether happy. To Godwin and his friends the memory of Mary Wollstonecraft was sacred, and a woman of no extraordinary talents may well have felt that she was being judged and found wanting in comparison with her predecessor. Indeed, some of Godwin's acquaintances were probably not over careful to hide their opinion of her inadequacy, and her own conduct rapidly confirmed their contempt.

At first she seems to have resorted to blunt inhospitality. Later she indulged in various mischief-making stratagems, including lies, tale-bearing and the deliberate provocation of quarrels by goading Godwin against his friends. In this way she was instrumental in causing temporary quarrels with Coleridge, Curran, Lamb and others. She had also an insatiable curiosity, and made herself unpopular by peering into the affairs of Godwin's friends and retailing in a scandalous manner all the information she could glean, filling in the gaps with her own suppositions. This characteristic resulted in Lamb caricaturing her as Priscilla Pry.

The result of all these unpleasant activities was to cause Godwin's friends to become much more infrequent in their visits. In September, 1802, Lamb wrote to Manning :

Godwin continues a steady friend, though the same facility does not remain of visiting him often. That . . . has detached Marshall from his house ; Marshall, the man who went to sleep when the "Ancient Mariner" was reading ; the old, steady, unalterable friend of the Professor.

A few months later matters seemed to become even worse, for he wrote again :

The Professor's Rib has come out to be a disagreeable woman, so much so as to drive me and some other old cronies from his house. He must not wonder if people are shy of coming to see him because of the "snakes."

Southey's hostility towards Godwin was increased because he chose to take such a woman for a wife while Mary Wollstonecraft's portrait hung in his house. Coleridge disliked Mary Jane, Curran described her as "a pustule of vanity," and even Crabb Robinson, who liked to be friendly with everybody, found her beyond his patience.

However, in time Mrs. Godwin's activities began to take on a less virulent form. She learnt to disguise her hostility towards Godwin's friends, and they in turn came to accept as necessary even such an evil as she must have appeared to them. But the

Godwin household was never harmonious, and there is no reasonable doubt that Mary Jane's attitude was the principal cause of this disharmony.

2

If Godwin imagined that re-marriage would be a cure for his economic insecurity, the event proved him wrong, and it is difficult to see how he could have calculated otherwise. Mary Jane's arrival brought three more mouths to the family table, and the unrecorded departure of Louisa Jones was soon offset by the birth of a new child into this strangely mixed household, William, the son of Godwin and his new wife.

His marital ventures had thus saddled Godwin with six dependants, whose demands, according to his revised theory of benevolence, had a prior claim on his activities before the rest of the world. So he had to relinquish the career he had planned for himself, of writing moral philosophy, and take to work which was devoted primarily to earning a living for his large and inefficiently managed household. Almost everything he wrote for more than twenty years was little more than good-class hack work. It was usually very conscientiously written and well-documented, and often had some temporary value, but it was not the kind of work for which Godwin felt he had a real vocation ; for this reason it lacks the quality of immediate and permanent value which characterises the major works of his preceding period. His books from 1800 until 1830 have all the appearance of being manufactured laboriously out of often inadequate materials. There is nothing in them of the feeling of organic necessity which strikes one in reading *Political Justice* or *The Enquirer*. Such books Godwin wrote because he enjoyed writing them and because they conveyed a teaching in which he believed with his whole reason. A book like *The Life of Chaucer*, on the other hand, is little more than a scholar's pastiche compiled to convey information and perhaps to earn money, but certainly not to stimulate an intellectual passion for justice and truth. Nevertheless, all this flat, and often useless, writing did not completely destroy Godwin's old spirit and his passion for justice. Here and there they come suddenly to the surface, and in the novels, where it was often possible to talk in allegory without destroying commercial value, the philosophy of universal benevolence still finds its place. Later, when economic distress had become less acute, Godwin was to return to his old themes in at least two books which were too substantial to be mere shadows of his former greatness.

The literary works which appeared under his name between 1802 and 1820 were six in number : *The Life of Geoffrey Chaucer* (1803), *Fleetwood ; or The New Man of Feeling* (1805), *Faulkener, a Tragedy* (1807), *An Essay on Sepulchres* (1809), *The Lives of Edward and John Phillips, Nephews and Pupils of Milton* (1809), and *Mandeville* (1818).

*The Life of Chaucer* was commenced in 1801, before his second marriage. Godwin was faced with the problem of making a profitably large book out of the scanty facts, which had been included comprehensively by Thomas Tyrwhitt in an eight-page biographical note to his *Canterbury Tales*, published three years previously. So Godwin decided to create a pageant of the age in which Chaucer lived, and something of the nature of its comprehensiveness can be gained from the full title : *The Life of Geoffrey Chaucer, the Early English Poet, including Memoirs of his Near Friend and Kinsman, John of Gaunt, Duke of Lancaster ; with Sketches of the Manners, Opinions, Arts and Literature of England in the Fourteenth Century.* Godwin set about his work with great assiduousness, reading in the British Museum, the Bodleian Library and the Record Office, and consulting Ritson, the pioneer vegetarian, who was also an authority on the fourteenth century. The result was a work of remarkable scholarship, which even today is readable for its fluency of style and the rich variety of its information on the fourteenth century. As a picture of the age of Chaucer it was excellent, although its value has since become somewhat obsolete. But as a life of Chaucer it was little better than Tyrwhitt's eight pages, for it contained no more information, and Godwin was forced to adopt the unfortunate device of padding it with suppositions of what Chaucer's actions or thoughts might have been under certain hypothetical circumstances. The literary criticism was not particularly brilliant, and was probably based on the opinions of Coleridge.

The book did not appear without difficulties, and at least one angry letter from Godwin to his publisher has survived :

I never did, and I never will thank any man for altering any one word of my compositions without my privity. I do not admit that there is anything indecorous or unbecoming in the statement which you have omitted. But that is not material. I stand upon the principle, not upon the detail. If the part omitted had been to the last degree solecistical and absurd, my doctrine is the same. " No syllable to be altered, without the author's privity and approbation." It is highly necessary, my dear Sir, that I should be explicit on this point. I am now writing a book, of which you are to be the publisher. It is to be " Godwin's Life of Chaucer," and no other person's. My reputation and my fame are at stake upon it. The moment therefore I find you alter a word of that book (and you cannot do it without my finding it) that instant the copy stops, and I hold our contract dissolved, though the consequence should be my dying in a jail. I know you have contracted that worst habit of the worst booksellers (the itch of altering) and I give you this fair and timely warning.

The book appears to have been produced without any further friction. Its appearance was greeted with mixed opinions. Scott and Southey attacked it in spiteful reviews. Lamb and Coleridge praised it in letters to Godwin, but failed to complete favourable reviews which they had promised. The *Anti-Jacobin Review*, strangely enough, praised it warmly and exposed the dishonesty of Scott's review. Taking into consideration Godwin's reputation, the sales were reasonably good, and he received £600, which he regarded as a " penurious " payment.

*Fleetwood* showed a further decline in his powers of novel writing. Godwin claimed that it was a story made out of " common and ordinary adventures," but, whatever this may have meant, it was certainly no realistic novel. In its most obvious aspect, it seems to have been intended as a condemnation of libertinism and jealousy, but the method of showing the sordid realities of life is by the end of the book so overloaded with sentimentality and rhetorical description that its purpose is not achieved. The individual at odds with society is again the central character, and there are many lesser themes of a characteristically Godwinian kind. The inadequacies of university education are exposed in the hero's youth at Oxford. In the section describing the youth of Ruffigny, the benevolent mentor who tried to save Fleetwood from his follies, there is an indignant passage on child labour which shows that Godwin was well aware of the terrible conditions in the English factories of his time. The literary world of London is portrayed in a descriptive passage in which the brilliant talker is compared unfavourably with the serious writer.

I am inclined to believe that no one ever uniformly maintained, in various companies, the first place in subtlety and wit, who has not cultivated this character with dishonest art, and admitted many unmanly and disingenuous subterfuges into the plan by which he pursued it. If so, the shining man of a company is to be put down in the lowest classes of persons of intellect.

Godwin, we are told by all his friends except Holcroft, was a dull conversationalist, and it is difficult not to see in this passage an attack upon those who had browbeaten him in debate. This was his answer to the Horne Tookes and the Coleridges. A recognisable projection of his idea of himself appears on a following page :

The man of genius, who has delivered the fruits of his meditations and invention to the public, has nothing naturally to do with this inglorious struggle. He converses that he may inform and be informed. He wishes to study the humours, the manners, and the opinions of mankind. He is not unwilling to take his share in conversation, because he has nothing to conceal, and because he would contribute, as far as with modesty and propriety he can, to the amusement and instruction of others. But his favourite place is that of the spectator. He is more eager to add to his own stock of observation and knowledge, than to that of his neighbours. This is natural and just : since he knows better his own wants, than he can know the wants of any other man ; and since he is more sure of the uses that will be made of the acquisitions he shall himself obtain.

Fleetwood is made to enter parliament, which Godwin himself once thought to do, and the opportunity is taken to deliver a lesson on the faults of representative assemblies. Finally, the domestic virtues are praised, though not with such vigour as in St Leon, and the heroine is once more a recognisable portrait of Mary Wollstonecraft, this time even to the name of Mary. However the details of Godwin's novels after Caleb Williams may have changed, the general pattern was always repeated.

Fleetwood met with less success than his former novels, and except for Mackintosh, few of his friends showed any great enthusiasm for it.

Faulkener, which Godwin had already begun to plan in 1801, and on which Lamb had given him advice, was based on a theme taken from Roxana, which Defoe in turn had written around a reported incident in the life of Savage. Godwin took several years to write it, during the intervals of producing The Life of Chaucer and Fleetwood, and it was finally completed in 1806. It was better than *Antonio*, as anything Godwin wrote in prose was inevitably better than anything he wrote in verse, although, as Coleridge said to Humphry Davy, Godwin considered himself an able poet. Nevertheless, it illustrated Hazlitt's contention that :

If a tragedy consisted of a series of soliloquies, nobody could write it better than our author. But the essence of the drama depends on the alternation and conflict of different passions, and Mr Godwin's *forte* is harping on the same string.

It was over *Faulkener* that Godwin and Holcroft had their great quarrel. Godwin sent Holcroft the manuscript for any criticisms and suggestions he thought might be of assistance in making the play more acceptable for theatrical performance. Holcroft, who had been a very successful playwright, mistook the request, and returned the play almost completely rewritten. Godwin was infuriated and evidently wrote back in anger, for we find a letter from Holcroft, dated September, 1804, who makes a reply singularly restrained and dignified for so irritable an individual :

I am sorry our feelings are not in unison. I am sorry that a work which cost me such deep thought, and was, in my own opinion, so happily executed, should excite in your mind nothing but the chaos of which you inform me. I came up to town with a high hope of having rendered my friend an essential service, with which, when he saw it, he would be delighted, and would perfectly understand all the emotions which passed in my mind, while stimulated by such an endearing reflection. I must bear my disappointment as well as I can, and have only to request that, since you think all conference must produce painful sensations, you will either adopt the piece as I have sent it you (which I by no means wish, since you think as you do), or put the whole of it into your own language. I don't in the least expect, after your long hesitation, that it corresponds with your ideas of good writing, for which I am sorry, but I hope that you will not think it unreasonable that I should object to that which your judgment shall direct, unless I could be made acquainted with it. I hope I have not spent my time wholly unprofitably, since you cannot be insensible that my zeal to serve you effectually has been great.

Godwin was implacable, and a great breach ensued, in which Mrs Godwin played so provocative a part that afterwards Holcroft always blamed her for the enstrangement which ensued between these two old friends and which lasted until a few days before Holcroft's death.

*Faulkener* was eventually accepted by Kemble for performance at Drury Lane Theatre. Lamb wrote to Manning, then in China :

The Professor has got a tragedy coming out, with the young Roscius in it, in January next, as we say—January last it will be with you—and though it is a profound secret now, as all his affairs are, it cannot be so much of one by the time you read this. However, don't let it go any further. I understand there are dramatic exhibitions in China. One would not like to be forestalled.

Owing to the temperamental protests of Betty, " the young Roscius," then a prodigy of thirteen, who took the part of Faulkener, the play was subject to many delays, and did not appear for a year after Lamb's letter. Lamb again wrote prologue and epilogue as poor as the play itself, and on December 16th, 1807, it was finally produced. It was not a complete failure, and it ran for six nights, but the profits were small, and the critics were not friendly, either to the performance or to the published script. Godwin learnt at last that, whatever he might think of himself as a dramatist, the world thought very little, and he does not appear again to have attempted the writing of plays.

*The Essay on Sepulchres* was a pious composition in honour of the great dead, recommending the building of monuments from public funds for those who had benefited humanity.

It is a debatable point whether Godwin's proposals are in strict accordance with the teachings of *Political Justice,* for they seem to give men an incitement to virtue other than the criterion of justice apprehended within their own hearts, and would also tend to give permanence to past systems of thought, which Godwin always wished to avoid. Nevertheless, the essay was written in admirable prose and contained some entertaining conceits.

Godwin had foreseen that its reception would not be enthusiastic, for he wrote in his preface, with a certain sardonic resignation to his fall from favour :

I am a man of no fortune or consequence in my country ; I am the adherent of no party ; I have passed the greater part of my life in solitude and retirement ; there are numbers of men who overflow with gall and prejudice against me (God bless them !), and would strenuously resist a proposal I made, though it were such as from any other quarter they would accept with thankfulness.

The pamphlet was not attacked, but virtually ignored, which

is worse. Nevertheless, Lamb liked it, thought it a " very pretty, absurd book," and told Godwin that it was "better than Harvey, but not so good as Sir T. Browne," which apparently offended him. Hazlitt said that it " contained an idle project enough, but was enriched with some beautiful reflections on old and new countries, and on the memorials of posthumous fame."

Of this and the other book which appeared in 1809, the *Lives of the Nephews of Milton*, Godwin remarked later to his daughter :

But these were not *me ;* I did not put forth the whole force of my faculties ; the seed of what peculiarly constitutes my individual lay germinating in the earth, till in its own time it should produce its proper fruit.

This certainly applies to the latter book, which is the dullest in style of all Godwin's non-dramatic writings. Its interest is chiefly antiquarian, as its subjects were of no abiding interest and contributed nothing of importance to the development of English literature. The sole interest to modern readers, as Kegan Paul has pointed out, lies in the pioneer appreciation of Cervantes, who had been misused and travestied by John Philips in his translation of *Don Quixote*.

For eight years Godwin produced no literary work under his own name. Then, in 1818, appeared a fourth novel, *Mandeville*. In the preface he again speaks sadly of the reception of his previous writings, and of the prevailing hostility towards him and his publications.

The most remarkable characteristic of *Mandeville* is its unrelieved and massive gloom. It is, like all Godwin's later novels, long drawn-out and over-rhetorical, but, although inferior to *St Leon* and *Caleb Williams*, it is an improvement on *Fleetwood* and holds its own among the novels of its age. Very little that Scott, for instance, wrote was any better.

*Mandeville* is another victim and enemy of society, condemned, in accordance with a foolish and primitive code of honour, to an unjustified ostracism for an action in which he had no responsibility. His sufferings turn him to an implacable hatred of society and of all his fellows, except his beautiful and virtuous sister, Henrietta. In particular, he hates a young man, Clifford, whose good fortune and natural capabilities give him the advantage over the unfortunate Mandeville in all the situations in which their lives are crossed. In the end Clifford takes from him even the one person he loves, his sister Henrietta, and he is left with only his hatred to protect him from the contempt and hostility of the world.

The familiar Godwinian themes occur again, of the rivalry between the individual and society, and of the injustices within a society governed by prejudice and positive institution. Mandeville's original condemnation illustrates the impossibility of a just verdict, because a judge can never know the full facts of the case or the intentions of the defendant. Mandeville is condemned to perpetual obloquy for having stood nobly in the place of the real culprit. The unhappiness which he subsequently endures is obviously intended to illustrate the misery which Godwin himself experienced when he was subjected to public abuse for actions which he calculated would be of benefit to humanity. But, just as the moral of *Political Justice* is that we should attempt to change society by persuasion and sweet reasonableness, so the moral of *Mandeville* is that, while society in its present state will oppose the individual who has acted against its conventions, this opposition should be met with forbearance and not hatred. Because of his hatred, Mandeville loses all the good which is left him, the love of his sister Henrietta.

Henrietta is yet another personification of the virtues of Mary Wollstonecraft, and during her reasonings with her brother she brings forward many Godwinian ideas.

Consider, that man is but a machine [she says]. He is just what his nature and his circumstances have made him ; he obeys the necessities which he cannot resist. If he is corrupt, it is because he has been corrupted. If he is unamiable, it is because he has been " mocked, and spitefully entreated and spit upon." Give him a different education, place him under other circumstances, treat him with as much gentleness and generosity as he has experienced of harshness, and he would be altogether a different creature. He is to be pitied therefore, not regarded with hatred ; to be considered with indulgence, not made an object of revenge ; to be reclaimed with mildness, to be gradually inspired with confidence, to be enlightened and better informed as to the mistakes into which he has fallen, not made the butt and object of our ferocity. . . .

I will tell you what a slave is, and what is a freeman. A slave is he who watches with abject spirit the eye of another ; he waits timidly, till another man shall have told him, whether he is to be happy or miserable today : his comforts and his peace depend on the breath of another's mouth. No man can be this slave unless he pleases. If by the caprice of fortune he has fallen as to externals into another's power, still there is a point that at his own will he can reserve. He may refuse to crouch ;

he may walk fearless and erect ; the words that he utters may be
supplied by that reason, to which the high and the low, the rich and the
poor, have equally access.  And, if he that the misjudging world calls a
slave, may retain all that is most substantial in independence, is it
possible, that he whom circumstances have made free should voluntarily
put the fetters on his own feet, the manacles on his own hands, and
drink the bitter draught of subjection and passive obedience ?

" What a wretched thing is anger, and the commotion of the soul !
If any thing annoys me, and interposes itself between me and the objects
of my desires and pursuit, what is incumbent upon me is, that I should
put forth my powers, and remove it.  How shall I do this ?  By the
exercise of my understanding.  Wherein does my power emphatically
reside ?  In the rational part of my nature.  To the employment of this
power, a cool and exact observation is necessary.  I must be like a great
military commander in the midst of battle, calm, collected, vigilant,
imperturbable ;  but the moment I am the slave of passion, my powers
are lost ;  I am turned into a beast, or rather into a drunkard ;  I can
neither preserve my footing, nor watch my advantage, nor strike an
effectual blow.

Mandeville, however, fails to conduct himself by Godwinian
principles, and comes to a sad end.

Of the minor themes of *Mandeville*, an interesting one is that
of the character of lawyers, sketched in *The Enquirer* and here
portrayed in the evil character of Holloway.  But perhaps the
most interesting speculation in the book is how far it was
influenced by Godwin's relationship with Shelley, which had
begun some years earlier, and will be discussed in a later chapter.
Many contemporaries asserted that Mandeville was meant to
represent Shelley, who seems to have been regarded by his
enemies as a gloomy, misanthropic character.  Godwin, however, must have known Shelley well enough not to have had this
impression of him, however much he may have disliked him
during their periods of estrangement, and it is reasonable to
say that if Shelley is portrayed at all in the book, he is Clifford
rather than Mandeville.  Clifford elopes with Mandeville's
sister, as Shelley with Godwin's daughter, and is thus the cause
of increased distress and shame to Mandeville, as Shelley's action
caused a temporary increase in the public notoriety attached to
Godwin's name.  The connection, it must be admitted, is
tenuous.

Shelley, it has been recorded, was an enthusiastic admirer of
*Mandeville*, and regarded Clifford as a particularly fine character.
But the book was, in general, too gloomy in its outlook and too

involved in its psychological development, to be enjoyed by many readers, and even Hazlitt, the admirer of most of Godwin's books, regarded it as a comparative failure.

3

One of the reasons for the slightness of Godwin's literary output between 1801 and 1820 was that there was little public response to the work of a writer who had been so abused and misrepresented. But the principal reason was that during this period his time and his pen were heavily engaged on more exacting labour.

Before Godwin had been married very long to Mary Jane Clairmont it became obvious that means must be found to increase the resources of his growing family. He had a small regular income from some property which had belonged to Mary Wollstonecraft, but apart from this, the family had to rely on the declining returns from his books and from the occasional translation work which Mrs Godwin undertook. Moreover, Godwin endeavoured to keep a liberal hospitality for those friends who still dared to approach his hearth, and he had many demands on his purse from outside sources. He frequently helped his brothers and sisters, of whom his mother said that she feared the streets of London would soon be full of begging Godwins, and gave money which he could ill afford to young disciples in difficulties or even to complete strangers of whose distresses he had heard indirectly.

It was in these circumstances that Godwin started upon the most disastrous venture of his life. In the spring of 1805 he had been considering a History of England, as large as that of David Hume. The negotiations with Phillips had already started, and Godwin was to receive £2,000 and a share of the copyright, the money to be paid in instalments over the time of writing. The book, however, was never begun. While the negotiations were in progress, Mrs Godwin produced a plan which seemed to Godwin more attractive, and, after hesitation, the idea of earning a certain £2,000 by some years of hard work was abandoned for a fascinating speculation, which required as much toil and which in the end, from Godwin's complete lack of business acumen, proved a disastrous liability rather than an asset.

The new scheme was " a magazine of books for the use and

amusement of children." While he was still undecided whether to relinquish his contract for the History of England, Godwin occupied himself with writing " the chief of a work which was to be the first-born child of our undertaking." This book was a collection of " Fables, Ancient and Modern."

As soon as it had been decided to adopt Mrs Godwin's plan, a further hundred pounds was borrowed from Thomas Wedgwood, and with this small capital the business was started. Premises were taken in Hanway Street, off Oxford Street, " a small street, but of great thoroughfare and commerce." Some rooms were let, which almost made up the rent, and " the coming in and fixtures were £60." It was necessary to conceal very carefully Godwin's connection with the new concern, if it were not to be damned from the outset, and a man named Hodgkins was established as manager and nominal proprietor.

Godwin now set to work industriously to write books for children, under various *noms-de-plume*. The book of Fables was published in 1805, under the name of Edwin Baldwin, who was the foreman of the shop where these books were printed. In the same year Godwin produced *The Looking Glass : a True History of the Early Years of an Artist*, by Theophilus Marcliffe. During 1806, two more books, *The Pantheon, or Ancient History of the Gods of Greece and Rome* and *The History of England*, appeared from the pen of Baldwin, and *The Life of Lady Jane Grey* under the signature of Theophilus Marcliffe.

These were pleasantly written little books, unmarred by the sentimentality and pious rhetoric which spoilt most of the children's books of the time. They erred on the side of pedantry, using modes of expression which would not be readily understood by young children. On the other hand, they avoided the great educational sin, which Godwin had condemned, of assuming children to possess an inferior order of intelligence. There was an air of equal discussion about them ; the tone was that of conversation rather than lecture.

Godwin might well have been engaged on much more important schemes for the general good of humanity, but these books were not without their value in improving the tone of educational literature, which at that time was very low. Besides being well written, they were of some practical use, and, if they have no intrinsic importance today, they are at least of interest in showing that Godwin's understanding of educational needs was not merely theoretical.

The superior quality of Godwin's school books was quickly realised by the reviewers, and, ironically, they were much better received than the serious books which he published during this period. Godwin carefully avoided expressions that might appear Jacobinical, and, except when he was led away into an occasional radical statement in his historical works, he managed to avoid censure or suspicion on these grounds.

The public followed the lead of the reviewers in purchasing freely at The Juvenile Library, as the bookshop was called. Even Christ's Hospital and the Charterhouse became substantial customers.

In spite, however, of this excellent response, the Godwins were soon in difficulties again. The business had started with too little capital to enable it to meet the current expenses of publication as well as to provide a margin for debts. As Mrs Godwin's activities were almost all engaged in the business of the bookshop, the household expenses were increased by the wages of a governess, a cook and sometimes a housemaid. Furthermore, there were still old, unpaid debts and impatient creditors who continued to make demands.

By 1807 the increased business made larger premises necessary, and in that year Godwin established himself at No. 41, Skinner Street, on the site of Snow Hill, off Holborn Viaduct. The house was large enough to serve as a residence, and the family moved down from the Polygon to rooms over the shop. The rent was high, but owing to the fact that the ownership of the premises was in dispute, Godwin managed to avoid meeting this liability for some long time. Nevertheless, even taking into account the fact that it was unnecessary for him to pay any rent, Godwin's financial position was still so bad that he was unable to establish himself without assistance.

In 1807 he borrowed £300 from Curran, and in the following year, with the willing assistance of Marshal, he set on foot a subscription among the wealthy liberals to gather enough money to give his business sufficient capital for its proper continuance. A draft of a letter of appeal, with a list of the principal subscribers, has survived, and is of some interest in showing Godwin's own opinion of his position at this time :

Mr William Godwin, a gentleman well known to the public by his various writings, but who in worldly circumstances partakes of the usual fate of authors, has lately digested a plan for providing for himself and family by entering into the business of a bookseller, principally in the mode of supplying books for schools and young persons. He has composed several works in prosecution of this plan under the feigned name of Edward Baldwin, an expedient to which he felt himself obliged to have recourse in consequence of the prejudices which have been industriously circulated against him. These books are so written as to be incapable of occasioning offence to any ; as, indeed, Mr Godwin would have held it an ungenerous and dishonourable proceeding to have insinuated obnoxious principles into the minds of young persons under colour of contributing to their general instruction. The books have accordingly been commended in the highest terms in all the reviews, and are now selling in the second and third editions respectively. A commercial concern, however, can only have a gradual success, and requires a capital greater than Mr Godwin can command. He has cheerfully devoted himself to this species of pursuit, that he might secure independence and competence to his family, and nothing can be more promising than the progress the undertaking has already made. But it is feared that it cannot be carried on to that maturity to which it naturally tends, unless such opulent persons as are impressed with favourable sentiments of the talents and personal character of Mr Godwin will generously contribute to supply him with those means which he does not himself possess.

Influenced by these considerations, and by the opinion that it is a much truer act of liberality to assist a man we esteem in giving effect to the projects of his industry, than to supply his necessities when such industry is no more, the undernamed gentlemen have respectively engaged to advance for the furtherance of Mr Godwin's project the following sums :

| Earl of Lauderdale | . | £100 | Rt. Hon. H. Grattan | . | £50 |
|---|---|---|---|---|---|
| Lord Holland | . | 100 | Rt. Hon. J. P. Curran | . | 100 |
| Duke of Devonshire | . | 50 | Hon. J. W. Ward | . | 50 |
| Earl Cowper | . | 50 | S. Whitbread, Esq., M.P. | | 50 |
| Earl of Thanet | . | 50 | W. Smith, Esq., M.P. | . | 50 |
| Duke of Bedford | . | 50 | R. Sharp, Esq., M.P. | . | 50 |
| Earl Grey | . | 50 | S. Rogers, Esq. | . | 50 |
| Earl of Rosslyn | . | 50 | Mr J. Johnson | . | 100 |
| Earl of Selkirk | . | 50 | Sir R. Phillips | . | 100 |
| Lord Kinnaird | . | 50 | Sir F. Baring | . | 20 |

Grattan, Curran and Samuel Rogers were personal friends ; Johnson and Phillips, it should be observed to their credit, were rival publishers ; most of the remaining subscribers were, as Godwin put it, " Fox's men."

The subscription brought in £1,200, which enabled Godwin

to pay off a few debts, and to get his business at Skinner Street properly started. His connection with The Juvenile Library having become known, it was no longer necessary for business to be transacted under another name, although Godwin still continued to write his children's books as E. Baldwin. Hodgkins was dismissed and the firm was established in the name of Mrs Godwin, as M. J. Godwin & Co. Premises next door were secured as a printing shop and warehouse, and for the first time the business was suitably equipped.

But although Godwin's financial difficulties had been suspended for a short time he was subject to other anxieties. His health, which had never been robust, was beginning to cause him anxiety, which was shown in a letter to his medical adviser, Dr Ash, in May, 1808, giving in characteristic detail the account of the disorder from which he was suffering. It appears to have been some kind of cataleptic seizure.

As this complaint has attacked me at many different periods of my life, I am inclined to suppose that it has a deep root in my frame, and that it may most usefully be explained by historical deduction.

Its first appearance was in the twenty-eighth year of my age ; the fits continued to visit me for some weeks and then disappeared. They did not return till 1800, after an interval of seventeen years.

In 1792 I had an attack of vertigo, accompanied with extreme costiveness, the only time at which I have experienced that symptom in an excessive degree.

In 1795 I first became subject to fits of sleepiness in an afternoon, which have never since left me, and occasionally seize me even in company.

In 1800 and 1803 my old disorder revisited me ; the attacks were preceded by a minute's notice, and each fit of perfect insensibility lasted about a minute. Air was of no service to repel a fit, but hartshorn smelled to, and a draught of hartshorn and water, seemed to drive them off, particularly in the last days of an attack. If seized standing, I have fallen on the ground, and I have repeatedly had the fits in bed.

It should be observed, that when first attacked in 1783, it was difficult to have been of more temperate habits than I was, seldom tasting wine or spirituous liquors. Since that time I have never been intemperate ; but for the last twenty years have indulged in the moderate regular use of both, not more than three or four glasses of wine in a day.

. . . The approach of the fit is not painful, but is rather entitled to the name of pleasure, a gentle fading away of the senses ; nor is the recovery painful, unless I am teazed in it by persons about me. . . .

It is interesting to observe that the symptoms of Godwin's " fits " were not unlike the physical manifestations which accompany certain so-called psychic phenomena. This form of disorder was to appear sporadically, and to an increasing extent, as he grew older. His sleeping in the afternoon became the subject of amusement to most of his acquaintances. Lamb and Southey mention it, Hogg recounts such an incident in his book on Shelley, and Hazlitt remarks, in *The Spirit of the Age* : " In common company, Mr Godwin either goes to sleep himself, or sets others to sleep."

This period was further saddened by the death of a number of people to whom he was closely attached, particularly his mother and Holcroft. From Holcroft he had been estranged for some years, since their great quarrel over *Faulkener*, but on his deathbed, according to Hazlitt's account, Holcroft :

expressed a wish to see Mr Godwin, but when he came, his feelings were overpowered. He could not converse, and only pressed his hand to his bosom and said, " My dear, dear friend ! " On Monday, he again wished to see Godwin, and all his friends that could be sent to ; but he had not strength sufficient to hold a conversation : he could only take an affectionate leave, and then he said, he had nothing more to do in this world.

Old Mrs Godwin died in August, 1809. Godwin attended the funeral, and wrote a letter home which showed that the death of his mother left a real emotional gap in his life :

The knot is now severed, and I am, for the first time, at more than fifty years of age, alone. You shall now be my mother ; you have in many instances been my protector and my guide, and I fondly trust will be more so, as I shall come to stand more in need of assistance.

The persistent mother fixation revealed in these lines is a complementary psychological element to the rivalry and hatred for his father which we have already observed as an important motive in Godwin's literary activities.

With his financial difficulties at least temporarily solved, and his business well established in its new premises, Godwin again turned to the production of new books for children ; 1809 was a very prolific year, for, in addition to two books under his own name, he wrote two under the name of Edward Baldwin, *The History of Rome* and a *New Guide to the English Tongue*. In 1811 he produced *The History of Greece*.

But The Juvenile Library did not confine itself to the publication of works by Godwin under various *noms-de-plume*. Several of his friends contributed, and among them the Lambs were the most prolific. In 1805 was published *The King and Queen of Hearts*, a small book of verse by Charles Lamb, and in 1807 appeared the most famous production of The Juvenile Library, *Tales from Shakespeare*, of which Mary Lamb wrote more than half. Charles Lamb later wrote three other small books, *The Adventures of Ulysses*, *Prince Dorus* and *Beauty and the Beast*, Mary Lamb wrote *Mrs Leicester's School ; or, the Histories of Several Young Ladies*, and they collaborated on two volumes of *Poetry for Children*. Hazlitt compiled an *English Grammar*, and Godwin's old friend Mrs Fenwick wrote a number of moral tales, and a curious advertisement brochure entitled *A Visit to The Juvenile Library*. Another famous writer who worked for The Juvenile Library was William Blake, in his capacity as an engraver. The plates which he made were, however, among his least successful work, and Lamb was justly indignant at the poor illustrations to *Tales from Shakespeare*.

Godwin's respite from financial difficulties was not of long duration. The public subscription did no more than pay off old debts and equip the new shop at Skinner Street. Indeed, it was probably insufficient even for these purposes, as Godwin must have laid out considerable capital on printing machinery, and it is probable that even at the time of the subscription he had to take out loans to meet all his expenses.

The productions of The Juvenile Library sold reasonably well, and should, theoretically, have made enough profit for the family to be clear of financial difficulty, especially as Godwin continued to pay no rent. But there was still difficulty in collecting outstanding debts from booksellers, and the prices of materials were high, owing to wartime conditions. Even so, it is not easy to account for the considerable debts which Godwin was forced to incur during the following years except on the supposition that he and his wife were singularly inefficient in the management of money. The difficulties certainly arose from no undue personal extravagance on Godwin's part. He maintained an unstinted hospitality and continued to give generously to all whose need was greater than his own, but in dress and personal comforts he was economical. Nevertheless, the amount of money required to maintain his large family at a comfortable standard must have been considerable, for it is reasonable to contend that it was for the comfort of others, rather than for his own interests, that Godwin was forced to devote so much of his time in the next few years to obtaining a continual series of loans which would enable him to keep his family from starvation and himself, with some ingenuity, from the debtor's prison.

Already, in 1811, he was involved deeply in the morass of economic difficulty, for we find an anxious letter written to Mrs Godwin, on holiday at Ramsgate, which already revealed an amazing tangle of financial obligations :

My Dearest Love,—Saturday was my great and terrible day, and I was compelled to look about me, to see how it could be provided for. I had less than £20 remaining in my drawer. I sent Joseph to Lambert and Macmillan : no answer from either : Lambert not at home. Bradley then undertook the expedition to Mercu and Jabart : he preferred Friday to Saturday : I therefore desired him to take Lambert on the way. This time I was successful : the good creature sent me £100, and at six in the evening Macmillan sent me £50, having, as you remember, brought me the other £50 on Tuesday last. This was something, but as there is no sweet without its sour, about the same time came a note from Hume desiring he might have £40 on Monday. . . .

I began to cast about how I was to comply with Hume's request. I was still £30 short for my bills—£30 and £40 are £70. I had, however, Place's bill in my possession, but who was to discount it ? I thought perhaps Toulmin would do it, I looked upon my list of discounters. By some oversight I had omitted to put the name to the discounter of one of Hume's bills. I thought by studying my journal I should be able to find it. I was unsuccessful. In the midst of this, however, my eye caught a bill of £140 of Place, that fell due next Friday. I had carefully put this out of my mind in the midst of the embarrassments of the present week, and had wholly forgotten it. Perhaps I never felt a more terrible sensation in my life, than when it thus returned to me. Lambert's and Macmillan's money had made me cheerful : I walked erect in my little sally to the Temple : I flung about my arms with the air of a man who felt himself heart-whole. The moment I saw the £140 I felt a cold swelling in the inside of my throat—a sensation I am subject to in terrible situations—and my head ached in the most discomfortable manner. I had just been puzzling how I could discount the £100 I had by me : what was I to do with £140 beside ? If Turner had not come in just then, I think I should have gone mad ; as it was, the morsel of meat I put in my mouth at supper stuck in my throat. . . .

This morning, however, the first thing I did was to send a note to Place, to state the circumstances, and to ask whether he must have the money to a day. He immediately came to me by way of answer, and told me he could wait till the 30th ! a glorious reprieve !

The post of today brought me £100 upon the house of Baring. It comes from the great American manager, with directions for me to furnish books, according to certain rules he lays down, at the rate of £100 per annum, this £100 being the earnest for the first year.   His letter is a very kind one :  I daresay he takes this step with a view to serve me in a certain degree ;  at any rate never did windfall come more opportunely.   I need not tell you that Theobald or anybody will discount a bill, when accepted, on the house of Baring. . . .

A little later, when Godwin's affairs had attained such a chaos that, with his own inaptitude for accurate accounting, he was quite unable to determine his indebtedness or how to escape from it, Francis Place undertook to assist the ordering of his finances.   Place, who later became famous as a champion of trade unions, had been an enthusiastic admirer of *Political Justice*, and, as an active member of the London Corresponding Society, had led the non-violent Godwinian faction against those who supported Thelwall and advocated political action and violent revolution.   He did not, however, meet Godwin until 1810. Then he soon became aware of the admired philosopher's financial difficulties and readily offered to help in his extrication.

The labour was more than Place had anticipated, and after four years he was bound to abandon his attempt, with a certain bitterness at Godwin's inability to act like a good business man.   He estimated that during the period of their connection, which extended until early 1815, he, together with Hume, Lambert, Taylor of Norwich and other friends whom he had interested in Godwin's plight, wasted in the neighbourhood of £2,500 in attempting to re-establish his financial stability.   In a note on their transactions he goes on to say :

In 1814 Mr Hamond and I made a statement from his own accounts which proved that he had received in money from various friends, upwards of £400 a year during each of the preceding *ten* years—and this account did not include,

1. Much money he had borrowed of which we were not informed.
2. Money received for his literary labours.
3. Profits from the bookselling business carried on by his wife.
4. Debts which he owed more than were owing to him.

And that thus he must have expended full £1,500 a year notwithstanding he had for the last four or five years paid no rent for the house he lived in, which was worth £200 a year.

Place concluded that, while he still admired Godwin as the author of *Political Justice*, he could not continue to associate with him as a man of business.   Yet he did not entirely blame Godwin :

Mr Godwin had however many good points, and no man could keep company with him without being benefitted. This was the case with Mr Hamond, Mr Lambert and myself. Mr Hamond almost adored him, and Mr Lambert admired him excessively. But Mr Godwin compelled us all three to give him up, as he had done many others. Had Godwin been placed in other circumstances, or had he had a prudent woman for a wife, instead of the Infernal devil to whom he was married, his good qualities would have preponderated, and he would have been a man of extensive influence as well personally as by his writings, and would have lived in ease in comfort and been a happy man.

As Place has hinted, there were others who shunned Godwin because of his habit of borrowing to meet his immediate needs. Crabb Robinson, who knew all the literary world, notes in his diary continual references to Godwin's distress and his unashamed borrowing. In the end Robinson, who became more conventional as he grew older, gave up Godwin's acquaintance, ostensibly because he regarded Godwin as unprincipled in matters of property, but in reality because he himself was somewhat mean and wished to avoid helping Godwin. At Godwin's death, when they had been unfriendly for many years, he wrote in his diary :

There died a few days ago another person who had a mighty influence on my early life—Godwin. I had lost all my personal respect for him. These are melancholy experiences in life. Godwin had no sense of *meum* and *tuum*.

Ever since, Godwin's lack of a " sense of *meum* and *tuum* " has been one of the principal weapons of his enemies. There seems to be a general tendency among critics, reared on the values of a property society, to assume that a man who does not or cannot pay his debts is necessarily dishonourable, and that what he says on paper, even if it criticises the institution of property, is for this reason to be regarded as nullified. Such an attitude has, of course, no logical basis, but it is common.

In Godwin's case it is not difficult to produce a justification of his actions which is much more convincing than any condemnation his enemies have constructed.

Firstly, it must be admitted that the continual concern with financial details, and the anxiety which it produced in Godwin's mind, tended to diminish his literary production and also to bring out some of the less pleasant traits in his character. Of this he was himself aware, for in 1813 he wrote to a Cambridge undergraduate named Patrickson (whom he had helped financially and whose suicide two years later caused him considerable grief) :

> Poverty, I assure you, is a very wretched thing. The prayer of Agur in the Bible is excellent, " Give me neither poverty nor riches, lest I be full and deny Thee, and say, who is the Lord ? or lest I be poor and steal, and take the name of my God in vain." I should not of course express the reasons of my wish in my own behalf, or in behalf of any one in whom I was interested, in so pious and religious a manner, but my sense would be nearly the same. Riches corrupt the morals and harden the heart, and poverty breaks the spirit and courage of a man, plants his pillow with perpetual thorns, and makes it all but impossible for him to be honest, virtuous and honourable.

But the fault of any corruption of this nature which Godwin may have suffered is surely as much in the money system itself as in Godwin for having been its victim.

With regard to the general question of Godwin's continual borrowings and unpaid debts, it must be remembered that his was an age when patronage was still in vogue, when there was an obligation on the wealthy to assist the talented poor, and when writers were regularly subsidised either by private patrons or by party caucuses. It was considered excusable that a man of talents should borrow widely and should neglect to pay the debts incurred by riotous living. Burke's unpaid debts were many times the few thousands which Godwin collected in small loans during the long period of his financial distress. Moreover, Burke's great spendings were caused by an extravagant standard of life, whereas Godwin himself lived humbly and spent most of the money he borrowed on the needs and comforts of his family and his poor friends. But Burke was a champion of the existing order, and therefore went unblamed, whereas Godwin was a critic, and therefore any argument was good enough to condemn him.

Those who base their case against Godwin on a supposed inconsistency between his financial behaviour and the doctrines laid down in *Political Justice* are on even less secure ground. In his references to property, Godwin states explicitly that the man whose need is great has a just claim to enough to maintain himself and his family, and that, for those who are engaged in work for the public good, other men who have a surplus of goods should be willing to provide. The reader who reverts to *Political Justice* will find an abundance of argument on this subject, but in order to prove our case at present it is sufficient to make two quotations. The first occurs in the chapter condemning the payment of pensions from public funds :

It has been deemed dishonourable to subsist upon private liberality but this dishonour is produced only by the difficulty of reconciling this mode of subsistence and intellectual independence. It is free from many of the objections that have been urged against a public stipend. I ought to receive your superfluity as my due while I am employed in affairs more important than that of earning a subsistence ; but at the same time to receive it with a total indifference to personal advantage, taking only what is precisely necessary for the supply of my wants.

The second occurs in the dissertation on property :

To whom does any article of property, suppose a loaf of bread, justly belong ? To him who most wants it, or to whom the possession of it will be most beneficial. . . . If justice have any meaning, nothing can be more iniquitous than for one man to possess superfluities, while there is a human being in existence that is not adequately supplied with these. . . .

Justice does not stop here. Every man is entitled, so far as the general stock will suffice, not only to the means of being, but of well-being. It is unjust if one man labour to the destruction of his health or his life, that another may abound in luxuries. It is unjust if one man be deprived of leisure to cultivate his rational powers while another man contributes not a single effort to add to the common stock. . . .

From these passages it is clear that Godwin would have found nothing contrary to his principles in living by loans from his friends when the earnings from his literary work did not suffice to keep him. Whether he wrote moral treatises, or produced children's books to further the cause of education, he was working for the common good and was entitled to subsidies from the superfluous means of other men. It should be remembered, moreover, that the passages which we have quoted were written not when Godwin had any need to live by borrowing, but at a time when he kept himself in frugal comfort on the proceeds of hard and conscientious literary work.

    .     .     .     .     .     .

For the remainder of the 1820's Godwin continued to work steadily at his publishing business, failing always to balance his receipts with his expenditure, and borrowing steadily to make up his losses. Shelley, whom he had encountered in 1812, replaced Place as the principal source of loans, but none of Godwin's more prosperous friends was immune from requests. On the

From the sketch by Daniel Maclise, 1834.

other hand, Godwin himself never refused a demand he could meet, and saved his old friend Marshal from the debtor's prison by raising a fund for his maintenance. As has been remarked by one of Godwin's defenders, had Shelley come to his house an impecunious youth, Godwin would have been as eager to open his purse to him as he was in the reverse situation to share what he erroneously imagined to be Shelley's unbounded riches.

By these various contrivances of hard work and borrowing, Godwin supported his family for a few more years. But in 1819 a new crisis developed. The dispute over the ownership of the premises was settled in favour of one of the claimants, and a judgment against Godwin was obtained for arrears of rent and costs, the total amount, Godwin estimated, being somewhere between £600 and £2,000.

Shelley, to whom he wrote immediately, recommended the abandonment of the business, which throughout its life had lost an unreasonable amount of money, but Godwin was convinced that with one last effort he would still be able to make it pay. Somewhat perversely, he insisted, " I consider the day on which I entered on this business as one of the fortunate days of my life."

Read, the owner of the premises, appears to have agreed to accept a sum of £500 in settlement of his claim, but Shelley would only loan this on the condition of Godwin's giving up the business. Godwin chose instead to procrastinate. In the beginning of 1822, however, the crisis developed rapidly. Read obtained a writ of ejectment, and was empowered to seize stock to the value of £135 to pay for costs. On May 3rd, 1822, the Godwins were forced to move out of Skinner Street with the remainder of their stock.

This day [wrote Godwin to his daughter] we are compelled by sum-mary process to leave the house we live in, and to hide our heads in whatever alley will receive us. If we can compound with our creditor, and he seems not unwilling to receive £400 (I have talked with him on the subject), we may emerge again. Our business, if freed from this intolerable burthen, is more than ever worth keeping.

It is doubtful whether by this time anyone but Godwin regarded his business as worth anything, but when his distress became known a number of his friends gathered spontaneously to his assistance. Lamb, who was himself in no good circum-stances, sent fifty pounds, and Murray the publisher, Henry

Crabb Robinson, James Mackintosh and the Whig Lord Dudley were among the other subscribers. In all, more than £200 was raised, and this enabled Godwin at least to pay his way in the new premises he had obtained at 195, The Strand. He still sold a few books, but he must have realised at last that The Juvenile Library could not provide him with a living, for in all this turmoil he began to write another massive literary work, *The History of the Commonwealth*.

Read continued to pursue him with litigation, and in July, 1822, he lost one of his few reliable helpers in Shelley's death by drowning in Italy. In 1823 Read obtained a final judgment for £500 and costs. Godwin's friends opened a public subscription in the hope of obtaining the £600 needed to save his affairs from immediate disaster. The amount was not raised, but a novel, *Valperga*, which Mary Shelley gave to her father, eventually brought in £400.

In 1824 the ill-starred venture of The Juvenile Library finally came to a close. Unable to satisfy his creditors, Godwin was declared bankrupt and his business dissolved. He was allowed to keep his personal belongings, books and literary materials, and returned to the writing from which he had been parted so long by this unhappy attempt to live by commercial methods which he had neither the mind to understand nor the cunning to make successful.

4

The main facts of Shelley's relationship with Godwin, and particularly the story of his elopement with Godwin's daughter Mary, are already sufficiently well known to the general reader. I shall not, therefore, attempt to give a detailed account of these events. Nevertheless, books on Shelley usually suffer from a sentimental bias which tends to portray Godwin as the villain in all transactions. The impression gained from such accounts is largely inaccurate and wholly unjust to Godwin. I shall therefore devote the present chapter to elucidating Godwin's actions and motives, and to demonstrating the great intellectual debt which Shelley undoubtedly owed him throughout his mature life. If I should err in partiality on the opposite side to that of Godwin's detractors, I hope I may be excused the fervour with which it is natural to defend those who are condemned unjustly.

Godwin first encountered Shelley in 1811, when the younger man, who had read Godwin's works during his college years, wrote him a strange letter of self-introduction, whose terms of admiration must have been very pleasant to Godwin in this time of unpopularity and anxiety.

You will be surprised at hearing from a stranger. No introduction has, nor in all probability ever will, authorize that which common thinkers would call a liberty. It is, however, a liberty which although not sanctioned by custom, is so far from being reprobated by reason, that the dearest interests of mankind imperiously demand that a certain etiquette of fashion should no longer keep " man at a distance from man," and impose its flimsy barriers between the free communication of intellect. The name of Godwin has been accustomed to excite in me feelings of reverence and admiration. I have been accustomed to consider him as a luminary too dazzling for the darkness which surrounds him, and from the earliest period of my knowledge of his principles, I have ardently desired to share in the footing of intimacy that intellect which I have delighted to contemplate in its emanations. Considering, then, these feelings, you will not be surprised at the inconceivable emotion with which I learned your existence and your dwelling. I had enrolled your name in the list of the honourable dead. I had felt regret that the glory of your being had passed from this earth of ours. It is not so. You still live, and I firmly believe are still planning the welfare of human kind. I have but just entered on the scene of human operations, yet my feelings and my reasonings correspond with what yours were. My course has been short, but eventful. I have seen much of human prejudice, suffered much from human persecution, yet I see no reason hence inferable which should alter my wishes for their renovation. The ill treatment I have met with has more than ever impressed the truth of my principles on my judgment. I am young : I am ardent in the cause of philanthropy and truth : do not suppose that this is vanity. I am not conscious that it influences the portraiture. I imagine myself dispassionately describing the state of my mind. I am young : you have gone before me, I doubt not are a veteran in the years of persecution. Is it strange that, defying persecution as I have done, I should outstep the limits of custom's prescription, and endeavour to make my desire useful by friendship with William Godwin ? I pray you to answer this letter. Imperfect as it may be, my capacity, my desire, is ardent, and unintermitted. Half-an-hour would be at least humanity employed in the experiment. I may mistake your residence. Certain feelings, of which I may be an inadequate arbiter, may induce you to desire concealment. I may not in fine have an answer to this letter. If I do not, when I come to London I shall seek for you. I am convinced I could represent myself to you in such terms as not to be thought unworthy of your friendship. At least, if any desire for universal happiness has any claim upon your preference, that desire I can exhibit. Adieu. I shall earnestly await your answer. P. B. Shelley.

Godwin replied in friendly terms, and a frequent correspondence was soon established, in which Shelley showed further signs of reverence for Godwin's achievements and of an intelligent comprehension of the principles of *Political Justice*.

It is now a period of more than two years since first I saw your inestimable book on *Political Justice ;* it opened to my mind fresh and more extensive views ; it materially influenced my character, and I rose from its perusal a wiser and better man. I was no longer the votary of romance ; till then I had existed in an ideal world—now I found that in this universe of ours was enough to excite the interest of the heart, enough to employ the discussions of reason ; I beheld, in short, that I had duties to perform. Conceive the effect which the Political Justice would have upon a mind before jealous of its independence and participating somewhat singularly in a peculiar susceptibility.

Shelley was delighted at the friendly interest which Godwin showed in him.

Godwin has answered my letters, and he is now my *friend* [he wrote to Elizabeth Hichener]. He shall be yours—share with me this acquisition, more valuable than the gifts of Princes. . . . It is with awe and veneration that I read the letters of this veteran in persecution and independence. He remains unchanged. I have no soul-chilling alteration to record of his character, the unmoderated enthusiasm of humanity still characterises him. He preserves those principles of extensive and independent action which alone can give energy and vigour.

Godwin regarded his new disciple with interest, but his approbation was soon qualified, when Shelley proposed to depart to Ireland in order to conduct a campaign for Catholic Emancipation. He wrote to the young poet a letter of mingled affection and remonstrance :

In the pamphlet you have just sent me, your views and mine as to the improvement of mankind are decisively at issue. You profess the immediate objects of your efforts to be " the organization of a society whose institution shall serve as a bond to its members." If I may be allowed to understand my book on Political Justice, its pervading principle is, that association is a most ill-chosen and ill-qualified mode of endeavouring to promote the political happiness of mankind. And I think of your pamphlet, however commendable and lovely are many of its sentiments, that it will either be ineffective to its immediate object, or that it has no very remote tendency to light again the flames of rebellion and war. . . .

Discussion and conversation on the best interests of society are excellent as long as they are unfettered, and each man talks to his neighbour in the freedom of congenial intercourse as he happens to meet with him in the customary haunts of men, or in the quiet and beneficent intercourse of each other's fireside.    But they become unwholesome and poisonous when men shape themselves into societies, and become distorted with the artifices of organization.    It will not then long be possible to reason calmly and dispassionately :  men will heat each other into impatience and indignation against their oppressors ; they will become tired of talking for ever, and will be in a hurry to act. If this view of things is true, applied to any country whatever, it is peculiarly so when applied to the fervent and impetuous character of the Irish. . . .

Shelley, however, persisted in his intention, and pointed out that *Political Justice* had not been so eminently successful that other methods might not be essayed :

I am not forgetful or unheeding of what you said of associations.  But *Political Justice* was first published in 1793 ; nearly twenty years have elapsed since the general diffusion of its doctrines.  What has followed ? Have men ceased to fight ?  Have vice and misery vanished from the earth ?  Have the fireside communications which it recommends taken place ?  Out of the many who have read that inestimable book, how many have been blinded by prejudice ;  how many, in short, have taken it up to gratify an ephemeral vanity, and when the hour of its novelty had passed, threw it aside, and yielded with fashion to the arguments of Mr Malthus ?

Godwin once again took up his pen, to save Shelley " and the Irish people from the calamities with which I see your mode of proceeding to be fraught."

You say, " What has been done within these last twenty years ? "   Oh, that I could place you upon the pinnacle of ages, from which these twenty years would shrink to an invisible point !  It is not after this fashion that moral causes work in the eye of him who looks profoundly through the vast and—allow me to add—venerable machine of human society.    But so reasoned the French Revolutionists.    Auspicious and admirable materials were working in the general mind of France ; but these men said, as you say, " When we look on the last twenty years, we are seized with a sort of moral scepticism ;  we must own we are eager that something should be done."    And see what has been the result of their doings.   He that would benefit mankind on a comprehensive scale, by changing the principles and elements of society, must learn the hard lesson, to put off self, and to contribute by a quiet but incessant activity, like a rill of water, to irrigate and fertilise the intellectual evil. . . .

I wish to my heart you would come immediately to London.    I have a friend who has contrived a tube to convey passengers sixty miles an hour :  be youth your tube.    I have a thousand things I could say, really more than I could say in a letter on this important subject.    You cannot imagine how much all the females of my family, Mrs Godwin and three daughters, are interested in your letters and your history.

This interest on the part of the Godwin females was to have serious consequences for all the members of both households.

Meanwhile, the poor reception Shelley encountered in Ireland combined with Godwin's persuasions to make him doubt the wisdom of his adventure. This expedition has been made the subject of the wit of his literary enemies and of some who appear as his friends. It was a serious effort to aid the Irish people. It may have been founded on a mistaken idea, but it is certain that neither Shelley, nor even Godwin in his most disapproving mood, regarded it merely as a boyish prank.

On March 18th Shelley wrote to tell Godwin that he had abandoned hope of achieving any good, and that he was about to leave Ireland.

It appears to me that on the publication of *Political Justice* you looked to a more rapid movement than has taken place. It is my opinion that if your book had been as general as the Bible, human affairs would now have exhibited a different aspect.

I have read your letters, read them with the attention and reverence they deserve. Had *I*, like you, been witness to the French Revolution, it is probable that my caution would have been greater. I have seen and heard enough to make me doubt the omnipotence of truth in a society constituted as that wherein we live.

The crisis of Shelley's intellectual life was past. From that day his mental activity came wholly under the influence of Godwin, and no other thinker of his own age ever rivalled Godwin as the mentor who shaped Shelley's aspirations and moulded the content of his poetry.

Godwin seems to have recognised an intellectual triumph, for on March 30th he wrote :

I can now look upon you as a friend. Before, I knew not what might happen. . . . Now, I can look on you not as a meteoric ephemeral, but as a lasting friend, who, according to the course of nature, may contribute to the comforts of my closing days. Now, I can look on you as a friend like myself, but I hope more effectually and actively useful, who is prone to study the good of his fellow men, but with no propensities threatening to do them extensive mischief, under the form and intention of benefit. . . .

In spite of this cordial relationship, Godwin and Shelley did not meet for some time. Shelley retired to Wales to express his Godwinian beliefs in his first long poem, *Queen Mab*. The correspondence continued, with frequent exchanges of letters, and in September Godwin set out to visit the Shelleys at Lynmouth.

After a slow journey, in which he visited Chepstow and Tintern, Godwin reached Lynmouth, only to find that the Shelleys had departed three weeks before for Wales. He took his disappointment philosophically, and made up for it by visiting Stonehenge and Salisbury on his way back.

Shelley and his girl-wife Harriet arrived a few days later, and were welcomed by Godwin, who appears to have been in his most pleasant mood, and by such of the curious female members of the family as were present, namely, Mrs Godwin, Jane, and Fanny. Mary was away in Scotland, and did not return until two days before the nomad Shelleys again set out abruptly on their travels. There is no record of what impression Shelley and Mary made on each other at this first meeting. Mary was still a gauche but pretty schoolgirl. In a letter to a correspondent who enquired after the daughters of Mary Wollstonecraft, Godwin describes her thus :

She is singularly bold, somewhat imperious, and active of mind. Her desire of knowledge is great, and her perseverence in everything she undertakes almost invincible. My own daughter is, I believe, very pretty ; Fanny is by no means handsome, but in general prepossessing.

After the departure of the Shelleys, the correspondence continued as cordially as ever, and Shelley compensated himself for the absence of Godwin by reading his books. In the summer of 1813 Shelley again returned to London, and social relationships were resumed, although not on so extensive a scale, for, like most of Godwin's friends, neither Shelley nor Harriet found themselves comfortable with his wife, whom Harriet described as "dreadfully disagreeable." Nevertheless, it would have required more than Mary Jane Godwin to separate Shelley from a philosopher whom he had taken as his intellectual master and whose philosophy had entered completely into the stream of his thought. He came more than ever to feel that to Godwin he " owed everything " in knowledge and inspiration ; to those who read his poetry at all thoroughly this will not appear an extravagant opinion.

It was during this visit to London that Shelley was joined by his friend and inaccurate biographer, Thomas Jefferson Hogg. Hogg met Godwin, and the account he gives of this encounter is one of the most vivid pictures of Godwin that have been left us. Hogg, who had expressed a desire to meet Godwin, was invited to dinner at the house of a common friend, where both Shelley and Godwin were expected. Godwin arrived, but Shelley did not appear :

I found a short, stout, thickset old man, with a very fair complexion, and with a bald and very large head, in the drawing-room, where he had been for some time by himself, and he appeared to be rather uneasy at being alone. He made himself known to me as William Godwin ; it was thus he styled himself. His dress was dark, and very plain, of an old-fashioned cut, even for an old man. His appearance, indeed, was altogether that of a dissenting minister. He informed me that our hospitable host and his family had been called away suddenly into the country, and that we should not have their company, but that Mr Shelley was expected every moment. He consulted several times a large silver watch, and wondered greatly that he had not come ; but he would doubtless be with us immediately. He spoke confidently on a subject which, to say the least, was doubtful. Bysshe, as was not uncommonly the case with him, never came near us. Why he made default, nobody ever knew, least of all did he know himself.

"Had Mr Shelley mistaken the day, the hour ? Did he not know the place ; surely he must know it, and know it well ? "

I could only say, on behalf of my absent friend, that he often failed to observe his engagements and appointments. It was his habit ; a disagreeable and most inconvenient one, certainly. Why and how he had formed it, I could not tell, although I was much interrogated and cross-examined on that head. It had been the way with him ever since I had known him, and it was only too probable that it always would be so. I could not explain, excuse, defend or justify it ; I could merely affirm that so it was.

At four o'clock I rang the bell, and ordered dinner. To this order there were objections and expostulations.

"We ought, in common civility, to wait awhile. Mr Shelley could not fail to be with us shortly."

The objections were overruled, and we two went to dinner ; and we two were a multitude, to judge from the number of dishes on the table. Vegetable fare was the rule of the house, and I observed the rule myself ; but meat of various kinds had been prepared in various ways for the cannibal guest. He dined carnivorously, but very moderately, paying little attention to the plate of vegetables, which he seemed to contemn, as well as the lore by which they were zealously and learnedly recommended.

William Godwin, according to my observation, always ate meat, and rather sparingly, and little else besides. He drank a glass or two of sherry, wherein I did not join him. Soon after dinner a large cup of very strong green tea—of gunpowder tea, intensely strong—was brought to him ; this he took with evident satisfaction, and it was the only thing that he appeared to enjoy, although our fare was excellent. Having drunken the tea, he set the cup and saucer forcibly upon the table, at a great distance from him, according to the usages of that old school of manners, to which he so plainly belonged.  He presently fell into a sound sleep, sitting very forward in his chair, and leaning forward, so that at times he threatened to fall forward ;  but no harm came to him.  Not only did the old philosopher sleep soundly, deeply, but he snored loudly.

Hogg seems to have regarded Godwin as a source of amusement, and he does not appear to have had any understanding of the teachings of *Political Justice*.  This was an attitude diametrically opposite to that of Shelley, who, in his moments of deepest annoyance at Godwin's personal conduct, never failed to reverence the philosopher whose writings had shaped the outlook of his own mind.

We have already referred to the money transactions for which Godwin has been condemned by Shelley's biographers.  As we have shown, Godwin did nothing in borrowing so extensively from Shelley that conflicted with his own principles of the distribution of property according to needs.  Shelley, for his part, never disputed that while he had money he was under an obligation to supply it.  The ill feeling that arose between them was due entirely to Godwin's misunderstanding of Shelley's actual means.

The second affair over which Godwin has been made the great anti-Shelleyan bogey, and the apostate from the doctrines of *Political Justice*, was the elopement of Shelley with Mary Godwin.

In the first two years of his acquaintance with Godwin, Shelley saw little of Mary, who was usually away during his visits to London.  It was during 1814, when Mary had grown into an attractive girl of seventeen, that they had the opportunity to become more closely acquainted.  By this time Shelley's marriage had disintegrated and a separation became inevitable.  Shelley fell in love with Mary, and she reciprocated with equal ardour.

During the early summer of that year they met secretly in St Pancras churchyard, by the grave of Mary Wollstonecraft.  At first their meetings were so carefully arranged that neither Godwin nor his wife was aware of anything amiss.  By June, however, Godwin had begun to suspect, and in that month his diary records a " talk with Mary," which might well have been devoted to her relations with Shelley.  Later, there was a talk with Jane Clairmont, and during July Godwin set to work energetically to make up the differences between Shelley and Harriet.

His efforts, however, were belated, and it is difficult to believe that, with the people concerned, they would have been any more successful if he had acted earlier. In the early morning of July 28th, Mary eloped with Shelley and set off for France. They were accompanied by Jane Clairmont. On the discovery of their departure, the Godwin household was in a flurry of disorder, and Mrs Godwin set off immediately for Dover. She crossed the Channel, and caught up with the trio at Calais. Her expostulations were unavailing, and she returned to England by the next boat, while Shelley, Mary and Jane set out on their odd journey across Europe, a pilgrimage that has been made familiar by many descriptions.

Godwin was angry with Shelley and Mary, and his attitude has been taken by his critics as a sign of inconsistency. Godwin argued against marriage in *Political Justice*. Therefore, according to his enemies, he had no right to condemn Shelley for deserting Harriet and running away with Mary. This form of argument, however, is grossly unfair to Godwin, who had very sound reasons for his attitude.

Firstly, his condemnation of marriage in *Political Justice* did not imply an advocacy of " free love." Godwin believed that we should free ourselves as far as possible from the trammels of sex, and certainly should not allow sexual considerations to divert us from the performance of our moral duty to consider the general good. Later, indeed, Godwin changed his attitude towards marriage and sex in general, but he never advocated " free love " as such. Secondly, the kind of furtive action that was involved in Shelley's meetings with Mary and in their elopement could not be held compatible with the teaching of sincerity contained in *Political Justice*. Thirdly, *Political Justice* taught that we should allow our actions to be guided, not by our own selfish desires, but by a consideration of the good of our fellows. Shelley and Mary certainly had little consideration for anything beyond their own pleasures, and Godwin, whose already uneasy position was rendered so much more difficult by their actions, had a right to complain.

Godwin's reputation had been unsavoury enough for the past twenty years, but by this time he was beginning to live down the misrepresentation he had suffered at the beginning of the century. His peculiar position, of living partly on credit and partly on the proceeds of a children's bookshop, made it necessary for him to keep a respectable reputation. In his own personal life he did nothing unrespectable—except for his complete inability to follow good business methods, and it was therefore all the more annoying that other people should give scandal the opportunity to render his situation precarious. For the immediate effect of the flight of Mary and Jane was that all the forgotten calumnies were revived and new ones added to them. Godwin, it was said, had sold the girls for eight hundred and seven hundred pounds respectively. Not unnaturally, he saw the prospect of a sudden and disastrous worsening of his situation. He avoided his friends, and many of them were glad to be shunned.

After some months of chaos and misery, Godwin managed to overcome his misfortunes and to present a stoical front. One member of his household, however, was more deeply affected. This was the devoted Fanny Imlay. Owing to the scandal over the elopement of Shelley and Mary, she lost her position as a teacher. She went back to live with her family, but became steadily more distressed at the misery of their life, which she felt as acutely as Godwin; she began to think herself an unnecessary burden on their attenuated material and moral resources. It is possible that Mrs Godwin, who had never liked her, was not backward in pointing this out. However that may be, Fanny left the house at Skinner Street one day in October, 1816, with the ostensible purpose of going to Ireland to visit her mother's sisters. She reached Swansea and there poisoned herself. Her last note was written on a scrap of paper from which she tore the signature as a final act of consideration for her beloved foster-father :

I have long determined that the best thing I could do was to put an end to the existence of a being whose birth was unfortunate, and whose life has only been a series of pain to those persons who have hurt their health in endeavouring to promote her welfare. Perhaps to hear of my death will give you pain, but you will soon have the blessing of forgetting that such a creature ever existed as . . .

In character she was undoubtedly the best of Godwin's family, and the only one among them who showed a really unselfish sympathy towards him in his difficulties.

It seemed to Godwin as if his misfortunes would never cease, and for a long time he kept her suicide a secret so that his enemies should not use it as a further weapon for their unscrupulous attacks.

The way for a reconciliation between Godwin and Shelley was eventually opened by the death of another actress in this unhappy real life melodrama. The miserable Harriet, who really loved Shelley far more than he understood, drowned herself in the Serpentine in December, 1816. This event made it possible for Mary and Shelley to marry, which they did in the following February. Godwin was delighted at this resumption of respectability, and saw with satisfaction that one of the greater scandals which his enemies could use against him had been removed. In his pleasure he wrote to tell his country brother Hull Godwin the news, in words which seem pathetic to those who know what had really happened :

I do not know whether you recollect the miscellaneous way in which my family is composed, but at least you perhaps remember that I have but two children of my own : a daughter by my late wife and a son by my present. Were it not that you have a family of your own, and can see by them how little shrubs grow up into tall trees, you would hardly imagine that my boy, born the other day, is now fourteen, and that my daughter is between nineteen and twenty. The piece of news I have to tell, however, is that I went to church with this tall girl some little time ago to be married. Her husband is the eldest son of Sir Timothy Shelley, of Field Place, in the county of Sussex, Baronet. So that, according to the vulgar ideas of the world, she is well married, and I have great hopes the young man will make her a good husband. You will wonder, I daresay, how a girl without a penny of fortune should meet with so good a match. But such are the ups and downs of this world. For my part I care but little, comparatively, about wealth, so that it should be her destiny in life to be respectable, virtuous and contented.

Godwin evidently chose to put the best appearance on his fortunes and wisely to forget past injuries when they were so gratifyingly mended.

The marriage led to a renewal of friendship between Godwin and Shelley, and for a while a cordial relationship persisted, with visits by Godwin to the Shelleys at Marlow, and letters in which Shelley praised Godwin's works admiringly and Godwin talked of Shelley's poems patronisingly. In 1817, Shelley wrote the second of his massive Godwinian poems, *The Revolt of Islam*. In the same year he wrote the rhetorical fragment which is said to have been addressed to Godwin :

> Mighty eagle ! thou that soarest
> O're the mighty mountain forest,
>     And amid the light of morning
> Like a cloud of glory hiest,
> And when night descends defiest
>     The embattled tempest's warning !

If the attribution is correct, this passage, although of little poetic value, at least reveals an undiminished admiration for Godwin's abilities.

Once again, Shelley assisted Godwin with money and guaranteed loans. But the money affairs led to misunderstandings, which soured their relationship, and during the last two years of Shelley's life they were on terms of more or less open hostility. These misunderstandings have been used by many writers on Shelley to discredit Godwin. But Shelley would have had little patience with such opinions. Even when he felt the greatest impatience with Godwin's actions, he never ceased to acknowledge the value of his work, the magnitude of his genius, or his own intellectual debt. In 1820, during the period of their bitterest animosity, he could still write, in his *Letter to Maria Gisborne* :

> You will see
> That which was Godwin, greater none than he ;
> Though fallen—and fallen on evil times—to stand
> Among the spirits of our age and land
> Before the dread tribunal of *to come*
> The foremost,—while Rebuke cowers pale and dumb.

When Shelley died in 1821 he was still as convinced a Godwinian as he had been during all the years since he first discovered *Political Justice*.

There is not sufficient space to discuss thoroughly the relationship between Shelley's poetry and Godwin's ideas. It is a subject on which a whole volume could be written without exhausting its intricacies. I will merely indicate the poetic manifestation of Godwin's philosophy as it matured in the course of Shelley's development. It is necessary to emphasise at the beginning that, while the debt to Godwin is less obvious in the later poems, this does not signify any lessening of Godwin's philosophical influence over Shelley's thought or his poetry. In the early works many passages are little more than crude versifications of points from *Political Justice*. In the later poems the literal statements of Godwinian arguments become less frequent and less crude, but beside this tendency to abandon the original form of Godwin's ideas, there is a continued preoccupation with their philosophical content. The principles of Godwin became gradually assimilated into the structure of Shelley's thought and poetry, so that in the end, although he now spoke with his own tongue rather than with Godwin's, the spirit of his works was such that it is impossible to understand them without reference to the background of *Political Justice*, the great mine from which Shelley drew the ore for his poetic gold.

*Queen Mab* was the first of the substantial Godwinian poems. The presentation of the thought is crude, yet the poem has a certain attractive vigour in its attacks on those ideas which Shelley regarded as the principal enemies of freedom. Government is the most concrete of these foes of progress, and Shelley tilts with great force at its representatives.

> Nature rejects the monarch, not the man ;
> The subject, not the citizen : for kings
> And subjects, mutual foes, forever play
> A losing game into each other's hands,
> Whose stakes are vice and misery. The man
> Of virtuous soul commands not, nor obeys.
> Power, like a desolating pestilence,
> Pollutes whate'er it touches ; and obedience,
> Bane of all genius, virtue, freedom, truth,
> Makes slaves of men, and of the human frame
> A mechanized automaton.

In particular, Shelley is preoccupied with the pernicious effects of influence over the opinions of men, especially the influence that moulds the child for an evil purpose.

> Kings, priests and statesmen blast the human flower
> Even in its tender bud ; their influence darts
> Like subtle poison through the bloodless veins
> Of desolate society . . .
> Let priest-led slaves cease to proclaim that man
> Inherits vice and misery, when Force
> And Falsehood hang even o'er the cradled babe,
> Stifling with rudest grasp all natural good.

Shelley goes through all the familiar Godwinian arguments and details in turn the curses to which man is subject, war, property, religion, and in the place of theological and political systems sets up the Godwinian conception of Necessity.

Spirit of Nature ! all-sufficing Power,
Necessity ! thou mother of the world !
Unlike the God of human error, thou
Requirs't no prayers or praises ; the caprice
Of man's weak will belongs no more to thee
Than do the changeful passions of his breast
To thy unvarying harmony . . .

The poem ends with a vision of the world when the rule of governments and religions has ended, and, serene under impartial natural law, mankind returns to contentment and peace.

To the end of this Godwinian vision is attached a series of prose notes, in which Shelley emphasises the teachings from *Political Justice*, already so obvious in the poem itself. These voluminous notes contain a number of quotations from Godwin, and refer to him in admiration.

*Queen Mab* was the work of Shelley's adolescence, and it might have been the detached fruit of a temporary enthusiasm, had not his meeting with Godwin made permanent the influence of that philosopher over his thought and writing.

It was in 1817, after he had known Godwin for some years, had discovered his personal faults, had quarrelled with him and been reconciled, that he wrote *The Revolt of Islam*, the first great work of his manhood. It showed how completely, in spite of personal disagreements, he remained under the intellectual influence of Godwin. This is clear, not only in the story around which the poem is built and the philosophy which it is intended to convey, but also in innumerable small details throughout the poem. In the dedication to Mary Shelley, for instance, there is one verse whose original version contained a deep tribute to Godwin. Shelley says to Mary :

> . . . thou canst claim
> The shelter, from thy Sire of an immortal name.
> A voice went forth from that unshaken spirit,
> Which was the echo of three thousand years ;
> And the tumultuous world stood mute to hear it,
> As some lone man who in a desert hears
> The music of his home : unwonted fears
> Fell on the pale oppressors of our race,
> And Faith and Custom, and low-thoughted cares,
> Like thunder-stricken dragons, for a space,
> Left the torn human heart, their food and dwelling-place.

Later, no doubt owing to a personal quarrel, he altered the verse slightly to make the reference to Godwin less direct.

The intention and plan of the poem are described by Shelley himself in words which make necessary no further exposition of its Godwinian character :

It is an experiment on the temper of the public mind as to how far a thirst for a happier condition of moral and political society survives, among the enlightened and refined, the tempests which have shaken the age in which we live. I have sought to enlist the harmony of metrical language, the ethereal combinations of the fancy, the rapid and subtle transitions of human passion, all those elements which essentially compose a Poem, in the cause of a liberal and comprehensive morality ; and in the view of kindling within the bosoms of my readers a virtuous enthusiasm for those doctrines of liberty and justice, that faith and hope in something good, which neither violence nor misrepresentation nor prejudice can ever totally extinguish among mankind.

For this purpose I have chosen a story of human passion in its most universal character, diversified with moving and romantic adventures, and appealing, in contempt of all artificial opinions or institutions, to the common sympathies of every human breast. I have made no attempt to recommend the motives which I would substitute for those at present governing mankind, by methodical and systematic argument. I would only awaken the feelings, so that the reader should see the beauty of true virtue, and be incited to those inquiries which have led to my moral and political creed, and that of some of the sublimest intellects in the world.

Fortunately for its poetic worth, *The Revolt of Islam* is not so strictly Godwinian as this prose description. In poetry Shelley raised the themes of *Political Justice* to heights of imaginary vision, but in prose he limped always behind Godwin, and spoke with his teacher's voice. Even the celebrated maxim, " Poets are the unacknowledged legislators of the world," was lifted almost word for word from *The Life of Chaucer*.

*The Revolt of Islam* is perhaps the greatest, certainly the most massive revolutionary poem in the English language. For revolutionary it is, and all its involved allegory and esoteric symbolism lead to the statement of an openly anarchist doctrine and a belief in the eventual triumph of freedom and peace.

Yet it would be foolish to contend that this is entirely a political poem. Its structure was clearly suggested by the historical events of the French Revolution, but it is also very much concerned with the struggle of ideas and impulses which was a permanent feature of Shelley's mind. The final apotheosis of Laon and Cythna is meant to symbolise the possibility of the final triumph of the human spirit, even in adversity and defeat, through the achievement of an inner peace that defies the tyrant.

But the beautiful words of Cythna in Canto IX have much more than a personal significance.

> Lo, Winter comes ! the grief of many graves,
> The frost of death, the tempest of the sword,
> The flood of tyranny, whose sanguine waves
> Stagnate like ice at Faith the enchanter's word,
> And bind all human hearts in its repose abhorred.

> The seeds are sleeping in the soil : meanwhile
> The Tyrant peoples dungeons with his prey,
> Pale victims on the guarded scaffold smile
> Because they cannot speak ; and, day by day,
> The moon of wasting Science wanes away
> Among her stars, and in that darkness vast
> The sons of earth to their foul idols pray,
> And gray Priests triumph, and like blight or blast
> A shade of selfish care o'er human looks is cast.

> This is the winter of the world ; and here
> We die, even as the winds of Autumn fade,
> Expiring in the frore and foggy air—
> Behold ! Spring comes, though we must pass, who made
> The promise of its birth,—even as the shade
> Which from our death, as from a mountain, flings
> The future, a broad sunrise ; thus arrayed
> As with the plumes of overshadowing wings,
> From its dark gulf of chains, Earth like an eagle springs.

> O, dearest love ! we shall be dead and cold
> Before this morn may on the world arise ;
> Wouldst thou the glory of its dawn behold ?
> Alas ! gaze not on me, but turn thine eyes
> On thine own heart—it is a paradise
> Which everlasting Spring has made its own,
> And while drear Winter fills the naked skies,
> Sweet streams of sunny thought, and flowers fresh-blown,
> Are there, and weave their sounds and odours into one.

> In their own hearts the earnest of the hope
> Which made them great, the good will ever find ;
> And though some envious shades may interlope
> Between the effect and it, One comes behind,
> Who aye the future to the past will bind— . . .

Our many thoughts and deeds, our life and love,
Our happiness and all that we have been
Immortally must live, and burn and move
When we shall be no more ;—the world has seen
A type of peace ; and—as some most serene
And lovely spot to a poor maniac's eye,
After long years, some sweet and moving scene
Of youthful hope, returning suddenly,
Quells his long madness—thus man shall remember thee.

Two years later Shelley wrote the poem in which his God-winism appeared in its most impressive form.   This is *Prometheus Unbound*, where the Godwinian nightmare of the individual pitted against the forces of society is raised to a gigantic level in the sufferings of the Titan chained and tortured by the angry Jupiter for his intervention in favour of mankind.   The parallel with *St Leon* is not difficult to detect.   Prometheus is saved from his torture, the gods are vanquished and mankind is set free by the action of Demogorgon, the unknowable principle from which springs all natural law, and which tends to the benefit of humanity.   The relationship between Demogorgon and the kind of life principle which Godwin postulated in *The Genius of Christianity Unveiled* will be shown in a later chapter.   It will suffice here to observe that Demogorgon, the god of the atheist Shelley, is directly derived from Godwin's idea of Necessity, and the descent can be traced through the verses on Necessity in *Queen Mab* and *The Revolt of Islam*.

Like these earlier poems, *Prometheus Unbound* contains its Godwinian visions of a golden age, written in great beauty of language.

And, behold, thrones were kingless, and men walked
One with the other even as spirits do,
None fawned, none trampled ; hate, disdain or fear,
Self-love or self-contempt, on human brows
No more inscribed, as o'er the gate of hell,
" All hope abandon ye who enter here " ;
None frowned, none trembled, none with eager fear
Gazed on another's eye of cold command,
Until the subject of a tyrant's will
Became, worse fate, the abject of his own,
Which spurred him, like an outspent horse, to death.
None wrought his lips in truth-entangling lines
Which smiled the lie his tongue disdained to speak ;
None, with firm sneer, trod out in his own heart

> The sparks of love and hope till there remained
> Those bitter ashes, a soul self-consumed,
> And the wretch crept a vampire among men,
> Infecting all with his own hideous ill ;
> None talked that common, false, cold, hollow talk
> Which makes the heart deny the *yes* it breathes,
> Yet question that unmeant hypocrisy
> With such a self-mistrust as has no name . . .

> The loathsome mask has fallen, the man remains
> Sceptreless, free, uncircumscribed, but man
> Equal, unclassed, tribeless and nationless,
> Exempt from awe, worship, degree, the king
> Over himself ; just, gentle, wise : but man
> Passionless ?—no, yet free from guilt or pain,
> Which were, for his will made or suffered them,
> Nor yet exempt, though ruling them like slaves,
> From chance, and death, and mutability,
> The clogs of that which else might oversoar
> The loftiest star of unascended heaven,
> Pinnacled dim in the intense inane.

In these verses we can see delineated all the Godwinian virtues, all the sincerity and integrity which underlie the social teachings of *Political Justice*. It is difficult to imagine how better the conclusions of that book could have been expressed in verse.

Shelley is careful to indicate that the end of tyranny and unhappiness must spring first of all from the man within, from what has become known as " the change of heart." It is on this theme that the poem ends, with Demogorgon, the Godwinian deity, declaring :

> To suffer woes which Hope thinks infinite ;
> To forgive wrongs darker than death or night ;
>   To defy Power, which seems omnipotent ;
> To love, and bear ; to hope till Hope creates
> From its own wreck the thing it contemplates ;
>   Neither to change, nor falter, nor repent ;
> This, like thy glory, Titan, is to be
> Good, great and joyous, beautiful and free ;
> This is alone Life, Joy, Empire and Victory.

There are those who see in such sentiments some kind of mystical advance beyond Godwinism. Yet it must be remembered that Godwin himself, after the failure of the Irish expedition, converted Shelley to the view that the fostering of the change within men was a surer way to freedom than the imposition of external changes.

The last of Shelley's important social poems is *Hellas*. In this the influence of Godwin is less openly manifest than in the three previous poems, partly because by this time Godwinism has become completely assimilated into Shelley's mental vision, and partly because the poem is concerned more with the contemporary uprising in Greece than with a general social theory. Indeed, there is evidence within this poem that Shelley might be returning towards a more directly revolutionary idea than that advocated by Godwin in his old age. The following passage in the preface was suppressed by the original publisher because of its revolutionary character :

This is the age of the war of the oppressed against the oppressors, and every one of those ringleaders of the privileged gangs of murderers and swindlers, called Sovereigns, look to each other for aid against the common enemy, and suspend their mutual jealousies in the presence of a mightier fear. Of this holy alliance all the despots of the earth are virtual members. But a new race has arisen throughout Europe, nursed in the abhorrence of the opinions which are its chains, and she will continue to produce fresh generations to accomplish that destiny which tyrants foresee and dread.

Yet even here there is a certain ambiguity, and the fact that Shelley identifies *opinions* as the chains which oppress men leads one to suppose that the passage may be nearer to Godwin than at first it appears. Within the poem there are many passages which clearly advocate the morality of *Political Justice*, such as the following :

> Revenge and Wrong bring forth their kind,
> The foul cubs like their parents are,
> Their den is in the guilty mind,
>     And Conscience feeds them with despair.

The final vision of a happy world is certainly less ample, and perhaps less confident than it had been before. Shelley talks of the Golden Age, but rejects the role of a final prophet.

> The world's great age begins anew,
> The golden years return,
> The earth doth like a snake renew
>     Her winter weeds outworn :
> Heaven smiles, and faiths and empires gleam,
> Like wrecks of a dissolving dream.

> Oh, cease ! must hate and death return ?
>   Cease ! must men kill and die ?
> Cease ! drain not to its dregs the urn
>   Of bitter prophecy.
> The world is weary of the past,
> Oh, might it die or rest at last !

Perhaps the most characteristic mood of this poem is its statement of the fundamental nature of thought in an evil and dissatisfying world. Thought continues, however empires may fall or tyrannies arise. There is reason to suggest that this was a conclusion reached by Godwin in the disillusionment of his old age, and it is certain from what we know of his respect for the intellect that Godwin would have agreed with the spirit of Shelley's beautiful lines :

> But Greece and her foundations are
> Built below the tide of war,
> Based on the crystalline sea
> Of thought and its eternity.

It was Godwin, after all, who declared that only through our thoughts and opinions can we be either slaves or free men.

### 5

After the final collapse of The Juvenile Library, Godwin lived on for some months in the expensive house at 195, The Strand. Then, in 1826, he moved to No. 44, Gower Place, a house at the relatively small rent of £50 a year. Here he worked quietly and industriously at his resumed literary labours.

Mary Shelley now spent much time with him, a few old friends and some belated disciples, like Robert Owen, came to visit him, and he still went out to social parties, to talk, to drink moderately, and to play cards.

He had outlived both the enthusiasm inspired in the heyday of fame and the unpopularity of his leaner years. His works were still read, or at least remembered, among the small remaining circle of radicals, but his reputation was only the shadow of what it had been thirty years before, and his enemies, wise in their own interests, had learnt that silence is more effective than abuse.

Hazlitt describes this condition of Godwin's fame in his *Spirit of the Age* essay, which was written with much sympathy :

Now he has sunk below the horizon, and enjoys the serene twilight of a doubtful immortality.  Mr Godwin, during his lifetime, has secured to himself the triumphs and the mortifications of an extreme notoriety and of a sort of posthumous fame. His bark, after being tossed in the revolutionary tempest, now raised to heaven by all the fury of popular breath, now almost dashed in pieces, and buried in the quicksands of ignorance, or scorched with the lightning of momentary indignation, at length floats in the calm wave that is to bear it down the stream of time.

Mr Godwin's person is not known, he is not pointed out in the street, his conversation is not courted, his opinions are not asked, he is at the head of no cabal, he belongs to no party in the State, he has no train of admirers, no one thinks it worth his while even to traduce and vilify him, he has scarcely friend or foe, the world make a point (as Goldsmith used to say) of taking no more notice of him than if such an individual had never existed ; he is to all ordinary intents and purposes dead and buried. But the author of *Political Justice* and *Caleb Williams* can never die ; his name is an abstraction in letters ; his works are standard in the history of intellect. He is thought of now like any eminent writer of a hundred-and-fifty years ago, or just as he will be a hundred-and-fifty years hence. He knows this, and smiles in silent mockery of himself, reposing on the monument of his fame.

This essay contained much friendly praise of Godwin's works, which must have been gratifying to the philosopher who, for years now, had become used to the blows of the world. But to us it is perhaps more interesting for its portrait of Godwin's personal habits and manners at this late period, and its brief and reasonably just analysis of his powers.

His forte is not the spontaneous, but the voluntary exercise of talent. He fixes his ambition on a high point of excellence, and spares no pains or time in attaining it. He has less of the appearance of a man of genius, than any one who has given such decided and ample proofs of it. He is ready only on reflection, dangerous only at the rebound. He gathers himself up, and strains every nerve and faculty with deliberate aim to some heroic and dazzling achievement of intellect : but he must make a career, before he flings himself armed upon the enemy, or he is sure to be unhorsed. Or he resembles an eight-day clock that must be wound up long before it can strike. Therefore, his powers of conversation are but limited. He has neither acuteness of remark nor a flow of language, both which might be expected from his writings, as these are no less distinguished by a sustained and impassioned tone of declamation than by novelty of opinion or brilliant tracks of invention. . . .

He lost this awkwardness with the first blush of popularity, which surprised him in the retirement of his study ; and he has since, with the wear and tear of society, from being too pragmatical, become somewhat too careless. He is, at present, as easy as an old glove. Perhaps there is a little attention to effect in this, and he wishes to appear a foil to himself. . . . He is not one of those who do not grow wiser with opportunity and reflection : he changes his opinions, and changes them for the better. . . .

In size Mr Godwin is below the common stature, nor is his deportment graceful or animated.  His face is, however, fine, with an expression of placid temper and recondite thought.  He is not unlike the common portraits of Locke.  There is a very admirable likeness of him by Mr Northcote which, with a more heroic and dignified air, only does justice to the profound sagacity and benevolent aspirations of our author's mind. . . .

The work on which Godwin was engaged for some years was his *History of the Commonwealth*, which appeared in four volumes between 1824 and 1828.  Like all his writings, it was compiled with care and painstaking research into the available records. Among those who assisted him in gathering facts for this work were two old enemies who had since become friendly, Isaac D'Israeli and Walter Scott.

The *History of the Commonwealth* enjoyed a great reputation in its day, although it has since become superseded by the works of writers who have had access to new material.  Godwin's analyses of the political causes of the civil war, and his criticisms of the actions of the participants are, on the whole, acute and impartial, and his assessment of Cromwell is a model of fair and reasonable observation.  The main fault of the work is, perhaps, its caution. It might well have been written by any liberal historian of the Victorian age, and only occasionally do the revolutionary sentiments of Godwin's prime appear in a recognisable form.  His treatment of Lilburne and the Levellers, although better documented and more copious than that of most historians, is by no means as favourable as they deserve.  There is evident an old man's distrust of the kind of " wild men " among whom Godwin himself had been at home in his earlier days.  The Diggers and Winstanley are dismissed with hardly any explanation at all, and Godwin seems to have failed completely to realise the close relationship between the social doctrines which Winstanley expounded and those developed in *Political Justice*.

It is not difficult to find reasons for this caution.  Godwin was growing old, and had become tired of persecution and poverty. Since the collapse of his business and the estrangement or death of his prosperous friends, he could earn money only by writing. Therefore he may well have felt it not worth risking a renewal

of popular hatred by recording history in a way more revolutionary than his readers might accept.

The unsatisfactory nature of the contents is reflected in the
form of the book. It is very much the conventional history, well
documented with battles and statutes, but paying little attention
to social and economic conditions and to the nature of popular
life. Twenty years before, in his *Life of Chaucer*, Godwin had
produced a fluent description of the way in which all classes of
the people lived in the fourteenth century. Had he done the
same for the seventeenth century, his *History of the Commonwealth*
would have been a more valuable and more interesting work.
As it was, its reliance on dry facts even broke up the natural
eloquence and vigour with which large sections are written, so
that, as Hazlitt put it, " his style creeps, and hitches on dates
and authorities."

The income from this work did not give him any provision
for leisure in his old age, and he was forced to continue working
steadily. He and his wife lived frugally. They rarely went out,
except occasionally to the theatre or to a whist party, and,
although they still welcomed visitors, their house was no longer
filled with friends. William, the last of their children to leave
home, was married and earning his living as a writer, but both
he and Mary visited the old people almost daily.

Two letters written during this period deserve quotation for
the picture they give of Godwin's quiet and penurious life. The
first is to Mrs Godwin, who had gone away on a visit, and it
gives an interesting indication of the persistence of ill feeling
between her and Mary Shelley.

My Dear Love. You are very wrong in saying I do not want your
society, and still more in supposing Mrs Shelley supplies the deficiency.
I see her perhaps twice a week ; but I feel myself alone ten times a day,
and particularly at meals, and after meals, which are the periods at
which, from nature or habit, I most feel the want of a human countenance to look at, and of a human voice with which to exchange the
accents of kindness and sympathy. . . .
There have been no letters from Vienna, or Moscow, or anywhere
else.
We go on quietly here. I am in good health, and working. I asked
Jane, previous to writing this letter, how she was, and she answers she
is very well now. Everything is smooth ; but I cannot take a frisk, as
I used to do with another servant, and give a dinner to Kenney or some
other fool. Jane had a visit from Mrs Eamer, who promises to bring

her her things the week after next.   She brought you two presents, a
pint bottle of ketchup, and a gallipot of nasturtiums. . . .

Do not, I intreat you, from any recollection of me, shorten your visit.
It is true, it is not good for man to be alone, and I feel it so.   But I can
summon philosophy to my aid, and can have consideration for some
one beside myself ;   especially when one can take the consolation to
oneself, this will soon be over.

The reference to a letter from Vienna or Moscow presumably
signifies Charles Clairmont, who, after working a time for Constable, the Edinburgh publisher, had gone to Austria, where he
became a tutor to the imperial princes.

The second letter, written in October, 1827, to Mary Shelley,
indicates the philosophical calm with which Godwin now lived
through his poverty and insecurity.

How differently are you and I organized !   In my seventy-second
year I am all cheerfulness, and never anticipate the evil day with dis-
tressing feelings till to do so is absolutely unavoidable.   Would to God
you were my daughter in all but my poverty !   But I am afraid you are
a Wollstonecraft.   We are so curiously made that one atom put in the
wrong place in our original structure will often make us unhappy for
life.   But my present cheerfulness is greatly owing to " Cromwell," and
the nature of my occupation, which gives me an object *omnium horarum*,
a stream for ever running and for ever new.

Early in 1830 he published his fifth novel, *Cloudesley*.   It is a
dull, sentimental story of a family intrigue in which a wicked
uncle deprives his nephew of the succession to an earldom, of the
youth's adventures as the supposed son of an English yeoman
living in Italy, of the final repentence of the wicked uncle and the
last-minute rescue of the changeling as he is about to be executed
for a bandit.

There are some redeeming descriptions of Italian scenery
which Godwin may have received at first hand from his daughter,
and an introductory section dealing with the adventures of one
of the characters in Russia, which may be connected with Arnot's
travels.   The inevitable virtuous and intelligent woman appears
in the person of Irene, the mother of the young hero Julian.   In
Borromeo, the blunt and rough-mannered friend of Cloudesley,
Julian's foster-father, we have a gruff exponent of a diluted
doctrine of universal benevolence.   The remaining characters
are mere pasteboard figures.   The writing is rhetorical and
verbose, the action being interrupted continuously for long

passages of soliloquy or moralising which have no real place in the story.

In spite of its faults, *Cloudesley* was fairly well received. Hazlitt took the opportunity to write in the *Edinburgh Review* a further long article on Godwin in which, although he could not praise *Cloudesley* very highly, he contrived to convey much approbation of Godwin's masterpieces. Even in criticising *Cloudesley* he spoke kindly, praising the language and referring sympathetically to the difficulties of living by writing, which were soon to bring his own untimely death.

A young critic who regarded *Cloudesley* with more thorough enthusiasm was Edward Bulwer, afterwards Lord Lytton. Bulwer was almost the last of the talented succession of young disciples who gathered round Godwin. He was introduced by Lady Caroline Lamb, who gained a permanent place in literary history by her infatuation for Byron, and who was an eccentric friend of Godwin in his last years. Bulwer had a real admiration for Godwin as a philosopher, but was most attracted to him as a novelist, and the influence of Godwin is very noticeable in his early books. Indeed, Godwin even helped him with some of his novels. He suggested the plot of *Paul Clifford*, and was full of praise when it appeared, saying to Bulwer :

There are parts of the book that I read with transport. There are many parts so divinely written that my first impulse was to throw my implements of writing into the fire, and to wish that I could consign all that I have published in the province of fiction to the same pyre.

Needless to say, Godwin did not burn his pens, or cease writing fiction. But his regard for Bulwer continued, and he gave him the idea of *Eugene Aram*, a theme on which he himself had contemplated writing a novel. Bulwer remarks : " I can well conceive what depth and power that gloomy record would have taken from the dark and inspiring genius of the author of *Caleb Williams*."

*Cloudesley*, according to Bulwer, sold " surprisingly well," and better than *Mandeville*, but the receipts do not appear to have given Godwin any permanent relief, for he wrote a really pathetic letter to his daughter in reply to an invitation to visit her at Southend, which showed the depressing anxiety over money by which he was still pursued :

I am miserable under the weight of this uncertainty, feeling myself able and willing to do eveything, and do it well, and nobody disposed to give me the requisite encouragement. If I can agree with these tyrants in Burlington Street for £300, £400 or £500 for a novel, and to be subsisted by them while I write it, I probably shall not starve for a fortnight to come. But they will take no step to bring the thing to a point, and I may go thither one, two or three times, and catch them if I can. I have no contention with them which is the nobler party, they or I ; but this dancing attendance wears my spirits and destroys my tranquillity. "Hands have I, but I handle not : I have feet, but I walk not : neither is there any breath in my nostrils." Meanwhile my life wears away, and " there is no work, nor device, nor knowledge, nor wisdom in the grave whither I go." But indeed I am wrong in talking of that ; for I write now, not for marble to be placed on my remains, but for bread to put into my mouth. In that sense, therefore, every day of which they rob me is of moment, since every day brings its cravings to be supplied.

Godwin's tiresome search for support continued for some time longer, and he had a discouraging experience with the publishers, who were evidently beginning to think that an old man could not really have the vigour of writing which Godwin in fact retained. In February, 1831, he wrote to Scott, whom he hoped would interest Cadell the publisher in a book on *The Lives of the Necromancers*, which he was then planning :

. . . I am conscious (if I do not greatly deceive myself) of powers undecayed, which I am most anxious to apply to the support of my life, and the procuring those slender comforts to which I have been accustomed. But the trade, or the disposition of the booksellers in London, is in such a state as to afford me nothing but discouragement. . . . With powers perhaps unimpaired, and a will to exert them, I find myself likely to be laid on the shelf, as a person whose name has been long enough before the public. . . . You will not, I think, refuse your sympathy to a person no longer active in his limbs, but who believes himself to be in the full vigour of his understanding. . . . I have a wife : I need the little house I live in to hold my books, and my literary accommodations ; I cannot live thus, considerably under £300 a year. My labour perhaps might be worthy of that reward, and with that I would be content.

But Scott was himself in no easy circumstances, and his credit with the publishers was not sufficient to enable him to help Godwin.

### 6

Shortly afterwards, Godwin succeeded in publishing his *Thoughts on Man*, a collection of philosophical and political essays. *Thoughts on Man* is the one book of Godwin's later years fully equal in merit to his earlier masterpieces. It is as readable and profound as *The Enquirer*, but at the same time it is more supple in its style and more kindly in its attitude to mankind. The title is significant of an important difference in outlook from Godwin's earlier period. *Political Justice* and *The Enquirer* were orientated towards a Reason which seemed to lie outside man. Man's conduct was to be guided by criteria of justice and morality abstracted from the world in which he lived, for, more perhaps that Godwin realised, his earlier thought tended towards a Platonic idealism, and the Godwinian criteria were in their nature hardly distinguishable from the Platonic forms. However closely applicable the contentions of *Political Justice* may have been to the concrete world of human affairs—and in this sense they represent perhaps the most effective union of idealist concepts with practical ideas of organisation of life—they were nevertheless built not around man himself, but around an idea of natural law which governed man's actions and shaped his character. *Political Justice* represented a philosophical attitude which was in its essentials pantheistic rather than humanist.

In *Thoughts on Man*, however, Godwin has come much nearer to complete humanism. Man is now his chief concern—he regards him as the noblest expression of the natural order, and the laws of nature as being manifest through man rather than through the necessities that govern his conduct. In reaching this attitude it seems to me that he resolved the last contradiction in the thought of *Political Justice*—the effort to reconcile a belief in philosophical necessity with a belief in the possibility of conscious and voluntary action for the improvement of human relationships. Man's actions are indeed involved in a necessary chain of cause and effect, but the human will is part of the series of causes, and man's actions become voluntary in so far as he can alter the direction of the chain, even if he cannot break it asunder.

Will [Godwin now admits] and a confidence in its efficiency, " travel through, nor quit us till we die." It is this which inspires us with invincible perseverance and heroic energies, while without it we should be the most inert and soulless of blocks, the shadows of what history records and poetry immortalises, and not men.

Free will is an integral part of the science of man and may be said to constitute its most important chapter. We might with as much propriety overlook the intelligence of the senses, that medium which acquaints us with an external world or what we call such, we might as well overlook the consideration of man's reason, his imagination or taste, as fail to dwell with earnest reflection and exposition upon that principle which lies at the foundation of our moral energies, fills us with a moral enthusiasm, prompts all our animated exertions on the theatre of the world, whether upon a wide or a narrow scale, and penetrates us with the most lively and fervent approbation or disapprobation of the acts of ourselves and others in which the forwarding or obstructing human happiness is involved. . . .

There is an old axiom of philosophy, which counsels us to " think with the learned, and talk with the vulgar " ; and the practical application of this axiom runs through the whole scene of human affairs. Thus the most learned astronomer talks of the rising and setting of the sun, and forgets in his ordinary discourse that the earth is not for ever at rest, and does not constitute the centre of the universe. Thus, however we reason respecting the attributes of inanimate matter and the nature of sensation, it never occurs to us, while occupied with the affairs of actual life, that there is no heat in fire, and no colour in the rainbow.

In like manner, when we contemplate the acts of ourselves and our neighbours, we can never divest ourselves of the delusive sense of the liberty of human actions, of the sentiment of conscience, of the feelings of love and hatred, the impulses of praise and blame, and the notions of virtue, duty, obligation, right, claim, guilt, merit and desert. And it has sufficiently appeared in the course of this Essay, that it is not desirable that we should do so. They are these ideas to which the world we live in is indebted for its crowning glory and greatest lustre. They form the highest distinction between men and other animals and are the genuine basis of self-reverence and the conceptions of true nobility and greatness, and the reverse of these attributes, in the men with whom we live, and the men whose deeds are recorded in the never-dying page of history.

But, though the doctrine of the necessity of human actions can never form the rule of our intercourse with others, it will still have its use. It will moderate our excesses, and point out to us that middle path of judgment which the soundest philosophy inculcates. We shall learn, according to the apostolic precept, to " be angry, and sin not, neither let the sun go down on our wrath." We shall make our fellow-men neither idols to worship nor demons to be regarded with horror and execration. We shall think of them, as of players " that strut and fret their hour upon the stage, and then are heard no more." We shall " weep, as though we wept not, and rejoice, as though we rejoiced not, seeing that the fashion of this world passeth away." And, most of all, we shall view with pity, even with sympathy, the men whose frailties we behold, or by whom crimes are perpetrated, satisfied that they are parts of one great machine, and, like ourselves, are driven forward by impulses over which they have no real control.

Reinforced with this more pragmatical view of human actions, Godwin surveys the nature of man in its many aspects. He commences with a panegyric on the human mind and body, and then, in a series of essays, " Of the Distribution of Talents," returns to his old subject of education. His theme is that the apparent inequality in mental powers among men, by which the few appear brilliant and the many dull, is unnatural, and is largely due to faults in education. Existing educational systems permit only a limited course in which talents can be developed, and the boy who cannot profit by their methods must appear dull. Godwin also blames the inequality of status between master and pupil, by which the pupil is made to feel his continual inferiority and his development is often halted permanently.

Godwin reiterates his theory of the natal equality of man, but in a modified form, for he now admits that, while all men can become capable and completely developed human beings, there is a divergence even at birth in the direction of their talents, which makes them adaptable to different vocations.

Education, therefore, should strive to develop the natural propensities of the child, by ascertaining carefully for what he is best fitted and then adapting instruction to that end. Uniformity of education is to be avoided, as well as any tyranny on the part of the teacher, and the pupil must above all be induced to reverence himself and his own talents.

In the remaining essays, Godwin deals with a wide variety of the aspects of human life and nature, from " The Durability of Human Achievements and Productions " to " Phrenology," from " Human Vegetation " to " Self-Complacency." In general, political subjects are avoided, but occasionally the familiar Godwinian social and moral ideas appear. Universal benevolence is defended fervently against the advocates of self-love, and perfect sincerity is once more recommended as the only condition in which human intercourse can be made satisfactory. The necessity for all men to have leisure for the cultivation of their natural talents is stressed, and again we are told of the importance of basing our actions on our own individual judgments. The evil effects of the unequal distribution of property are indicated, and the courts of kings are shown to be the abodes of lying and hypocrisy.

The book ends with a tribute to the potentialities of man, which is remarkable in that it is written by one who had received more justification than most men to be cynical and contemptuous of human virtues.

Let then no man, in the supercilious spirit of a fancied disdain, allow himself to detract from our common nature. We are ourselves the models of all the excellence that the human mind can conceive. There have been men, whose virtues may well redeem all the contempt with which satire and detraction have sought to overwhelm our species. There have been memorable periods in the history of man, when the best, the most generous and exalted sentiments have swallowed up and obliterated all that was of an opposite character. And it is but just, that those by whom these things are fairly considered, should anticipate the progress of our nature, and believe that human understanding and human virtue will hereafter accomplish such things as the heart of man has never yet been daring enough to conceive.

It does great credit to Godwin's own virtue that, at the end of a life during which he had endured so much persecution for having sought the happiness of his fellow men, he should still have sufficient respect for his species to speak of it in such noble terms.

7

Before his own death, Godwin was to be troubled by a last tragedy in his unfortunate family. In 1832, his son William, who had become a competent journalist and a brilliant illustrator, was infected with cholera, and died in a few hours, while Godwin and his wife watched at the bedside. He left a novel, *Transfusion*, which, like Mary Shelley's works, was in the gloomiest Godwinian style, and which his father later published with a short memoir.

In that year the Reform Bill was passed, and an indirect result of this was Godwin's own emancipation from financial anxiety, for when the new ministry was established, there were some of the Whigs who did not forget the services he had rendered the cause of freedom. In April, 1833, at the instance of many of his old friends, Lord Grey offered Godwin the post of Yeoman Usher of the Exchequer. It was almost a sinecure, carrying a house in New Palace Yard, fuel, lighting and an income of about two hundred pounds a year. Godwin, who in his time had condemned salaries, accepted the offer. It is impossible to blame the old man, who had experienced so much poverty, and so little benefit from the private generosity which he had hoped would replace public employment.  If he had refused, at the age of seventy-seven, his last years would have been made hideous by increasing poverty and incapacity, whereas now he could end his days in the assurance of an income sufficient for his needs.  When the Reform Parliament began to abolish the sinecures, it was agreed by all parties that Godwin should be left in peace until his death.

His last few years, though happily untroubled by the anxieties that had poisoned the previous decades, were not inactive.  His restless brain continued to speculate as he waited serenely for death, and his pen was not laid down until the last weeks of his life.

In 1833 he published his last novel, *Deloraine*.  It was a dry, wordy book, and received little attention.  The old Godwinian theme of the individual at odds with society was repeated, but perhaps the most interesting feature of the book was the last portrait of Mary Wollstonecraft as the hero's wife, Emilia.  The description of the relationship between man and woman is a recapitulation of the great passion of Godwin's life.  The length of the passage on this subject and the sincerity of the tribute leave no doubt that Godwin intended this as a testament to his past. Many paragraphs recall sentences in the *Memoir of Mary Wollstonecraft*, and the following passage is a good example of this renewed picture of the life of Godwin and Mary :

The frankness we exercised was perfect.  We talked to each other, as a man talks to his own soul.  We did not utter all our thoughts : for thought is endless ; its process is such as no words can follow ; but we uttered every thing worthy to be recited, and to which a precise or intelligible form could be given.  The sound of our own voices encouraged us ; our mutual answers, replies and rejoinders gave an indescribable animation to our dialogue.  We led each other on ; we gave breath to each unfinished conception.  There was no fear on either side that an uncandid advantage would be taken of trips and mistakes that might be incurred.  We rather resembled what has been affirmed of certain animals, who are said by their parental assiduity and care to complete the conformation of their half-finished progeny. . . .

The habit of entire and unhesitating explicitness which we cultivated towards each other, removed us as it were into another class of beings from the human creatures with which we were surrounded.  We had no distrust.  Our hearts were ever on our lips.  We considered the faculty of speech as given us to express our thoughts.

The final parallel with Godwin's own history comes when

Emilia dies in childbirth, and the husband perceives a revolution in his view of life :

I looked around me ; the outline of things, though obscure and dim, was the same : but where was now the grace that so lately animated them, the ornament that had tingled in all my veins and shot through my soul ?

Thus the memory of Mary Wollstonecraft stayed with Godwin to the end of his days. There may have been much of exaggerated sentimentality in his attitude, but there was also enough of abiding love and sorrow to disprove entirely the statements of those who have sought to deny him the virtues of feeling and to portray him as a monster of cold intellectuality.

In 1834 he published at last his *Lives of the Necromancers*, a long and scholarly work, embracing a very wide range of persons and subjects connected with sorcery and the occult :

If we would know man in all his subtleties, we must deviate into the world of miracles and sorcery. To know the things that are not, and cannot be, but have been imagined and believed, is the most curious chapter in the annals of man. To observe the actual results of these imaginary phenomena, and the crimes and cruelties they have caused us to commit, is one of the most instructive studies in which we can possibly be engaged. It is here that man is most astonishing, and that we contemplate with most admiration the discursive and unbounded nature of his faculties.

Godwin did his best to upset what he considered credulous superstition and did not hesitate to attack the more improbable miracles of the Bible. For this reason, his book was not popular. In some ways his study was inadequate, for he does not appear to have understood fully the rationalistic basis of magic and other occult practices, but on the whole his conclusions were sound. Yet, although he condemned ideas he regarded as erroneous, he showed a surprising tolerance for the man who fell into such errors, realising perhaps that no man can be wholly free from faults :

One useful lesson which we may derive from the detail of these particulars is the folly in most cases of imputing pure and unmingled hypocrisy to man. The human mind is of so ductile a character that, like what is affirmed of charity by the apostle, it " believeth all things, and endureth all things." We are not at liberty to trifle with the sacredness of truth. While we persuade others, we begin to deceive ourselves. Human life is a drama of that sort, that, while we act our part, and endeavour to do justice to the sentiments which are put down for us, we begin to believe we are the thing we would represent.

His remaining years were passed in quiet study and an increasing consciousness of the approach of death. He still went out occasionally to the houses of his friends, and Carlyle records having met him at a whist party whose frivolity seems to have shocked the Scots more than the English philosopher. Of Godwin Carlyle noted :

He is a bald, bushy-browed, thick, hoary, hale little figure, taciturn enough, and speaking, when he does speak with a certain *epigrammatic* spirit, wherein, except a little shrewdness, there is nothing but the most commonplace character. (I should have added that he wears spectacles, has full gray eyes, a very large, blunt, characterless nose, and ditto chin).

His letters surviving from this period are few, and show a quiet equanimity at the peaceful ending of an agitated life. In August of 1834 he wrote to his wife, away on one of her frequent visits, and gave a brief picture of his life :

My health is better. I have had no return of the sick feeling which obstinately pursued me for three weeks after my journey to Harrow. I have written at my manuscript for four days, a little at a time, and feeling as if I were too old to do much. But it cheers me.

Mrs Shelley dined with me on Friday 22nd, and I with her the following Monday. She spent the evening with me yesterday. We should meet oftener, but I rather decline going to her evenings. The evenings are now dark, and the walk across the park at a late hour is anything but pleasant.

I am afraid to say how much I wish to see you, lest you should call me selfish. Do, however, stay longer, if you think it will do you good. I have still £50, the produce of the Necromancers.

The manuscript to which he referred was his book of essays in religious criticism, which he intended to entitle *The Genius of Christianity Unveiled*. In writing this book he was fulfilling an intention expressed in his notes more than thirty years before. He was also, perhaps, making his last philosophical reckoning with reality, before the personal end of which he was becoming steadily more conscious.

It was at this time that, having read through the diaries of the preceding decades, he wrote in a loose sheet certain reflections to be pasted on the last page of his journals when he felt his end was near. The sheet was written on August 21st, 1834, but it was not put in place until March 26th, 1836, a few days before he actually died :

With what facility have I marked these pages with the stamp of rolling weeks and months and years—all uniform, all blank. What a strange power is this ! It sees through a long vista of time, and it sees nothing. All this at present is mere abstraction, symbols, not realities. Nothing is actually seen : the whole is ciphers, conventional marks, imaginary boundaries of unimagined things. Here is neither joy nor sorrow, pleasure nor pain. Yet when the time shall truly come, and the revolving year shall bring the day, what portentous events may stamp the page ! What anguish, what horror, or by possibility what joy, what Godlike elevation of soul ! Here are fevers, and excruciating pains " in their sacred secundine asleep." Here may be the saddest reverses, destitution and despair, detrusion and hunger and nakedness, without a place wherein to lay our head, wearisome days and endless nights in dark and unendurable monotony, variety of wretchedness ; yet of all one gloomy hue ; slumbers without sleep, waking without excitation, dreams all heterogeneous and perplexed, with nothing distinct and defined, distracted without the occasional bursts and energy of distraction. And these pages look now all fair, innocent and uniform. I have put down eighty years and twenty-three days [he must have written in his age when he actually inserted the leaf in his diary], and I might put down one hundred and sixty years. But in which of these pages shall the pen which purposes to record, drop from my hands for ever, never again to be resumed ? I shall set down the memoranda of one day, with the full expectation of resuming my task on the next, or my fingers may refuse their functions in the act of forming a letter, and leave the word never by the writer to be completed.

Everything under the sun is uncertain. No provision can be a sufficient security against adverse and unexpected fortune, least of all to him who has not a stipulated income bound to him by the forms and ordinances of society. This, as age and feebleness of body and mind advances, is an appalling consideration " a man cannot tell what shall be," to what straits he may be driven, what trials and privations and destitution and struggles and griefs may be reserved for him.

Fortunately, Godwin's few remaining years were less filled with " trials and privations " than most of his preceding life, and he does not appear to have been more eager than his father to leave " this sublunary scene." Harriet Martineau visited him at home and found him preoccupied with death :

He was so comfortable that he had evidently no mind to die. Three times in the course of that evening he asked questions or made a remark on the intended length of my absence, ending with " When you come back, I shall be dead," or " When you come back, you will visit my grave," evidently in the hope that I should say " No, you will see me return."

But Godwin regarded the approach of death with much more philosophical equanimity and detachment than Miss Martineau supposed. He never seems to have deceived himself with false hopes of personal immortality, and his honest fearlessness is shown to its best effect in a letter he wrote in reply to the father of a young admirer who had died towards the end of 1834. During his last illness the boy had been converted to faith in Christianity, and his wish was that after his death the story of his conversion should be told to Godwin and his other friends. Godwin replied with kindness, but also with a dignified assurance of his own attitude towards death :

I do most sincerely condole with you on the death of your son, who had many good qualities that awakened my esteem. I know how fervently you were attached to him, and, considering all things, am almost glad that he died in a manner that could best afford you consolation under the afflicting dispensation that has taken from your age its greatest comfort.

As to my own creed, to which you refer, that is a totally different thing. It has been deeply reflected on, and has been the fruit of as much patient and honest research as your own. I am now in my seventy-ninth year, and am not likely to alter in a matter of so much moment. We must be contented with different results, and should entertain charity for each other. If I am in error, I am in the hands of God, and I humbly trust that he will see the integrity and honesty of my enquiries.

8

The book on which Godwin worked during these years was his *Genius of Christianity Unveiled*, which represented a last attempt to establish his own view of the universe and his attitude towards religion. No doubt it was intimately connected with his consciousness of impending death, and represented something in the form of a reckoning with the world.

He left the book with a message to his daughter, which shows the importance he attached to its contents :

I am most unwilling that this, the concluding work of a long life, and written, as I believe, in the full maturity of my understanding, shall be consigned to oblivion. It has been the main object of my life, since I attained to years of discretion, to do my part to free the human mind from slavery. I adjure you, therefore, or whomsoever else into whose hands these papers may fall, not to allow them to be consigned to oblivion.

Unfortunately, Mary Shelley was much more solicitous for her father's repute than he would have wished and, realising the storm that would be roused among the faithful by his attacks on the Church and its dogmas, chose in her timidity to suppress *The Genius of Christianity Unveiled* for nearly forty years. When at last it was published, in 1873, it appeared under the undescriptive title of *Essays Never Before Published*, and the force of its arguments was largely spent because by this time other criticisms had already weakened the dogmas Godwin attacked. Nevertheless, it remains a brave and vigorous work, and one of the most intelligent of the early books of religious criticism.

Godwin begins with a discussion of the theory that it is necessary to delude the common people in order to keep them, by the promise of reward or the fear of punishment, to the strict path of morality. He condemns this theory, and the whole idea of dual esoteric-exoteric aspects for the purpose of maintaining ignorance among the masses :

The question is the same as that of political liberty and slavery. There was a time when it was held that it was only a privileged few that were to be the masters of their own actions, while the great majority was to be held in chains, and to move this way and that merely as they are ordered by their imperial lords. This is, of all considerations, the most vital to the community of mankind. So long as we were divided into two classes, the master and the slave, both parties were corrupted —the lower by the condition of their existence being precluded from the influence of almost every generous motive, every impulse of a loftier sort, and the higher impelled from the first hour of their moral existence to the practice of tyranny and despotism. But that time is happily gone by. All men are acknowledged to partake of a common nature, to have a right to deliberate, to conduct themselves accordingly. This is the most important revolution that has occurred in the history of the world. The equality of human beings as such, opens upon us the prospect of perpetual improvement. It is of consequence not true that the mass of our species is to be held for ever in leading strings, while a few only are to have the prerogative of thinking and directing for all, but that the whole community is to run the generous race for intellectual and moral superiority. This idea lies at the foundation of all improvement. It opens to us the prospect of indefinite advancement in sound judgment, in real science, and the just conduct of our social institutions.

Here are an eloquence and a frankness of speech not inferior to those of *Political Justice*.

Godwin indicates that he is not necessarily opposed to all religion, but the degree of religion he admits would certainly not satisfy any Christian sectarian. It consists in an almost mystical " religious sense " :

I have always been of opinion that a certain portion of what may be called the " religious sense " is necessary to the sound and healthy condition of the human mind. . . . That we should behold the works of nature with wonder and awe, that we should stand astonished at the symmetry, harmony, subtlety, and beauty of the world around us, is natural and reasonable ; and that we should feel how frail and insignificant a part we constitute of the great whole, can alone inspire us with a proper sobriety and humility, and make us sensible of our real state and condition.

But I think that religion encroaches too far on the human understanding, when it proposes to deprive us of our sense, or prohibits in whatever direction the use of our reasoning powers.

Godwin finds this fault in all organised religion. The fundamental beliefs of the churches, and in particular the underlying sanction of eternal damnation, are certainly the reverse of beneficial. When men believe, they become cowardly and their characters are weakened. Those who do not believe with full sincerity but accept the form of the doctrine are equally unfortunate :

The sort of belief and no belief which is nearly inseparable from the profession of the Christian faith, renders every man in some degree a hypocrite. Truth is no longer sacred and inviolable to our thoughts. We juggle with the powers of our understanding, and " palter in a double sense." Each of us becomes, in some sort, a double man, and is encumbered with limbs and articulations that make no proper part of ourselves. Truth is the proper element of the human soul, and frankness its becoming habit. We can never be what under advantageous circumstances we might be expected to become, till our word shall be as sacred as our oath, till ingenuousness is our daily habit, till by self-examination we come to know what we think and what we are, and till we are ready to render to every man an undisguised account of the results of our judgment upon every momentous subject, and the reasons on which our judgment rests for its support.

The doctrine of eternal punishment makes God appear a tyrant, and Godwin shows the inconsistency between this terroristic religion and the beneficial ethical teachings of Christianity. He traces this to the difference between the religion of the Old Testament, the systematised form of a primitive anthropomorphism, and the excellent teachings of disinterestedness and benevolence which occur among the sermons of Christ. From the beginning, these simple teachings of self-denial and brotherhood were overlaid with irrelevant supernatural ideas, and the Kingdom of God on earth which Christ preached was almost immediately replaced in men's minds by the Kingdom of God in Heaven, after death and judgment. Because of its present nature, Christianity is useless and almost wholly harmful to the development of human potentialities.

Godwin makes no attempt to formulate an alternative religion. His moral order rests on the single principle of reason, and he needs no faith beyond. Nor does he choose to delve deeply into the nature of the universe :

> I do not consider my faculties adequate to pronouncing upon the cause of all things. I am contented to take the phenomena as I behold them, without pretending to erect an hypothesis under the idea of making all things easy.

Nevertheless, Godwin declares his faith in a " principle, whatever it is, which acts everywhere around me. The principle is not intellect ; its ways are not our ways," but, although it is not endowed with human or superhuman attributes, this principle " in the vast sum of instances, works for good, and operates beneficially for us. . . . We have here a secure alliance, a friend that so far as the system of things extends will never desert us, unhearing, inaccessible to importunity, uncapricious, without passions, without favour, affection or partiality, that maketh its sun to rise on the evil and the good, and its rain to descend on the just and the unjust."

There is a temptation to see in this unintellectual guiding principle the same complex of natural laws which Godwin chose to call Reason in his earlier works. It is also, as H. N. Brailsford has pointed out, interesting to compare Godwin's view of the guiding force with Shelley's idea of Demogorgon in *Prometheus Unbound*, a power whose shape cannot be seen or whose attributes described :

> I see a mighty darkness
> Filling the seat of power, and rays of gloom
> Dart round, as light from the meridian sun.
> Ungazed upon and shapeless ; neither limb,
> Nor form, nor outline ; yet we feel it is
> A living Spirit.

But, Godwin concludes, this belief in an impersonal guiding principle implies no approbation of dogmatic religion, which has always delayed the development of the human mind :

We know what we are : we know not what we might have been. But surely we should have been greater than we are but for this disadvantage. It is as if we took some minute poison with everything that was intended to nourish us. It is, we will suppose, of so mitigated a quality as never to have had the power to kill. But it may nevertheless stunt our growth, infuse a palsy into every one of our articulations, and insensibly change us from giants of mind which we might have been into a people of dwarfs.

This was Godwin's testament to his age. With a complete doubt of his own personal survival, but a sublime confidence in the progress of mankind towards the happy continent he had charted for them, he prepared to face his death.

It came in the spring of 1836, when he had just completed his eightieth year. Throughout the previous winter he had been in poor health, and had suffered from serious colds. On March 26th he entered the last note in his diary :

Malfy, fin. Call on Hudson, Trelawney calls, cough, snow.

This entry finished the last page of the thirty-second notebook of his diary, and, with a premonitory gesture, he pasted on to the cover the leaf which he had written more than two years before for that purpose.

His evident foreboding was not unfounded. The cough he had mentioned brought him to bed the next day with a fever. During ten days of illness his strength passed gently from him, and he died calmly on April 7th, 1836.

In accordance with his own wish, expressed in a will written nine years before, he was interred with Mary Wollstonecraft in the burial ground of Old St Pancras Church. Some years later, when this churchyard was disturbed by the building of railways out of London, the bodies of William and Mary were disinterred and carried to Bournemouth Churchyard, where they were buried in the same grave as Mary Shelley.

## PART VII

# The Reckoning With Time

### I

GODWIN died in obscurity. His ideas were familiar only to a restricted group of people with literary interests, and his social writings became the gospel of no political group. Indeed, among the socially active elements of the 1830's, the Chartists and the Owenites, who came mostly from the artisans and the lower middle class, his name was probably unknown, or, at best, the echo from a dead age.

The general neglect of Godwin has persisted. Never, in the nineteenth century, was he among the revered political writers. So far as I know, *The Enquiry Concerning Political Justice* was not reprinted during that century, and even in the twentieth century it has been published only once, in an eccentrically abbreviated American edition. Godwin's teachings against political parties and other collective activities made him unsympathetic to the majority of socialists and reformers, and the general tendency of left-wing movements to base their organisation on Jacobin patterns, modernised by Blanqui and Marx, ensured his continued neglect.

Lesser men, like Saint-Simon, Fourier and Engels, acquired a much greater influence in the socialist movement. The English liberal theorists, like John Stuart Mill, H. T. Buckle and Herbert Spencer, who went so far in the same direction as Godwin, made no recognition of the value of his thought, and appear to have been too much under the influence of Bentham to be able to appreciate him fully. Even the anarchists, whose ideas were nearest to Godwin's, gave him little acknowledgment, and chose as their prophets men like Proudhon, Bakunin, Tolstoy and Kropotkin, whose leading ideas had already been outlined in *Political Justice*.

This almost universal neglect has led to the creation of a completely distorted picture of Godwin among people who have gained their knowledge from anything but a direct study of his work. He has become known less for his own writings than for his connection with contemporary men and women, almost all of whom are undeservedly more valued by posterity. He is the husband of Mary Wollstonecraft, the father-in-law of Shelley, the friend of Coleridge, an amusing character in the essays of Hazlitt and Lamb, and an unpleasant one in the diaries of Crabb Robinson.

Both his character and his works have been misrepresented by the interested and the irresponsible. The biographers of Shelley have, in general, been among the worst offenders. In order to whitewash Shelley, they have blackened Godwin's character and lied about his actions, and most of them, probably through ignorance of his work, have completely failed to estimate his intellectual influence over Shelley. Two exceptions are H. N. Brailsford, the author of *Shelley, Godwin and their Circle*, and F. A. Lea, author *of Shelley and the Romantic Revolution*, both of whom have been just in their discussion of the motives behind Godwin's actions and have shown considerable knowledge and appreciation of his work.

The general lack of knowledge of Godwin's writing has bred many curious misconceptions of his ideas. De Quincey, as we have shown earlier, was responsible for the legend that Godwin retracted all his fundamental beliefs in the second edition of *Political Justice*. Most students of literature who have not studied Godwin directly, accept this legend as true, and it has passed unexamined into the stock-in-trade of many political writers.

Moreover, this neglect of a great writer has given rise, not only to misapprehensions of his character and his teachings, but also to a failure to appreciate fully either the influence his writings have actually wielded, or the relevance they may have for those who are concerned with the perennial problems which afflict society as acutely today as in Godwin's own age.

2

In estimating the influence of Godwin's teachings, it can be said that, although unrecognised by the participants in social movements, they have wielded an unobtrusive but steady influence on English social thought which has contributed towards its libertarian tendency, a tendency still surviving in an attenuated form in spite of authoritarian influences. On the continent the distinction between libertarians and authoritarians has been marked clearly since the split in the First International. In England all socialists, except the extreme Marxists, have a libertarian tendency which makes them distrust authoritarian ideas, even when they give way to them, and which is shown even in the peculiar structure of the Labour Party, as compared with continental Socialist parties.

Godwin's ideas came to the English labour movement, not so much through the political theorists, as through the trade union and co-operative movements. Francis Place, who took a leading part in the agitation for repeal of legislation against Trade Unions, was a devoted follower of Godwin, and inherited his distrust of political methods and demagogic appeals. But perhaps the most important agent for the spreading of Godwinian ideas was Robert Owen.

Owen came into contact with Godwin when the philosopher's name was already sinking into obscurity, and their personal intercourse appears to have been scanty. But he was a devoted reader of Godwin's writings, and in his own plans for the regeneration of mankind his debt to them is manifest.

Owen strove to demonstrate Godwin's contention that the rich can be converted to a realisation of the need for virtue, and that because of this it is unnecessary to indulge in violent revolution or political agitation. Himself a rich manufacturer who had risen from poverty, he set about using his wealth for the general good, by endeavouring to educate men to a state of mind, where they would voluntarily abandon government and property and elect to live in small, self-governing communities, linked by a beneficial intercourse and co-operation which would know no barriers of race or nation. The fundamental ideas on which he built his teachings were derived from *Political Justice*, and remained constant throughout his life. They were, that man is made evil by his environment, that he can be changed not by punishment but only by the building of a society founded on social justice, and that most of the misery and evil in the world are due to bad institutions and could be removed easily if men were educated rationally under conditions of freedom and equality.

Owen began by reforming his own factory in order to give his workers just conditions. It was from his experience here that he learnt to modify his Godwinism by admitting the need for co-operation in material affairs. Owen's theory of co-operation became, many years later, the complement of Godwin's insistence on individual liberty, in the Anarchist Communism put forward by Kropotkin and Elisée Reclus.

Owen, like Godwin, was an outspoken critic of political methods. Years before it was achieved, he prophesied that Parliamentary Reform would bring no benefits to the poor. This attitude lost him the support of the politically-minded liberals, to whom his ideas seemed merely reactionary, but he continued to insist that the real revolution must be in human relationships rather than in the form of government, that it must be economic rather than political, and that only by education and the alteration of environment could men be made free.

Nothing could be closer to Godwin's ideas than Owen's statement that education, " so far at least as depends upon our operations, is the primary source of all the good and evil, misery and happiness, that exist in the world."

Man, Owen maintained, was moulded by the environment in which he lived from birth, and his differences from others arose largely from differing social circumstances. Bad institutions and erroneous opinions were the cause of all human unhappiness and evil :

. . . the members of any community may by degrees be trained to live without idleness, without poverty, without crime and without punishment ; for each of these is the effect of error in the various systems prevalent throughout the world. They are all necessary consequences of ignorance.

Thus we can realise the injustice of the punishment of people whose erroneous actions are due to the circumstances in their development that were beyond their own control :

How much longer shall we continue to allow generation after generation to be taught crime from their infancy, and, when so taught, hunt them like beasts of the forest, until they are entangled beyond escape in the toils and nets of the law ? when, if the circumstances of those poor unpitied sufferers had been reversed with those who are ever surrounded with the pomp and dignity of justice, these latter would have been at the bar of the culprit, and the former would have been at the judgment seat.

Owen's general approach had been summarised by one of his biographers, Frank Podmore :

He was a prophet of the tradition of Rousseau ; his gospel, the essential goodness of human nature : all wrong, all crime and suffering proceeded from the governments and other circumstances created by the perversity of man in the past. Let those governments be abolished, those circumstances re-created, give the natural instincts full play, and man will rise to his full stature and perfection. Happily, there was none to hinder. Reason showed us the way ; man had but to will, and it was done.

Here, as Podmore indicates, was a gospel identical in every important point with that of Godwin and Shelley, and it was according to this libertarian doctrine that Owen's varied activities for the rest of his life were continued. In whatever work he engaged, whether in co-operatives, trade unions, exchange banks or his ill-fated communities, he had always before him the vision of a free society similar to that foreseen by Godwin, and the causes he furthered appeared only as the means to this great end.

Owen's sole major difference from Godwin lay in the emphasis he placed on co-operation. Godwin, in his extreme anxiety for the integrity of the individual, had always tended to distrust co-operation between men except in the most necessary aspects of life. Yet, in one sense, co-operation was an integral part of Godwin's teachings, for he held that our actions must be directed above all by a regard for the general good. In this sense there is an apparent paradox in Godwin's teachings which is, however, easily resolved ; mutual aid between human beings is a necessary part of political justice, but in co-operation we must be careful that our contact with individuals does not obscure our vision either of the general good or of the natural laws of justice and truth.

Owen carried his Godwinian ideas into the co-operatives and the trade unions and left upon these movements a tendency to distrust political activity and to rely on their own forms of organisation which has persisted to this day. But his characteristic vision of society, the system of Villages of Co-operation, was really an attempt to state in precise terms Godwin's conception of a decentralised society of self-governing parishes. Godwin was perhaps wiser in not giving a detailed description of a world which would obviously develop in a way inconceivable to those who dwelt among governments and exploitation.

Owen's principles continued unchanged throughout his life, and in the *Book of the New Moral World*, which began to appear in 1836, and which he seems to have regarded as a definite statement of his social beliefs, he sets out a criticism of existing society and a sketch of the principles for a just order, which we can be sure would have been endorsed almost completely by Godwin.

He gives an interesting list of eighteen causes of the evils that afflict the world. I quote Podmore's abridgement, which retains the full significance of the various items. The causes are :

1. The Religions, so-called, of the world.
2. The Governments of the world, under every form and name.
3. The professions civil and military of all countries.
4. The monetary system of all nations.
5. The practice of buying and selling for a moneyed profit.
6. The practices which produce contests, civil and military, individual and national.
7. The present practice of forming the character of man.
8. The present practice of producing and distributing wealth.
9. Force and fraud, as now prevalent in every department of life, in all countries.
10. Separate interests and consequent universal disunion.
11. Isolated families, and separate family interests.
12. The practice of educating women to be family slaves, instead of superior companions.
13. The artificial and indissoluble marriages of the priesthood.
14. The falsehood and deception, now prevalent over the world.
15. Unequal education, employment and condition.
16. The strong oppressing the weak.
17. The levying of unequal taxes, and expending them upon inefficient measures for good, when they might be applied, most efficiently, to produce wealth, knowledge and permanent prosperity for all the people.
18. The practice of producing inferior wealth of all kinds, when the most superior would be more economical, and far more to be desired.

All these items, with the exception of the seventeenth, were favourite subjects of Godwin's reasoning, and can be found discussed elaborately in *Political Justice* or *The Enquirer*.

I have discussed at some length Godwin's influence on Owen's ideas, because Owen occupies a position of peculiar importance in the British labour movement.  But there were other men whose contribution was not inconsiderable, and who derived many of their ideas from Godwin.  Among these were not only Francis Place, but also William Thompson, whose economic theories of value were later borrowed by Marx, Thomas Hodgskin and John Gray.

The tendency represented by these men was opposed to the Chartist ideas, which descended from the teachings of Godwin's Jacobin opponents.  The Chartists saw the solution of social problems in a change of political institutions rather than in freedom from coercion and government.  They never renounced the conception of authority, and later, when the socialists of the end of the nineteenth century turned towards the ideas of a socialist state, imposing its changes from above, the authoritarian character of political action became more clearly defined.  From the Jacobins sprang not only the Communists and the parliamentary socialists, but also the Fascists and the Nazis.  Indeed, it can be said that the turning of the socialist movement away from the ideas of Godwin and Owen and towards the ideas of Babeuf, Marx and the Fabians, led directly to the rise of Fascism.

While the main bodies of the radical and labour movements became involved, in England and to a greater extent on the continent, in a growing preoccupation with political methods and the idea of gaining power to institute a form of authority known as " the dictatorship of the proletariat," there persisted a trend away from authoritarian politics.  This trend based itself on the complementary ideas of the independence of the individual and the co-operative organisation of functions within society on a libertarian basis, ignoring political government as an unnecessary evil that would only impede any attempt to achieve real freedom or equality.

In England this tendency continued in a more or less direct line from Godwin, through Owen and Place, into the Trade Unions and the Co-operative movement, which for many years eschewed contact with political radicalism and looked to the foundation of a co-operative society without political interference. The Grand National Consolidated Trades Union, founded in

1834 under the influence of Owen, had as one of its declared objects,

> bringing about a DIFFERENT ORDER OF THINGS, in which the really useful and intelligent part of society only shall have the direction of its affairs, and in which well-directed industry and virtue shall meet their just distinction and vicious idleness its merited contempt and destitution.

Right up to the last quarter of the nineteenth century the British labour movement looked with distrust on political parties and governmental action, and it was not until the advent of Marxist ideas through the Socialist Democratic Federation and of political radicalism through the Fabian Society that the trade unions and the co-operatives turned away from their old traditions and began to take part in political action.

Among individual socialists a distrust of the state and of political parties has persisted. William Morris, in *News from Nowhere*, portrayed a society of individual freedom with which Godwin could have found no fault, while Oscar Wilde, in *The Soul of Man Under Socialism*, and Hilaire Belloc, in *The Servile State*, indicated the evils of authoritarian socialism in terms which have been amply justified in our own day. These men may not have been influenced directly by Godwin, but certainly their ideas were in the libertarian tradition that sprang from Godwin's writing. Among the workers themselves the tendencies against authoritarian socialism were represented by such movements as the Syndicalist Education League of Tom Mann and Guy Bowman, and the various anti-political groups which have continued, particularly in Scotland, right down to the present day.

On the Continent, Godwin's influence was not so openly manifest as in the tradition of the English labour movement. Nevertheless, Godwin was translated into French and German, and a number of continental writers, including Benjamin Constant, showed considerable admiration of his work. On the Continent also a division occurred between the two tendencies of the labour movement, but here the difference became obvious at a much earlier date and was much more pronounced.

The social thinker from whom the libertarian movement arose was Pierre Jean Proudhon, who marked the distinction between libertarian and political thought quite clearly when he said :

All parties without exception, in so far as they seek for power, are varieties of absolutism, and there will be no liberty for citizens, no order for societies, no union among working men, till in the political catechism the renunciation of authority shall have replaced faith in authority.  No more parties, no more authority, absolute liberty of man and citizen—there is my political and social confession of faith.

I have discovered no external evidence that Proudhon was a student of Godwin.  But there is so great a similarity between his own practical schemes and those of Owen that it is highly probable that Godwin's ideas reached him through such an indirect contact.  Owen's reputation was widely known on the Continent, he visited France several times, and in 1848, when the national workshops were set up in revolutionary Paris, he visited that city and met a number of the leading Socialists.  It is likely that he and Proudhon, whose ideas had so much in common, met and discussed social topics.

The differences between the libertarians and the authoritarians were emphasised in the great struggle in the First International between the followers of Bakunin and the Marxists.  The split that ensued left the two movements clearly demarcated.  From the libertarian fraction sprang the anarchist and syndicalist movements.  From Marx sprang the authoritarian social-democrats and the communists.

Bakunin, who was a disciple of Proudhon, had probably not read Godwin ; he was too active and restless a figure to be a great student.  But Kropotkin, the theorist of latter-day anarchism, read and praised Godwin's work, and also expressed a number of theories which bore a striking resemblance to those set forth in *Political Justice*.  A later anarchist, Pierre Ramus, wrote a treatise, *William Godwin, der Theoretiker des Kommunistischen Anarchismus*, in which he accepted Godwin as the precursor of anarchist thought, and modern anarchists in general have since agreed in giving Godwin an honoured place among their thinkers.

3

As we have already indicated, Godwin's ideas failed to make headway against those of the radicals who were concerned with political action, and the English liberal movement became committed to a political struggle for authority which Godwin would have regarded with the greatest distrust. In a similar manner, on the Continent the teachings of Proudhon and Tolstoy, in America the teachings of Thoreau, were set aside for political doctrines and programmes based, not on the functional co-opera-tion of free men, but on governmental systems imposed from above.

All political doctrines based on the idea of government derive their nature from a widespread idea that man must be made to do what a ruling élite consider is good for him. The fundamental sanction behind the most democratic government is coercion, and because of this no governmental system is moral. It is based, not on a criterion of right action, but upon the fear of punish-ment or the hope of reward, neither of which are moral incen-tives. Governmental societies, and movements based on ideas of political organisation, therefore tend to elevate expediency above morals. When we do anything because it is expedient, we begin to lose our power to do anything because it is right, and thus moral conceptions lose their value, and continue to exist only as pretences that hinder growth rather than as living and real forces which can produce continual progress on human society.

Thus Godwin argued, and events have confirmed his argu-ments. The political movements and associations which he regarded with so much distrust have had their logical termination in such organisations for mass deceit as the Nazi, Fascist and Communist parties. The steady and ever-increasing growth of the state under the influence of political interests, has led to the appearance of social monstrosities whose main object is to depress all men into a sad uniformity of mind and body where their individual natures are destroyed and they become mere ciphers in an abstract pattern of organisation created for the benefit of small classes of rulers as denaturised as their unfortunate subjects. Out of the development of the state during the last hundred years have sprung all the evils of modern war, of large-scale economic exploitation and of the persecution of individuals for their ideas or races, which form the most terrible charac-teristics of our fantastic modern society and which, in spite of all our optimistic prophets, are likely to continue so long as the State in its present form dominates the affairs of men.

This is not the place to develop an indictment of the modern

State or of political parties. It is sufficient to point out that up to now the State has failed signally to provide men in general with peace, security and a sufficiency of material well-being, the primary social requirements from which men can build their individual and co-operative lives and achievements. It has produced only inequality, oppression, physical want and moral insincerity, and the political movements which have based themselves on the method of government have failed signally to cure any of the important defects of modern society.

It is time that we asked ourselves whether there is an alternative to a system which, in all its forms, has brought about, or at best failed to prevent, such colossal miseries among the human race. The benefits of authority have not been so great in our age that we should feel any sentimental reluctance to exchange them for the possible advantages of an alternative system.

The alternative to authority is liberty. The alternative to a system of government is a society based on the co-operation of free men, working and living together voluntarily and without coercion. That such a society is possible has been the contention of many men of considerable knowledge and intellectual power, since the days of the Stoics and the great Chinese sages. That it is not possible has never been proved, because such a form of society has never been attempted in a community with all the amenities of industrial civilisation, although free and co-operative societies have flourished among primitive men and simple agricultural communities. This latter fact is a proof that no inherent factor in human nature prevents men from living together in peace and amity without a coercive organisation. On the other hand, the history of modern man would seem to suggest that the two most important factors of our present society, coercion and privilege, play a great part in preventing men from living in brotherhood, and, further, have consistently hindered the resources of human knowledge and natural wealth from being exploited in such a way as to give to all men the material abundance and the freedom from irksome toil which scientists have long agreed to be possible in a constructive society.

The continuance of war and social crisis proclaims the inadequacy of the patterns by which men live today. We cling to our authoritarian political theories, not because we have any faith that they will attain the goal we desire, but because we fear to try methods that negate the assumptions on which we have acted in the past.

Yet perhaps our only hope of avoiding complete social tragedy is to have the courage to put aside the social concepts that have failed us so often and in so many forms, and to attempt to found our society on a completely different pattern, a pattern of freedom instead of authority, of equal and voluntary co-operation instead of privilege and force, a pattern centred on the concrete reality of the individual instead of the abstract collectivity of the State.

There is, in fact, an increasing tendency among thinking men of all types to turn towards such a libertarian view of society. And at such a time it is not inappropriate to look back to those neglected prophets of individual freedom who were unheeded and forgotten during the era of political struggle. That is my principal reason for writing this study of Godwin. For Godwin was not only the first man to present an elaborated criticism of political institutions as such and to produce a justification for a libertarian society. He was also endowed with a profound social vision which gave his work a permanent value. His teachings apply not merely to social institutions in his own day, but to society in general, and most of *Political Justice* can be read with as much profit today as in the eighteenth century.

With modern political developments, Godwin's clear-sighted judgments have been demonstrated time and again, and I can think of no other book of social theory that was written so long ago and contains so many ideas relevant to the problems that afflict us today. From a study of Godwin we can gain much that will assist us in evolving a workable alternative to the social chaos in which we live today. But I am not contending that we should accept Godwin as the infallible prophet of a new social cult. None would have been more opposed to this than Godwin himself, for he always believed that men must gain the truth through individual judgment, and must accept nothing on trust. I can think of no better ending to this book than his own exhortation :

" No doubt man is formed for society. But there is a way in which for a man to lose his own existence in that of others that is eminently vicious and detrimental. Every man ought to rest upon his own centre and consult his own understanding. Every man ought to feel his independence, that he can assert the principles of justice and truth without being obliged treacherously to adapt them to the peculiarities of his situation and the errors of others."

THE END

# BIBLIOGRAPHY

*Books concerning Godwin*

The indispensable source book for all studies of Godwin is Kegan Paul's *William Godwin : His Friends and Contemporaries* (1876). This is more a collection of letters and parts of his journals and other personal documents, linked by short pieces of narrative, than a real biographical study, but the information it contains is invaluable, and I have used this freely in my own study. The only biography proper in existence is that by Professor Ford K. Brown, *The Life of William Godwin* (1926). It adopts a rather patronising attitude towards Godwin and, like Kegan Paul's book, presents no adequate discussion of his works and the ideas expressed in them. Nevertheless, it gives a valuable picture of Godwin's relationships with some of his contemporaries.

A short, but sound, discussion of Godwin's ideas is included in H. N. Brailsford's little book, *Shelley, Godwin and their Circle* (1913). Mr Brailsford shows clearly the extent of Shelley's debt to Godwin, and deals fairly with Godwin's part in the differences that marred their relationship. The only other writer on Shelley who has avoided misrepresentation of Godwin in this matter is Mr F. A. Lea, whose recent book, *Shelley and the Romantic Revolution*, is a most useful aid to the study of Godwin's influence on Shelley.

The essay on Godwin in Hazlitt's *The Spirit of the Age* and his article in the " Edinburgh Review " on *Cloudesley* (1830) give together a good contemporary account of Godwin, while the chapter on Godwin in Gilfillan's *Literary Portraits* (1845) fills in some of the details of his character.

*Books by Godwin*

In the following list I have given merely the dates of the first editions, except for *Political Justice*, where there are important differences between the three editions.

*The Life of Chatham.* London, 1783. (anon.)

*An Account of the Seminary that will be opened on Monday the Fourth Day of August at Epsom in Surrey.* London, 1783 (anon.)

*The Herald of Literature.* London, 1784 (anon.).

*Sketches of History, in Six Sermons.* London, 1784.

*An Enquiry concerning the Principles of Political Justice, and its Influence on General Virtue and Happiness.* 2 vols. London, 1793.

      Second Edition. 2 vols. London, 1796.

      Third Edition. 2 vols. London, 1798.

*Things as They Are ; or, the Adventures of Caleb Williams.* 3 vols. London, 1794.

*Cursory Strictures on Lord Chief Justice Eyre's Charge to the Grand Jury.* London, 1794 (anon.)

*Considerations on Lord Grenville's and Mr. Pitt's Bills.* London, 1795. (by " A Lover of Order.")

*The Enquirer : Reflections on Education, Manners and Literature.* London, 1797.

*Memoirs of the Author of a Vindication of the Rights of Woman.* London, 1798.

*St Leon : a Tale of the Sixteenth Century.* 3 vols. London, 1799.

*Antonio : a Tragedy in Five Acts.* London, 1800.

*Thoughts Occasioned by Dr Parr's Spital Sermon, etc.* London, 1801.

*The Life of Geoffrey Chaucer.* 2 vols. London, 1803.

*Fleetwood ; or, The New Man of Feeling.* 3 vols. London, 1805.

*Fables, Ancient and Modern.* 2 vols. London, 1805. (*pseud.* Baldwin).

*The Looking Glass : a True History of the Early Years of an Artist.* London, 1805. (*pseud.* Marcliffe).

*The Pantheon, or Ancient History of the Gods of Greece and Rome.* London, 1806. (*pseud.* Baldwin).

*The History of England.* London, 1806. (*pseud.* Baldwin).

*The Life of Lady Jane Grey, and of Guildford Dudley, her Husband.* London, 1806. (*pseud.* Marcliffe).

*Faulkener ; a Tragedy.* London, 1807.

*The History of Rome.* London, 1809. (*pseud.* Baldwin).

*A New Guide to the English Tongue.* London, 1809. (*pseud.* Baldwin).

*An Essay on Sepulchres.* London, 1809.

*The Lives of Edward and John Phillips, Nephews and Pupils of Milton.* London, 1809.

*The History of Greece.* London, 1811. (*pseud.* Baldwin).

*Mandeville : a Tale of the Seventeenth Century in England.* 3 vols. Edinburgh, 1817.

*Of Population : an Enquiry concerning the power of Increase in the Numbers of Mankind ; being an Answer to Mr Malthus's Essay.* London, 1820.

*History of the Commonwealth of England, from its Commencement, to the Restoration of Charles the Second.* 4 vols. London, 1824-8.

*Cloudesley.* 3 vols. London, 1830.

*Thoughts on Man, his Nature, Productions and Discoveries.* London, 1831.

*Deloraine.* 3 vols. London, 1833.

*The Lives of the Necromancers ; or, An Account of the Most Eminent Persons in Successive Ages, who have claimed for themselves, or to whom has been imputed by others, the Exercise of Magical Power.* London, 1834.

*Essays.* London, 1873.

The above list does not include the three romances and the pamphlet mentioned by Godwin in his own autobiographical notes, but of which no other trace has survived.

As far as I have been able to trace, only three of Godwin's books have been reprinted recently. *Political Justice* was published by Alfred A. Knopf (New York) in 1926, in a slightly abridged edition, while the section on *Property* was published by Allen & Unwin (London) as a separate volume, edited by H. S. Salt (1890). *The Memoirs of Mary Wollstonecraft* were reprinted in Constable's Miscellany in 1928, edited by John Middleton Murry, and there has also been a recent American edition. *Caleb Williams* was reprinted by Routledge in 1903, and by George Newnes in 1904. All these editions are now out of print and difficult to obtain.

# INDEX